Dönitz, U-boats, Convoys

Dönitz, U-boats, Convoys

The British Version of His Memoirs from the
Admiralty's Secret Anti-Submarine Reports

Jak P. Mallmann Showell

FRONTLINE BOOKS, LONDON

DÖNITZ, U-BOATS, CONVOYS
The British Version of His Memoirs from the
Admiralty's Secret Anti-Submarine Reports

This edition published in 2013 by Frontline Books,
an imprint of Pen & Sword Books Ltd,
47 Church Street, Barnsley, S. Yorkshire, S70 2AS
www.frontline-books.com

ISBN: 978-1-84832-701-6

CIP data records for this title are available from the British Library

For more information on our books, please visit
www.frontline-books.com, email info@frontline-books.com
or write to us at the above address.

· Printed and bound by CPI Group (UK) Ltd, Croydon, CR0 4YY

Typeset in 11/13 Celeste by M.A.T.S. Typesetters, Leigh-on-Sea, Essex

Contents

List of Plates

1. Admiral Dönitz.
2. Dönitz addressing U-boat men.
3. Type VIIC U-boat with modified conning tower.
4. The bows of a Type VIIC U-boat with 88mm gun.
5. Layout of the conning tower of an early Type IX.
6. Victor Oehrn, commander of *U37* in May 1940.
7. Dönitz greeting survivors from the sunken supply ship *Belchen*.
8. The mansion and wooden huts at Bletchley Park.
9. Admiralty Operational Intelligence Centre in London.
10. A U-boat wireless operator.
11. British signalman eavesdropping on U-boat signals traffic.
12. H/F D/F and Type 276 radar aerials.
13. Escort in heavy weather in the North Atlantic.
14. A Catapult Aircraft Merchant Ship.
15. Escort carriers HMS *Biter* and HMS *Avenger*.
16. Swordfish aboard HMS *Chaser*.
17. The ocean-going Type IXB U-boat *U123*.
18. Accommodation aboard a U-boat.
19. Meals aboard a U-boat.
20. A storm in the North Atlantic.
21. The four-wheel Enigma machine introduced on 1 February 1942.
22. U-boats iced-up in a Baltic port, winter 1941/42.
23. Temporary anti-aircraft machine guns aboard a U-boat.
24. The Metox radar detector and its 'Biscay Cross' antenna.
25. Later retractable aerial for Metox.
26. Meeting of the Naval War Staff for the Baltic Command.
27. The 'Castle' class corvette HMS *Pevensey Castle*.

Introduction

Karl Dönitz
16 September 1891 – 24 December 1980

Karl Dönitz (U-boat Chief, Supreme Commander-in-Chief of the German Navy and finally Hitler's successor) must rank as one of the most mis-understood leaders of the Second World War. There has been a widespread tendency to over-estimate his pre-war powers and, after he had been promoted to Supreme Commander-in-Chief of the Navy, to reproach him for not having acted like a rebellious junior officer. At the start of the war, he was at the bottom of a long command chain and in what many people considered to have been an undesirable and unimportant post. As Flag Officer for U-boats (Führer der Unterseeboote), he held the position of Captain and Commodore and was responsible for running a small opera-tional control department. This carried approximately the same authority as a cruiser captain. The real power in submarine command was wielded by the U-boat Division of the Supreme Naval Command in Berlin, with which Dönitz had virtually no contact. The U-boat Division did not seek his opinions and Dönitz did not influence submarine development, con-struction programmes, training schedules or naval policies. His isolation can be illustrated by the position of the submarine training flotilla, which came under the jurisdiction of the Torpedo Inspectorate and not under the Flag Officer for U-boats. This state of affairs did not change until after the start of the war.

Dönitz's promotion on 30 January 1943 to Supreme Commander-in-Chief of the Navy was most extraordinary. Grand Admiral Erich Raeder was 67 years old when he resigned, after having served as Chief of the Navy for just over 14 years. Both his immediate predecessors (Paul Behnke appointed in 1920 and Hans Zenker appointed in 1924) were 54 years old when they took command and remained in the post for four years. In view of Raeder's age and length of service, one might have thought that the Naval Command (or Admiralty) would have had several deputies in the running for this high office. Yet no one was ready to step into Raeder's shoes. He nominated the 58-

year-old Admiral Rolf Carls (Commander-in-Chief of the Naval Group Command North) as his most suitable successor, but also suggested Dönitz to Hitler if the Führer wanted to emphasise the importance of the U-boat war.

Dönitz's appointment was a great personal triumph and a terrific boost to the sagging morale of the U-boat arm, but there were some distinct disadvantages. Dönitz, who had never been trained as a staff officer, was not familiar with the delicate intricacies of the Naval High Command and, in addition, had been incarcerated within the narrow confines of the U-boat operations headquarters for eight years. For the last two he had been in France, a long way from the general naval hubbub, and furthermore he had several major disagreements with the departments he was now to command. To make matters worse, he took over from Raeder at a most difficult stage of the war. All fronts were falling: the battle in the Atlantic had been lost; the Battle of Stalingrad had ended in disaster; the North African campaign was in full retreat and the naval leadership had no alternative other than to become fully involved in political struggles. Despite this, he was one of the few officers who openly opposed Hitler and often put forward alternative proposals when he did not agree with the Führer's directions. On several occasions he even refused to carry out Hitler's orders.

Dönitz was also more than democratic when dealing with the men under him. Commanders and men were allowed to leave their U-boats, without having to give reasons, as soon as replacements were found and more than one commander was relieved of his position because the lower ranks objected to his presence. In May 1943, when the more than forty U-boats were sunk, Dönitz went as far as instructing flotilla commanders to hold a secret ballot among crews. Everybody, including the lowest ranks, should vote whether to give up or continue with the struggle. It was the over-whelming support to continue going to sea that induced him to re-group what remained and to have another fling against powerful opponents.

At the time when Dönitz wrote his memoirs, it was exceedingly difficult to find information about the war at sea. Many German naval records and log-books were captured at the end of the war and immediately classified as 'top secret' by the victorious Allied powers. This ruling was so tight that neither Dönitz, Raeder nor their defence lawyers were allowed access to these vital documents after the start of the Nuremberg Trials. A few senior officers were allowed to view the logs for a period of a few days before the trials started but without knowing the charges which were likely to be made. This cloak of tight secrecy remained until the early 1990s, when the British Admiralty finally returned captured documents to Germany. By that time, American authorities were already more open to scrutiny and the US National Archives had made a good number of German logbooks available on 35mm microfilm. The absurdity of the Admiralty's dogged tightness can be further illustrated by the fact that copies of a number of the logs in their possession could be viewed in the United States and in German libraries while those in London were still closed to the public.

During the war about half-a-dozen or so copies were made of each log for distribution to a variety of departments and this duplication assured that one set of the U-boat Command's war diary remained in Germany, to be used by Dönitz as source for *Ten Years and Twenty Days*. Very few other authors of the period would have access to such valuable records.

Ten Years and Twenty Days was one of the first U-boat books to be published after the war and was written at a time when it was virtually impossible for the average person to find out even the most basic information about U-boats; who commanded which boat, what type any U-boat might have belonged to or any other relevant information. This led to numerous inaccuracies in many books because the majority of historians often had to make calculated guesses as to which piece of highly contradictory information might be correct.

Dönitz had one more significant advantage over other authors of the period. That came in the form of help from his son-in-law, the ex-U-boat commander and staff officer Günter Hessler. Immediately after the end of the war, the Royal Navy commissioned him to write a German account of the U-boat war and this was printed for limited circulation, but remained so highly classified that the majority of historians didn't even know of its existence. This was not released until 1989, when Her Majesty's Stationery Office published all three volumes as one book. Hessler did have some limited access to German papers, but it is unlikely that he saw Allied classified documents. Yet the writing of this account must have generated a considerable volume of useful information for his father-in-law. 'Illegal' carbon copies of this typescript and some of the original Indian ink diagrams were passed on by Hessler, although it is now too difficult to trace the history of this material or determine how much of this had been available for the writing of Dönitz's book.

Over the years reviewers have made the point that Dönitz's *Ten Years and Twenty Days* and Raeder's memoirs are somewhat different to other academic histories, but very few people have explained that considerable volumes of history were not generated until after the end of the war. Several different channels were responsible for creating these post-war additions to history.

First, immediately after the war the Allied forces of occupation introduced massive and highly intensive re-education programmes to make sure that any positive points about the Third Reich were quickly forgotten and that the Allied version of events should be accepted as the only 'true' history of the war. This has resulted in much of what has been written about the Second World War being based on powerful misinformation generated very cleverly by the Allied propaganda systems rather than on what happened during the conflict. This propaganda has since been embellished with the imagination of historians and further decorated with heavy doses of hindsight to produce many misleading insights. At the same time, events not so palatable for the Allies were suppressed to the point that a number have now been almost forgotten.

Secondly, a number of stories were concocted for war crimes trials, where wrongdoings were brought to the court's attention, without having to be supported by proof. There were cases where people making such claims were not allowed to be cross-examined by defence lawyers and this led to a chain of fantastic stories being made up. It would appear that anyone coming up with fabricated stories of war crimes was rewarded during those incredibly harsh years. Some stories even featured prominently at the Nuremberg Trials and then afterwards formed the basis on which history books were written; although there is no evidence that the events ever happened.

Lastly, people who served the post-war German government created other stories of dreadful happenings to boost their promotion prospects and other people, so-called eyewitnesses, invented their own stories to make themselves more attractive for television interviews or to get their own books into print. Although such stories have been regurgitated by historians, embroidered and often repeated by the media to such an extent that they have become common knowledge, it is possible to prove with naval logs that many events couldn't have taken place.

Dönitz lived long enough to see a number of stunning revelations about the U-boat war being published by his former adversaries, when, long after the war, the British Official Secrets Act allowed people to speak out publicly. The most shattering was that Bletchley Park in England read much of the secret U-boat radio code, something he found difficult to digest. Dönitz was most open-minded, taking considerable trouble to help historians and throughout this remained at the hub of new information as it became available. Yet his book has the terrific advantage that it was written before much of this secret information leaked out and was therefore written with hardly any hindsight and without the many post-war fabrications.

Karl Dönitz, the U-boat chief and named as successor to Hitler, finally died at the age of 89 on 24 December 1980 and was laid to rest on 6 January 1981 in the Waldfriedhof (Woodland Cemetery) at Aumühle (Bergedorf), close to where he ended his days. He was not given an official state funeral and men from the Federal German armed forces were not allowed to attend in uniform, yet he was honoured by many of his ex-colleagues. Shortly after this, in 1983, more than a hundred prominent Americans of high rank contributed towards the book *Dönitz at Nuremberg: A Re-appraisal* (Institute for Historical Review, Torrance, California; edited by H. K.

Thompson and Henry Strutz), whose dedication states, 'To Karl Dönitz – a naval officer of unexcelled ability and unequalled courage who, in his nation's darkest hour, offered his person and sacrificed his future to save the lives of many thousands of people.' (The figure actually ran into several million rather than many thousands.)

During more than forty years of research I met several men who said that they were no great 'Dönitz fans' but, at the same time, none of them said anything negative about him. Some stated that they didn't particularly like him, but then reeled off a number of personal experiences praising his command. Trying to assess his character today is more than difficult because no one can recreate the thought-patterns of the Dönitz years and no one from the modern generation will ever understand the restraints and the freedoms under which people of those times lived. In any case, Dönitz's character and his private life are hardly significant. What is important is how this one small person managed to keep the world's most powerful navies on the defensive for such an incredibly long period of time and how he managed to fight such a powerful war with what amounted to a relatively small and untrained force of men.

The essence of this is that from a force of 1,171 commissioned U-boats, twenty-five attacked and at least damaged twenty or more ships, thirty-six U-boats attacked between eleven and nineteen ships, seventy U-boats attacked between six and ten ships, and 190 U-boats attacked between one and five ships. This makes a total of 321 U-boats. A few more can be added to allow for calculation errors. Three hundred U-boats were never sent on missions against the enemy because they were used for training, experiments or they were not fully operational before the end of the war. Of the 870 U-boats sent on missions against the enemy, 550 did not sink or damage a target, many never getting close enough to an opponent to launch an attack.

When looking at this from a slightly different angle, by considering ships to have been sunk by men rather than machines, one comes to an even greater contrast. About 2,450 merchant ships were sunk or seriously damaged by U-boats in the Atlantic and this total rises to about 2,775 when other theatres of war are added. Eight hundred of these ships were sunk by thirty commanders. In other words 2 per cent of the U-boat commanders were responsible for sinking almost 30 per cent of the shipping. Eight of these commanders joined the navy before 1927, nineteen joined in the period 1930–4 and three belonged to the 1935 class. Therefore, thirty older men who joined the navy before Hitler came to power made a significant impact by reintroducing submarines and national conscription sank almost 30 per cent of all Allied shipping lost to submarines.

Jak P. Mallmann Showell, Folkestone, 2013

Sources for this Book

The information in this book headed ::Dönitz:: is a résumé from his memoirs *Ten Years and Twenty Days.* This was first published in 1958, two years after he had been released from Spandau Prison.

The heading ::JS: refers to comments from the author/editor, and ::The British Side::, unless otherwise stated, to the secret Monthly Anti-Submarine Reports. Other sources are listed in the Bibliography.

Most of the British information in this book has been extracted from the Monthly Anti-Submarine Reports, released by the Anti-Submarine Warfare Division of the Naval War Staff at the Admiralty. This has the advantage that it was not written for public consumption. Distributed only to leading officers hunting U-boats, it stated very clearly on the front of each copy:

<u>Secret</u>
Attention is called to the penalties attaching to any
infraction of the Official Secrets Acts.
Monthly
Anti-Submarine Reports
Secret
This book is intended for the use of the recipients only,
and for communication to such Officers under them
(not below the rank of Commissioned Officer)
who may be required to be acquainted with its contents in the course
of their duties.
The officers exercising this power will be held responsible that
such information is imparted with due caution and reserve.
Note. – At the discretion of the Commanding Officer, Warrant and
Subordinate
Officers may also be acquainted with the contents of this book.
Anti-Submarine Warfare Division of the Naval Staff
The Admiralty, London

Despite the limited circulation, the reports still contain large doses of propaganda, possibly to help keep up morale in difficult times. However, the readers were leading front-line officers and were well aware of what was really going on. This made it difficult to pull the wool over their eyes. So these reports are ideal for reflecting, balancing and supplementing what Dönitz has written. They certainly cannot contain any 'hindsight' or tales made up after the war by zealous historians, 'eyewitnesses' and authors.

Each monthly edition contained short summaries entitled 'The U-boat Offensive' and 'U-boat Countermeasures', which form the basis of this book. This material obviously lacked basic facts from the German side and some of this has been added in square brackets to make reading easier. It is important to remember that the events of one month could often not appear until the edition of the following month or sometimes even one or two months after that.

The problem with using the Monthly Anti-Submarine Reports is that a complete set of bound volumes is so heavy that I could only just lift them as long as they were inside a box so that individual volumes wouldn't fall from my arms. It would appear that these books were recalled by the Admiralty after the war and then pulped before being de-classified. Hardly any copies remain, making access most difficult, yet they make such a vital contribution to history that they must not be overlooked or forgotten. Sadly, we do not know much about the authors, who were probably serving naval officers, and we are most grateful to the British National Archives for permission to use this material in this book.

It is highly unlikely that the authors of these secret Anti-Submarine Reports knew about Special Intelligence and some topics, such as information about British acoustic torpedoes, conspicuous by not being mentioned at all.

Most of the information from the Monthly Anti-Submarine Reports used in this book comes from four volumes reprinted between 2001 and 2003 by the German U-boat Museum (formerly the U-boat Archive) with help from The Royal Navy Submarine Museum (Gosport) and The Bletchley Park Trust (Milton Keynes). The Military Press (www.militarypress.co.uk) published these for limited circulation with permission from Her Majesty's Stationery Office. Copyright for all this material remains with Crown Copyright/Ministry of Defence. The original text was photocopied and then passed through an OCR (Optical Character Recognition) program (Textbridge) and misreadings corrected by the author of this book. This text has been modified slightly by writing ship names in italics, rather than in inverted commas as in the original. Since the original was written exclusively for naval officers, a few extra words have been added to make the understanding of specialised terms easier for modern, non-naval readers. Much of the technical information has been omitted and this has resulted in a few awkward connections between passages. However, for the most part the text has been left exactly as it was written during the war.

The reason why this highly-significant document has gone unnoticed by so many historians is that the classified copies were recalled by the Admiralty after the war and apparently destroyed. This happened shortly before Commander Richard Compton-Hall was appointed as Director of the Royal Navy's Submarine Museum in Gosport. In those days the museum occupied nothing more than a couple of rooms within the naval base and acted as a 'regimental collection' for HMS *Dolphin*, but it was filled with fascinating relics, papers and books, all interesting enough for the public to be allowed limited access. Shortly after being appointed, Commander Compton-Hall received a reminder from the Admiralty to return the still classified books and since they could not be found, he replied that his predecessor must already have done this. Then, many years later, when the documents had been declassified, they were discovered among a pile of rubbish under the stairs. As a result several copies were put back into what was now becoming a substantial library. I am most grateful to 'Sea-Aitch', Richard Compton-Hall, for lending me a complete set for several months and I must also thank 'Professor' Gus Britton and Margaret Bidmead for helping to unravel much of the technical terms. The original Yearbooks for the German Submarine Museum (In those days still the German U-boat Archive) would not have been produced had it not been for their help. Photographs in this book, unless otherwise indicated, come from the author's collection or the German U-boat Museum in Cuxhaven-Altenbruch and I am most grateful to its founder and director, Horst Bredow, for all the help he has given. This book would never have been started had it not been for his unfailing support. Thanks must also to the staff of the British National Archives in Kew (London) for their help and for permission to reproduce the texts from the secret Anti-Submarine Reports. I am grateful for the help from Bruce Taylor.

Chapter 1

The Start of the War –
September 1939 to June 1940

:: Dönitz ::

The signal 'Start hostilities against England immediately' arrived at the U-boat Command in Wilhelmshaven at 13.30 hours on 3 September 1939; a short time after Britain had declared war on Germany. This was followed by a meeting at Neuende Radio Station between Dönitz, Admiral Alfred Saalwächter (Commander of Group Command – West) and Admiral Hermann Boehm (Fleet Commander). Dönitz mentions the seriousness of the situation of having to face a powerful opponent with almost unlimited resources and then he describes the first air attack during the following day; saying a number of aircraft sacrificed themselves without any great gain but the pilots flew low, displaying considerable tenacity and guts.

:: The British Side ::

This first air attack is described exceedingly well by Constance Babington Smith, saying it came about as a result of some fairly good reconnaissance photographs taken by Sidney Cotton a few days before the outbreak of hostilities. Her account about the beginnings of the Royal Air Force's Photo Reconnaissance Unit is interesting and valuable and she wrote that the raid provided dreadful evidence that the British Blenheim aircraft were not capable of bombing in daylight against serious opposition. The Bomber Command War Diaries state that a minimum of three bombs hit *Admiral Scheer* but failed to explode. This pocket battleship was lying in the harbour approaches with much of her machinery dismantled, awaiting a major refit. It would appear that most of the damage was caused by one of the five aircraft to be shot down crashing into the bows of the light cruiser *Emden* and causing the first German casualties of the war. This attack, made by flying over the North Sea because belligerent military aircraft were not allowed to cross the neutral territory of Holland and Belgium, illustrated another incredible weakness in RAF preparation. The attack came in two waves, with the other group dropping bombs on Brunsbüttel at the southern end of the Kiel Canal, but instead of hitting this target some of planes bombed Esbjerg in Denmark, 110 miles to the north, suggesting their navigation was way off beam.

Chapter 2

The First Ten Months

:: JS ::

Dönitz describes the goings-on after the outbreak of the war when U-boats made a considerable effort to obey the Prize Regulations. While writing this, he used the British official history (*The War at Sea* by Stephen Roskill) for reference. This work has the advantage over books published during the war years inasmuch that the author deals with basic facts rather than filling his pages with propaganda.

:: The British Side ::

The U-boat Offensive – November 1939

The degree of intensity of the U-boat campaign at the beginning of October appears to have been dependent on the political situation. As long as the Germans felt there was even a remote chance of their peace proposals being accepted, they avoided hardening British opinion against them by prosecuting the campaign against Allied trade. Consequently, though submarines were still despatched to the Western Approaches, they seem to have been ordered not to attack merchant shipping until they received the signal to do so. In the first eleven days of the month only two British ships, one of them a destroyer, were attacked. On the 12th of October, however, the U-boat campaign flared up again – in the next forty-eight hours six Allied ships were sunk. Thereafter the sinkings settled down to a fairly steady rate.

[JS – It is interesting that 'peace proposals' are mentions because this suggests the general public in Britain was aware of the fact that several peace proposals were under discussion but all these efforts seem to have been lost in time and are now almost totally forgotten. Also note that these reports provide a different view to the one presented by some post-war authors, who mention that the sinking of the first ship of the war, the liner *Athenia* by *U30* under Fritz-Julius Lemp, provided Britain with the indication that Germany had started 'unrestricted submarine warfare' right from the beginning.]

Parallel to this campaign at sea another developed on paper, the German Government seeking to justify an intensification of the U-boat campaign. On the 6th October, a German broadcast stated that the British Admiralty had ordered cargo steamers to ram German submarines on sight. This was followed a few days later by the argument that while it was legal to arm merchant ships, should the merchant ships use their guns, they rendered themselves liable to treatment as warships. The German attitude in these respects was not consistent from day to day, but there seems to have been a motive to it, every article in the newspapers being designed as propaganda for unrestricted submarine warfare.

On the 30th October an important article appeared in the *Völkischer Beobachter*, the official organ of the National Socialist Party. It stated:

> A neutral observer reports that the crews of British passenger steamers are trained to fight submarines by gunfire and aggressive manoeuvres. This procedure constitutes a grave risk to the lives of passengers. German submarines have sunk several British warships camouflaged as merchant ships. The statement of Mr. Churchill, that Britain was not using so-called 'Q ships' is, thus, untrue. Maritime warfare is, therefore, being waged on a reciprocal basis. If Great Britain scraps all rules of international warfare the responsibility for an intensification of commercial warfare at sea must be attributed to Britain.

Whilst the attitude of the German press is not as yet entirely reflected in the behaviour of individual U-boat Captains, there have been indications that the earlier acts of courtesy have become more rare. There has also been less regard for the safety of crews of ships sunk.

U-boat activities took place in four areas:

(1) Off the east coast of England, largely in the Humber district, where it appears likely that the casualties were mainly due to mines. Most of the victims in this area were neutrals and no ships in convoy were either sunk or damaged. Attempts have been made to clear these mines, but so far without success. It is suspected that they are magnetic.

(2) In the Western Approaches; U-boats worked farther out than they did in September, i.e., beyond the points of dispersal of convoys for Africa and America, 200 miles WSW of the Fastnet. The activity in this area was confined to four days in the middle of the month during which four British and three French ships were sunk.

(3) At least two submarines were operating about 150 miles NW of Cape Finisterre, and on the 17th October three ships of an

unescorted convoy were sunk and several others were attacked.

(4)   In the Approaches to the Straits of Gibraltar, one U-boat claimed three victims on the 24th October. All the ships were British.

In addition to these known operations rumours persisted throughout the month that submarines were working in the Atlantic in the neighbourhood of the Azores and also of the North and South American coast, but no ships were attacked and it seems probable that the reports were groundless.

The majority of U-boats seem to have proceeded to their operational areas round the north of Scotland. The outward-bound submarines appeared to be passing through the Fair Island Channel, and the homeward-bound ones round Muckle Flugga, often a long way out. [Muckle Flugga is the northern tip of the Shetland Islands.]

Some U-boats, however, certainly tried to pass through the Dover Barrage and at least three were mined in the attempt. If the Dover Barrage continues to be so effective, it means that the small 'Nordsee Enten' ['North Sea Ducks', 250/300-ton boats] can only operate in the North Sea and not in the Channel, because their endurance is believed to be too small for them to be able to proceed North about.

The whole statement must be accepted with reserve, as little reliable information is available.

Throughout the month of November the main effort of the German High Command seems to have been centred upon a mine-laying campaign on the East coast, particularly in the Thames estuary. It is impossible, however, to be certain that ships reported as having been mined were, in fact, not sunk by torpedoes, or to establish whether the mines themselves were laid by aircraft, surface ships or submarines, but there are indications that U-boats laid lines of mines across the fairways off the East Coast. [Both U-boats and small surface vessels undertook mining operations close to British harbours during the first winter of the war.]

In the Western Approaches it appears that an average of only two or three U-boats were operating during the month. This small number may have been due to a temporary shortage having been produced by the destruction of a considerable proportion of the German ocean-going U-boats.

[U-boats lost so far were:

U39 IXA	(Kptlt. Gerhard Glattes)
U27 VIIA	(Kptlt. Johannes Franz)
U40 IXA	(Kptlt. Wolfgang Barten)
U42 IXA	(Kptlt. Rolf Dau)
U45 VIIB	(Kptlt. Alexander Gelhaar)
U16 IIB	(Kptlt. Horst Wellner)

U35 VIIA   (Kptlt. Werner Lott)
U36 VIIA   (Kptlt. Wilhelm Fröhlich)

IXAs were large, ocean-going types, VIIAs medium sea-going types and IIBs small coastal boats.]

On our western and southern coasts there was some activity off the entrances to harbours. It seems possible that here also the enemy were laying mines or trying to emulate what Kapitänleutnant Prien did at Scapa Flow, for on one occasion our motor anti-submarine boats attacked two contacts in the Firth of Clyde and another U-boat was detected attempting to penetrate deep into the Bristol Channel. [There were numerous mining operations by U-boats and small surface craft such as destroyers throughout the dark winter nights.]

There were also apparently two U-boats on patrol between the Bay of Biscay and the Straits of Gibraltar at the beginning of the month. Four neutral ships were stopped and their papers were examined. One of the U-boats responsible was described as displaying the skull-and-crossbones on its conning tower. It is possible that the French destroyer *Siroco* accounted for both these boats. [They were not sunk.]

At the end of the month, when the German High Command realised that the presence of pocket battleship *Deutschland* would probably bring our heavy ships into the Northern Approaches, a patrol line of U-boats seems to have been placed between the Shetlands and the Norwegian coast. It was one of these U-boats [*U47* under Kptlt. Günther Prien], which unsuccessfully attacked HMS *Norfolk* on the 28th November, and another [*U35*, Kptlt. Werner Lott] was destroyed by the *Kingston* and *Kashmir* on the following day.

Further reports of U-boat activities much farther afield, in the Canaries and in the West Indies, are being continually received. Since no attacks have taken place south of the Straits of Gibraltar, these reports are in all probability false.

There is evidence that the Germans use the Fair Island Channel when outward bound; the interrogation of survivors of *U35* tends to confirm this.

It is very difficult to make any estimate of the total number of U-boats sunk, but it is noteworthy that two of the survivors of *U35* stated that, in their opinion, the U-boats could not be considered as a decisive weapon.

German U-boats are no longer divided into flotillas, but grouped as the strategical situation demands. [U-boat flotillas became administrative units, responsible for looking after men in port and equipping boats for their next operational voyage. The flotilla commanders' operational control was limited to their immediate coastal waters and U-boats at sea were controlled by radio from the U-boat Command, headed by Dönitz.]

U-boat Tactics: Information from Survivors of U35

[*U35* under Kapitänleutnant Werner Lott was sunk on 29 November 1939. The previous seven sinkings had yielded no more than about three survivors, while the entire crew of *U35* was saved. Lott became one of the few Germans to have been imprisoned in the Tower of London for some time.]

The officers of *U35* all said that it was found necessary to dive continually in order to avoid being sighted and reported by aircraft. They also said that aircraft made it impossible to send a prize crew on board a neutral vessel and to obtain fresh provisions, unless they went alongside the ship or compelled the crew to bring supplies in their own boat. They added that they did not fear bombing from aircraft very much, as it was usually possible to dive to a safe depth before the aeroplanes could attack. They thought there is always a danger, however, in low visibility, and more especially when the sky is half covered with clouds, as it is then that aeroplanes may surprise them.

U-boats have standing instructions to dive on sighting aircraft, as firing recognition signals takes far too long. Six men are apparently kept on the bridge as aircraft lookouts. The Captain of *U35* said he thought that, if they were sighted by a merchant vessel, aircraft would probably be on the spot in twenty minutes.

A submarine sighted by a U-boat while in her operational area is not attacked, unless she is definitely proved by her silhouette to be hostile.

When attacked, U-boats go to 70 metres (230 feet) if it is not possible to bottom. It is noteworthy that depth charges, which exploded below *U35*, were much more feared than those which exploded above. The Germans know, however, that our depth charges can be set to 500 feet, which is greater than any depth to which their U-boats can go.

The Captain of *U35* stated that he had learnt to distinguish between destroyers sweeping with Asdics and destroyers in contact. In his experience the destroyers usually lost contact after firing depth charges. He said he would have been unable to attack the destroyers, which hunted him because they always remained bows on.

This officer also stated that if a single British destroyer were picking up the survivors of a U-boat she had sunk, a second U-boat in the vicinity would probably not attack the destroyer, if it was obvious that rescue work was going on; but, if the second U-boat could not see why the destroyer had stopped, because of the range or the visibility, an attempt to torpedo the destroyer would certainly be made. He added that his advice to an unaccompanied destroyer in these circumstances, would be to steam round two or three times to make sure that there was not a second U-boat about and only then to stop and pick up the survivors of the first U-boat. Note that the Admiralty has definite indications that two

U-boats are unlikely to be so close that such an attack is possible.

The U-boat Offensive – March 1940

There was a marked lull in U-boat activity throughout the whole month, such activity as occurred being concentrated around the Shetlands and Orkneys in the last ten days of March. The most striking feature was the absence of all enemy submarines in the Atlantic waters after about the 12th. This disappearance of U-boats, although no doubt temporary, was certainly complete.

In the first week of the month two British ships were sunk off north Cornwall, a vicinity in which torpedoing had not previously occurred; this attack and other evidence indicated that one or even two U-boats may have been to the southward of Ireland in the beginning of the month.

In the Western Approaches proper, the only casualty was the sinking of the Dutch *Eulota* [by *U28*, Kptlt. Günter Kuhnke] on the 11th of March; it is believed that after this date all U-boats westward of the British Isles were recalled.

Only one U-boat appears to have passed through the English Channel during the month, and it is probable that her passage was made during the final week. This U-boat may have been the subject of a severe attack carried out by two trawlers off Bull Point but there is no evidence of its destruction.

During the last ten days nine unescorted neutrals and one British tanker were lost. Four Danes were torpedoed in the Moray Firth, two Danes torpedoed west of the Shetlands, one Dane and one Norwegian were torpedoed north-west of the Sule Skerry. The British tanker and a Norwegian vessel were torpedoed east of the Orkneys. In only one instance was any warning given by the U-boat.

A patrol of small U-boats was probably maintained in the Skagerrak during the latter part of the month, following the success achieved by British submarines on contraband control in that area.

U21 [Kptlt. Wolf-Harro Stiebler] went aground on the southern coast of Norway on the 26th of March, and was interned.

In the face of the declaration of unrestricted warfare on the 18th February 1940, an increase in sinkings during March was to be expected, but this did not occur.

In reply to a protest, the German Government stated they were entitled to attack all Neutral Shipping that –

(1) Sailed in Allied convoys.
(2) Are without ordinary lights or nationality marks.
(3) Use their wireless to give military information.

(4)   Refuse to stop when called upon to do so.

All the Danish ships sunk during the month were attacked without warning and in complete disregard of the above declaration.

The U-boat Offensive – April 1940

Early in the month every available U-boat left Germany to take up patrol positions for the operations against Norway, which were then imminent. The small U-boats were disposed between Norway and the Orkneys and Shetlands, with the exception of two stationed to the eastward of North Rona. The larger boats occupied positions north-east of Shetlands and off the Norwegian coast, extending as far north as Lofoten Islands, Vest Fiord and Vaags Fiord.

The number of U-boats off Norway was at its maximum in the second week and thereafter dwindled. There were at the beginning of the month eleven U-boats in German bases, which, as they became available for service, probably relieved other boats during the month.

One U-boat is known to have been sunk in the Norwegian operations and two or three more may have been sunk or damaged.

The U-boat Offensive – June 1940

The recrudescence of U-boat activity, which commenced about 20th May continued throughout the month of June. The tonnage lost during the month reached the highest point since the war began, namely, 260,479.

In the North Sea there was very little activity, and only one ship, the *Astronomer* was sunk [by *U58*, Kptlt. Herbert Kuppisch]: this vessel was torpedoed in the Moray Firth on the 1st of June, and was not a victim of sabotage as was at first suspected.

The area of greatest activity has been that enclosed by the parallels of 45°N and 51°N and the meridians of 8°W and 15°W, but on the 11th, a U-boat operating somewhat farther south distinguished itself by stopping and threatening the United States Liner *Washington*. On the 21st and 25th, ships were sunk as far south as the latitude of Lisbon and Cape St. Vincent respectively. On two occasions also, a U-boat appeared further West, as far out as 17°–18°W.

A further feature, peculiar to this month, was that of evacuation from West France, U-boats worked close in to the coast in the Bay of Biscay.

During the month, the German 'Ace' Kapitänleutnant Günther Prien [*U47*] cruised to the southern Western Approaches. Leaving Germany on 10th he went as far south as 45°N, followed a convoy north-eastward towards Ushant and returned northabout to claim a record tonnage of 66,587. The ten ships sunk by this U-boat included the *Arandora Star*, carrying German and Italian internees, which was destroyed without warning with heavy loss of life. This cruise conformed in duration to the normal 24–28 days.

Three Armed Merchant Cruisers were sunk – the *Carinthia* [by *U46* – Kptlt. Engelbert Endrass] West of Ireland on the 6th, the *Scotstoun* [by *U25* – Kptlt. Heinz Beduhn], West of the Hebrides on the 13th, *Andania* [by *UA* – Kptlt. Hans Cohausz] near Iceland on the 15th – and the *Canton* was missed by a torpedo. [*Canton* – 5,779 GRT – was sunk by *U30* under Kptlt. Fritz-Julius Lemp on 9 August 1940 near Tory Island.]

Convoys have been attacked with greater boldness than in earlier periods, advantage being taken of the paucity of escorts rendered inevitable by the exigencies of an urgent phase of surface warfare and by the demands of the military evacuation. The total number of ships sunk in escorted convoys was eight.

A very considerable number of torpedoes were fired, of which quite a proportion missed, and several ships, even when hit fairly and squarely, succeeded in reaching port in tow; the *Athel Prince* was brought in under her own steam with two holes in her side, caused by torpedoes fired West of Finisterre [from *U46* under Kptlt. Engelbert Endrass].

The U-boat Offensive – July 1940

During this month there were two distinct phases of U-boat activity. Up till the middle of July the most active area was still the Western Approaches between the latitudes of 48° North and 51° North. After the re-routeing of convoys through the North Channel the enemy lost no time in re-organising his U-boat patrols to meet the increased traffic in the North-Western Approaches.

Prior to mid-July such attacks as were made on shipping off the North of Ireland resulted from encounters with U-boats on passage to or from their patrol areas further south. Thus, on 2 July, the *Arandora Star*, carrying prisoners of war and internees to Canada, when North of Ireland, passed across the homeward track of Kapitänleutnant Prien [*U47*], and was sunk by the last torpedo remaining to him, after eight successful attacks carried out during a cruise which began on the 10th June. No other ship was attacked in the North-Western Approaches until 16th July.

During this month a very important innovation in U-boat strategy occurred: Lorient, a port to the South-East of Brest, and possibly also Brest itself, began to be used as a base for U-boats. For the most part U-boats which go to France appear to spend only a very few days in port and to use the base as an intermediate port of call for renewing supplies and, in particular, for replenishing torpedoes. No actual sighting of a U-boat in port was effected during the month, but the presence of at least two U-boats at

9

Lorient for a day or two in each case, in the last week of July, was established by two German broadcasts which narrated, in a garbled form, the exploits of Kapitänleutnant Rollmann and Kapitänleutnant Kretschmer [*U23* and *U99*]. The former was possibly the first U-boat Commander to enter a port of North-West France, and the occasion was celebrated by a broadcast, the commentator standing on the quay as Rollmann came in on 22 July. His successful attack on the destroyer *Whirlwind*, which he sank on 5 July, South-East of Ireland, was loudly proclaimed. [Full name is: Wilhelm Rollmann of *U34*. The first boat to refuel in a French Biscay port was *U30* under Fritz-Julius Lemp. She arrived in Lorient on 7 July 1940. Rollmann sank the destroyer *Whirlwind* on 5 July 1940 and the submarine *Spearfish* on 1 August. Thus he was responsible for sinking a warship at the beginning and end of the same cruise.]

With the elimination of France from the Allied Countries and the absorption of a considerable additional volume of former Neutral and Allied tonnage into the British register, the tendency is for the British totals to increase and Allied and Neutral to decrease.

Although the total tonnage lost in July fell to 213,938 from the 267,000 tons reached in June, the British proportion of the loss went up to 150,619 tons and touched the highest point in the present war. This was 13,541 tons above the previous highest point reached in September 1939. The Allied losses fell to 12,196 and Neutral to 51,123 tons.

Enemy attacks on convoys resulted in the loss of 29 ships in July. Eight of these, all British, were sunk by U-boat, 2 by mines, 18 by aircraft. The loss of the Dutch ship *Alwaki*, which sank as a result of several explosions on board, is thought to have been due to sabotage. [*Alwaki* was sunk by *U69* – Kptlt. Jürgen Oesten – on 9 July 1940.]

No attacks on British fishing vessels were reported during July.

Chapter 3

The Battle in the Atlantic Phase 1: July – October 1940

(Note that Dönitz considered the first phase of the Battle of the Atlantic to have started in July 1940.)

:: Dönitz ::
Disastrous torpedo breakdowns during the Norwegian Campaign of spring 1940 left the U-boat Command poised on a knife edge with the possibility of open rebellion in the minds of many officers. Dönitz wrote that the depressing failures could only be overcome by some successes, but it took a while before the next wave of U-boats would appear in the Atlantic. Many needed urgent repairs and the heavy action off Norway had assured that there were long queues in the shipyards. The first boat of the next wave, *U37* under Kapitänleutnant Victor Oehrn, left Wilhelmshaven on 15 May and shortly afterwards reported five torpedo failures, where the magnetic detonators apparently malfunctioned. As a result Dönitz prohibited the use of this magnetic head and insisted that only contact pistols be used. These were theoretically less effective because they resulted in a huge hole being blown on the side of the ship and watertight compartments could well prevent a sinking. The magnetic variety exploded under the ship, breaking it in two and thus assuring that the majority were likely to sink. Only a few well-built tankers survived such a hammering by having one-half of the ship remaining afloat.

Despite Oehrn's initial failures, he returned on 9 June 1940 after twenty-six days at sea, having sunk over 43,000 GRT. Dönitz was especially thankful to Oehrn for this splendid performance because the good news assured that the next crews went to sea in much better frames of mind, convinced that the Norwegian disasters had been finally been overcome.

Several historians have stated that Oehrn was sent out to restore the dreadful morale within the U-boats Arm, but this is definitely not true. He was sent out because *U37* was the first boat ready to put to sea. Werner Hartmann, Commander of the 6th U-boat Flotilla (Flotilla Hundius), had been given command of this boat at the outbreak of the war because it was one of only two special Type IXA boats, carrying additional communications equipment for leading a group of boats into action. Various difficulties meant that it was not possible to set up wolf packs until the late summer 1940. Oehrn took over *U37* so that Hartmann could continue with the increasingly important role of running the flotilla. As it turned out, Oehrn made a considerable contribution to the restoration of U-boat morale, but that was not reason why he had been selected to command *U37*.

U37's success was largely due to some accurate calculated guesswork sending the boat to the right area where plenty of shipping was available. The radio monitoring service, the B-Dienst under Heinz Bonatz, was providing a good number of decrypted messages from the Royal Navy, but the majority arrived too late to act upon. It was not until September that messages were deciphered quicker and this then led to the first major group attack on the 10th, when five ships were sunk during heavy seas with a force eight gale. (According to Jürgen Rohwer four ships were torpedoed during the early hours of 11 September by *U28* – Kptlt. Günter Kuhnke and *U99* – Kptlt. Otto Kretschmer, but only one these went down. The other three were damaged.)

Following this, the B-Dienst deciphered a number of signals about mid-ocean meeting points where escorts from Britain were due to make contact with east-bound convoys, after having escorted a westbound group into the Atlantic. This presented the U-boat Command with the unique opportunity to hit fully-laden ships and the night of 21/22 September proved most decisively that Dönitz's pre-war plans had been correct. Fifteen ships were attacked from Convoys OB216 and HX72. This was bettered one month later, when thirty-four ships of Convoy SC7 were attacked. The first attack was especially noteworthy because all the boats at sea were running short of torpedoes.

The high sinking figures were achieved despite one and sometimes two of the leading commanders being detailed to act as weather reporters, where their only duty was to send meteorological data back to Germany to help the Luftwaffe with forecasting conditions for their bombing raids on Britain. The U-boat Command's biggest problem at this time was the finding of convoys. As a result the reporting of targets took priority over virtually everything else. So, some U-boats with all their torpedoes expended were able to leave their frustrating weather-forecasting duties to shadow a convoy and direct other U-boats to their targets. It is important to stress that most of these were group attacks rather than wolf packs or patrol lines. A U-boat shadowing a convoy called in other boats for a mass attack, but in many cases these boats had not been searching for the convoy by having formed a line abreast in its expected path.

It is probably unnecessary to mention here that these successful attacks resulted in what the German called their 'Happy Time' and the carnage continued until the seasonal bad winter weather made it difficult for U-boats to operate in the North Atlantic. Many of the successes were due simply to U-boats running into a good number of targets and attacking these at night on the surface, where it was difficult to spot the low silhouette of submarines from higher vantage points. U-boats also developed a technique of closing in to almost point-blank range, where one torpedo could almost be guaranteed to hit. The Royal Navy had been expecting submerged attacks, when it would be necessary to shoot a salvo of perhaps three torpedoes from a range of several miles.

:: The British Side ::
The most pertinent account as to why U-boats were so incredibly successful during the autumn of 1940 has got to be Patrick Beesly's *Very Special Intelligence*. He was Deputy Head of the secret Submarine Tracking Room at the Royal Navy's Operational Intelligence Centre in London and has written what must still be the best and most accurate book about British naval intelligence. He said it is now amazing that British forces were taken so much by surprise, especially as Dönitz had outlined his ideas in a pre-war book. Trade protection did not feature strongly in Britain during the inter-war years and a combination of putting too much confidence in the new invention of Asdic and a failure to study the effects of Germany's unrestricted submarine warfare of the First World War made the naval leadership think the next onslaught would come from surface ships instead of U-boats. It would appear that the British Naval Staff had not even studied the U-boat offensive of the First World War in depth by 1939. (Asdic, a name derived from Allied Submarine Detection Investigation Committee, is now called sonar and could detect only submerged submarines. It failed to work when the boat was on the surface.)

The other contributing factors to Germany's successes were:

1. A long disagreement between the Navy and the RAF meant that two years of war passed before suitable aircraft and weapons for operating at sea were built. At first there were many instances of both surface ships and U-boats being attacked with bombs which failed to explode. One of the first attacks [against *U30* (Kptlt. Fritz-Julius Lemp)] even resulted in two aircraft being brought down by their own bombs without inflicting any damage on their target.
2. The remark earlier in this book about the first attack on Wilhelms-haven on 4 September 1939 coming about as a result of photos taken by Sydney Cotton shortly before the outbreak of hostilities, gives a

slightly misleading picture. British air reconnaissance was most ineffective during the early part of the war and the first aerial photos of Kiel were not taken until 7 April 1940. So air reconnaissance did not play a significant role until later in the war.

3. British radio direction finder stations were still being set up and they were hardly working during the autumn of 1940. In addition to this, U-boats maintained radio silence for much of the time, making it exceedingly difficult to get accurate fixes on their transmissions for working out their positions.

4. Being able to gain an insight into British radio traffic because the Royal Navy was using an old-fashioned cipher system helped the Germans quite considerably.

5. The British Operational Intelligence Centre with its secret Submarine Tracking Room at the Admiralty in London had only just been set up and did not yet make any noteworthy contribution to the winning of the U-boat war.

One other contributing factor to the U-boats' high success rate could well have been that merchant ships were not being accompanied by warships as a defence against U-boats, but to prevent the rather high proportion of neutrals, sailing under the British flag, from attempting 'home runs' back to their own country. It would have been quite easy for Norwegian, Danish, Dutch and other ships to abscond and run home instead of making for a British port.

According to the Secret Anti-Submarine Reports, the high casualty rate among merchant seamen was due to their ships still not having been provided with adequate lifesaving equipment, although by this time the war was more than a year old.

The U-boat Offensive – August 1940

During this month, activity was closely concentrated in the North-Western Approaches and attacks on shipping, which were constant, took place almost exclusively in this area. It was also during August that the U-boats started to use new tactics, attacking, in the majority of cases, at night, presumably firing from, and certainly withdrawing on the surface.

Many loud boasts have been made about the glorious triumphs of U-boats, and grains of truthful information have been extracted from the broadcasts but, as yet, no picture of the events of the month can be drawn with sufficient clarity to define the respective movements and actions of individual U-boats.

The unrestricted U-boat warfare against Merchant Shipping continued, unabated, throughout August. The total tonnage sunk, 251,000, was not quite as high as the highest figure of 267,000 tons reached in June, but the British proportion of this loss was the highest recorded since the war began, namely 187,000 tons. The previous highest losses were 151,000 tons in July and 136,000 tons in September 1939. The losses of our Allies were 22,000 tons, compared with 83,000 tons in June and 12,000 tons in July. Neutrals suffered to the extent of 42,000 tons compared with 63,000 tons in June and 44,000 in July.

The highest neutral losses occurred in February when some 81,000 tons of their shipping was sunk. [A good number appeared to be coming from or making for British ports.]

On 15th August the German Government proclaimed a complete blockade of the British Isles, and called upon Neutral Governments to forbid their vessels to sail through the Anglo-German war zone. They further declared that every Neutral vessel in this region in future would run the risk of being destroyed.

There is no doubt that U-boat activity was considerably intensified after this date, some 21 British ships totalling 110,000 tons being sunk between 23rd and 31st August. Allied and Neutral losses were, however, more or less normal.

Twenty-eight vessels were sunk inward bound to United Kingdom and 22 outward bound; of the remaining two, one was sunk in the Mediterranean and the other off the West Coast of Africa.

The occupation of French North-Western ports, enabling the enemy to extend his operations in the Atlantic still further West, resulted in the sinking of *Yew Crest* [by *U37* under Kptlt. Victor Oehrn] on 25 August, in position 55°10'N 25°02'W.

The U-boat Offensive – September 1940

The U-boats appear to have displayed greater boldness in their attacks during September, and several cases have occurred of attacks being made from the surface by gunfire. The scene of greatest activity was again in the North-Western Approaches. Of the 59 ships attacked in this area 40 were in convoy; 71 per cent of the total were night attacks. The period of greatest activity was between 16th and 22nd September, when a concerted attack by several U-boats is thought to have been made on Atlantic convoys. This was the period of, and immediately following the full moon.

There were no attacks on shipping by U-boats in the North Sea.

No ships in the Irish Sea were attacked in September, and although U-boats were known to be operating in the Bay of Biscay during the month no ships were attacked in this area. Evidently the Germans still consider that the English Channel may be too dangerous for them, as no U-boat is known to have passed through.

On 21st of September the 'Halifax' Convoy HX72 suffered the severe loss of 11 ships, when attacked at night by at least two U-boats, one of which may have been hit and damaged by a shot from SS *Harlingen*.

Italian U-boats were known to be operating in the Bay of Biscay during September, but they made no attacks.

For the third time in four months the monthly total of mercantile losses due to U-boat action exceeded a quarter of a million tons, the actual figure for September being 264,502 tons. Although the total losses did not quite reach the peak figure of 267,180 tons in June, the British tonnage loss of 194,151 tons was the highest yet recorded. Our Allies lost some 38,000 tons, which was more than in each of the two preceding months, hut less than half their losses in June. The Neutral total was down to approximately 33,000 tons, which was lower than any of the three preceding months.

The U-boat Offensive – October 1940

During October, Lorient was the principal U-boat operational base, but no defined patrol zones appear to have been observed. The average time U-boats spent at sea was between two and three weeks.

Once more activity was confined to the North-Western Approaches, but the casualties were not heavy except during the four days 17th–20th October, when two inward bound convoys were very heavily attacked. During 18th–19th alone, 31 ships were hit. [Mainly from Convoys SC7 and HX79.]

An important feature of U-boat tactics during October was the concentration of aggressive operations into the middle phase of the 'Hunter's moon'. [The first full moon in October after the Harvest Moon. The Harvest Moon was the full moon nearest the autumnal equinox of 22–23 September.] Every night attack on a convoy was made during moonlight, and the period of greatest activity followed the 15th when the moon was full. At this time, when the hours of moonlight were the longest, conditions were most favourable to U-boats for prolonged chases, also for manoeuvring before, after and between attacks. Logically enough the enemy employed his boldest and most skilful commanders.

Günther Prien took part in the assaults and claimed to have sunk eight ships out of two convoys. It is believed that he returned to Germany round Muckle Flugga, and that he was the target for a strong attack by three 'Hudson' aircraft off Egersund on 25 October. That the U-boat suffered damage is proved by the fact that she took two full days to travel 150 miles into the Skaggerak, and preferred to creep in by the back door, rather than risk further air attack by continuing on her way to Wilhelmshaven.

U-boat Tactics

By Day

U-boats continued to make their attacks from periscope depth; there are indications that, in some cases at least, they made use of high-submerged speed in order to escape after making their attacks.

By Night

Tactics vary with the individual Captain, but the normal plan of recent attacks is believed to have been as follows:

The U-boat gains contact with the convoy during the day, either as a result of reports from long range German reconnaissance aircraft, by reports from other U-boats or by sighting smoke, and then proceeds to shadow at visibility distance on the bow or beam. When darkness has fallen, the U-boat, trimmed down on the surface, closes the convoy and endeavours to reach a position broad on its bow. She keeps very careful watch for the escorts and endeavours to pass astern of those stationed on the bow of the convoy. The attack is pressed home as close as the U-boat Captain dares, and it is possible that, in some cases, a firing range of about 600 yards has been achieved. Having reached a firing position on the beam of the convoy, most U-boats increase to full speed, fire a salvo of four torpedoes, turn away still at full speed, firing stern tubes if fitted, and retire as rapidly as possible in the direction considered safest. U-boat Captains have been advised not to dive after making night attacks but to evade our forces on the surface.

If their retreat is unseen, they will continue along the line of advance of the convoy some miles off and, if weather permits, reload their torpedo tubes on the surface. Subsequent attacks may then be made on the same convoy, in the same manner, at intervals throughout the night.

No U-boat has yet been known to make such attacks at intervals of less than one hour. [Due to the time taken to reload torpedo tubes.]

With the exception of the attack by *U32* [Kptlt. Hans Jenisch] on Convoy HX66A no conclusive evidence exists to show that any U-boat has made an attack on a properly formed convoy, from a position within the convoy, nor that any U-boat has ever been between the columns of a convoy on the surface at night.

It is now known that some U-boats carry nine electric and two air torpedoes. The range of the former is believed to be 3,000 yards with a possible 1,000 yards over-run. This provides corroborative evidence that long range attacks are not normally made at night. [Both the G7a 'air' and the G7e 'electric' torpedo were exactly the same size and could be mixed in any proportion. The 'a' refers to Type A and is not an abbreviation of 'air'. The number carried by a Type VIIB and C was as follows: In bow torpedo tubes = 4; in stern torpedo tube = 1; under the floor in bow compartment

17

= 4; on top of the floor in bow compartment = 2; between electro motors in the stern = 1; in external storage tube in bows = 1; in external storage tube in stern = 1; total = 14.]

These German tactics indicate the paramount importance of vigilance by night lookouts, particularly on bearings abaft the beam.

With U-boats on the surface, echo contact cannot normally be expected, but U-boats are believed to have passed escorts at night at such a distance and such a speed that detection by hydrophone effect should have been obtained.

The U-boat Offensive – November 1940

U-boats were much less active. At the beginning of the month, Kapitän-leutnant Otto Kretschmer was operating in the North-Western Approaches, and sank the armed merchant cruisers *Patroclus* and *Laurentic*, also a merchant ship SS *Casanare*. He was then awarded the Oak Leaves to the Iron Cross; this very special distinction is reserved for U-boat Commanders who have sunk, or claim to have sunk, 200,000 tons of shipping.

Kretschmer then attacked Convoy HX83 on the 5th of November, sinking the *Scottish Maiden*. He followed this convoy towards Ireland, when some 10 hours later he was attacked by HMS *Beagle*. It is possible that the U-boat suffered damage, as she then went back to her base at Lorient, arriving on the 8th.

This incident, combined with the excellent results from attacks by *Antelope*, *Harvester* and *Highlander*, seriously depleted the enemy's U-boat strength in the North-Western Approaches.

No ships were sunk until the 13th, when the *Cape St. Andrew*, a straggler from Convoy OB240, with engines disabled, who was being towed back to port by *Salvonia* and escorted by *Hurricane*, was torpedoed north-west of Bloody Foreland, by a small U-boat probably commanded by Wohlfahrt. It is believed that this U-boat then sank SS *Planter* on the 16th and SS *St. Germain* and *Veronica* on the 17th, all north of Ireland. She then returned to Germany northabout. [This was *U137* under Kptlt. Herbert Wohlfahrt.]

A German U-boat left Lorient and went south as far as Freetown. During her operations in that area she sank four ships in three days, afterwards returning to Lorient. [This was *U65*, a Type IXB, under Kptlt. Hans-Gerrit von Stockhausen and the long voyage was possible because the U-boat was refuelled by the tanker *Nordmark*.]

On the 21st of November, a U-boat [*U103* under Kptlt. Viktor Schütze] attacked the ocean Convoy OB244 and sank two ships, SS *Victoria* and *Daydawn*. The corvette *Rhododendron* sighted the U-boat an hour later and counterattacked. In spite of the very rough weather, the attack is believed to have been successful. [*U103* survived.]

Convoy SC11 was attacked twice on the night 22nd/23rd, by a U-boat believed to have been commanded by Joachim Schepke; the first time in position about 13°W, when three ships were sunk, and again early on the 23rd in about 9°W, when a further three ships were torpedoed, one of which reached port.

In the second half of the month, two or three Italian U-boats were operating in the North-Western Approaches, but they do not appear to have made any attacks.

Casualties to Shipping

For the first time since the intensified U-boat warfare began, the monthly losses due to U-boat action have shown an appreciable fall, and the losses in November, 133,542 tons, approximate closely to the figure for the second month of the war [October 1939] when some 136,000 gross tons were sunk.

U-boats appear to have given up attacking fishing vessels, as there have been no such attacks since the two reported in September.

U-boat Countermeasures – August 1940

Since the transfer of shipping routes to North-Western Approaches, aircraft have escorted convoys further into the Atlantic; therefore, the time spent on this duty exceeds the previous month's return by 849 hours.

Of the 12 sightings made without attack, in six instances U-boats dived before an attack could be delivered: on four occasions the aircraft sighting were on convoy A/S duty and reported to surface escort vessels who took action. One sighting was by an aircraft that was not suitably armed, and another failed to relocate the U-boat, owing to low visibility.

Naval depth charges, modified for use in Sunderland aircraft, are believed to have obtained their first success on August 16th, when a U-boat is thought to have been sunk by an aircraft of 210 Squadron in position 24° St. Kilda, 164 miles. A further possible sinking is recorded on the 29th August when a Sunderland of the same squadron delivered an attack in co-operation with HMS *Mackay*, in position 277° Oban 130 miles. In view of the initial successes obtained by Sunderlands, modifications are in progress to other Coastal Command aircraft, which will enable them also to carry depth charges, when it is expected the lethal value of air attack against U-boats will be considerably increased. [No U-boats were lost during this period.]

U-boat Countermeasures – September 1940

The main pre-occupation of our naval forces in Home Waters was the threat of sea-borne invasion. This necessarily confined large numbers of our destroyers to the East and South Coasts. As Enemy U-boat activity was concentrated almost exclusively in the North-Western Approaches, this re-acted unfavourably on our Anti-Submarine operations.

In spite of this, however, the increase in the numbers of A/S vessels available for convoy escort duties in the North-Western Approaches, which was recorded in August, was maintained. This was largely due to the number of new corvettes and new or converted A/S trawlers, which came into service during the month. In the middle of the month these increases suffered a temporary setback due to the withdrawal, for anti-invasion duties, of a number of trawlers from the Belfast trawler force, however, the net increase at the end of the month was 11 ships.

The fitting of depth charges instead of bombs in aircraft engaged on operations is being continued as rapidly as possible.

Forty-nine attacks on U-boats or supposed U-boats were made; thirty-two being carried out by warships, nine by submarine, six by aircraft and two by merchant ships, who had previously been unsuccessfully attacked.

U-boat attacks on convoys during the month were, in nearly every case, made at night. There is strong evidence that the attacks have been made on the surface, generally from a position broad on the bow of the convoy, and that the U-boat has then withdrawn on the surface, at high speed, in the direction of her original approach.

The measures taken to counter these new tactics included re-disposition of the convoy escorts in positions down each wing, and at a greater distance from the convoy than heretofore, and the issuing of instructions to the escorts concerning their action in the event of attack. These instructions directed escorts to proceed outwards from the convoy at full speed, firing star shell to illuminate the area where the U-boat might be, in an attempt to sight or force her to submerge and improve the chances of Asdic detection.

Another change made during this month was the taking over by the Admiralty of responsibility for the routeing of all ocean-going convoys, thus enabling emergency changes to be made without delay, when, information was obtained of the presence of U-boats near convoy routes.

In order that the efficacy of our counter-measures may be continually kept under review and improved without delay, a weekly meeting at the Admiralty, attended by Officers responsible for the organisation and administration of convoy escort forces in the North-Western Approaches, was instituted. The first meeting was held on 1st October.

U-boat Countermeasures – October 1940

Thirty-five attacks on U-boats or supposed U-boats were made during the month. Eighteen of these by surface ships, four by submarines and thirteen by aircraft.

This month has been devoted to developing and improving measures taken to counter day and night U-boat attacks on convoys. To this end changes have been made both in the dispositions of convoys and of their escorts.

Great efforts are being made to equip all convoy escorts with apparatus, which will enable them to locate a U-boat on the surface at night outside visibility distance. As more ships are fitted, dispositions will be changed so as to make the maximum use of this aid. [This appears to be the first mention of radar being used and it is strange that a name has not been attached to the new aid.]

This new equipment has also been fitted into aircraft of Coastal Command and Fleet Air Arm. It will detect U-boats on the surface up to a range of 15 miles, and will be especially valuable for detecting U-boats on the surface at night.

It is hoped that depth charges will be carried by the aircraft, but in any event the enemy can be forced under and kept submerged until the arrival of Asdic-fitted ships, or until he is compelled to surface to re-charge batteries.

The transfer of all convoy routes to the North-Western Approaches in July led to considerable difficulty in the provision of air escorts for convoys, owing to the lack of adequate landing ground facilities in that area; these difficulties are being surmounted and it is now becoming possible to operate aircraft at night for convoy escort work. It is intended to provide the maximum air escort for three hours before darkness falls, as this is the period in which U-boats take up their shadowing positions, preparatory to night attack.

The high percentage of hits recently obtained by U-boats in night attacks has made it necessary to increase the distance apart of convoy columns from three cables to five cables. [One cable's length was originally 100 fathoms, which equalled 182 metres. However, the British military tended measure one cable as being 608 feet or 185.3 metres, while the United States took one cable to be 720 feet or 219.5 metres.] This materially reduces the theoretical chances of more than one ship being hit by a salvo.

The latest German methods of attack are described in the volume about The U-boat Offensive and the following measures are employed by convoy escorts against the enemy tactics:

By Day
On an attack being made, escorts on each side of the convoy form on line of bearing on the mean line of advance of the convoy, ships 2,500 yards apart, then move to a position three miles in rear of the convoy, turn outwards together 90° and sweep in line abreast for one hour. All ships drop

depth charges on the initial turn and further depth charges every two miles of the sweep. If by this time no contact has been obtained, escorts re-join the convoy.

By Night
Escorts are disposed in line ahead 3,000 yards apart at visibility distance from the convoy. In the event of attack, all ships on the engaged side, or on both sides if the side of attack is in doubt, turn 90° outwards together and proceed at full speed for a distance of 10 miles from the convoy, firing star shell to illuminate the area. Destroyers are stationed in van and rear positions where possible.

Coastal Command Operations

Coastal Command Operations	September	October
Total hours flown by Coastal Command	13,787	11,858
Total miles flown by Coastal Command	1,792,310	1,541,540
Hours on purely Anti-Submarine Patrol	1,792	1,811
Miles on purely Anti-Submarine Patrol	224,770	235,430
Hours on Convoy duty	5,986	5,700
Number of convoys provided with escort	778,180	741,000
U-boats sighted	18	18
U-boats attacked	10	10

September: The flying time during September was divided between Anti-Invasion Patrols, reconnaissance and offensive operations. In six cases of submarine sightings the aircraft either carried no A/S bombs or was in the vicinity of a convoy and summoned surface hunters. In two cases the U-boat dived too quickly for an attack to be made.

October: The decrease in the total of hours flown in October is mainly attributed to longer hours of darkness. Some promising attacks on U-boats were made during this month by aircraft of the Command.

The Photographic Reconnaissance Unit has contributed valuable information concerning the location and activity of various enemy submarine bases and building yards. The ensuing bombing attacks may curtail enemy submarine.

U-boat Countermeasures – November 1940

Twenty-six attacks on U-boats or supposed U-boats were made during November. Nineteen of these by surface ships, four by submarine and thirteen by aircraft. [In the original, the number 26 has been corrected by pen to 36.]

Day

No great change has taken place or is envisaged in the tactics to be adopted against U-boats by day.

Night

At night escorts are disposed in line ahead 3,000 yards apart at visibility distance from the convoy. Thus a U-boat attempting an attack may well be sighted or heard by hydrophone effect before she reaches a firing position. If she gets through the escort unobserved and undetected, the first intimation that an attack has taken place, is generally the flash or noise of a torpedo explosion.

The effect of this explosion varies considerably, and cases have occurred in which escorts only a short distance away from a U-boat victim, have not seen or heard anything, and also when men in torpedoed vessels have not been awakened by the explosion.

For this reason, the vital importance of the torpedoed ship firing a white rocket to announce that she has been struck, has been impressed on the captains of merchant vessels. Some merchant ships have been unable to determine on which side they have been hit, or even worse, have been convinced that they have been hit on the opposite side to the true one – the use of red and blue flares has, for this reason, been discontinued.

The action to be taken by escorts in the event of a night attack on a convoy remains as established. That is to say, all escorts on the engaged side, or on both sides if the side of attack is in doubt, turn 90° outwards together and proceed at full speed for a distance of ten miles from the convoy, firing starshell over the whole arc away from the convoy to illuminate the area.

These tactics have been carefully worked out as the best measures to overcome the present methods practised by the U-boats, but it is obvious that immediate action and close co-operation by escorts and merchant vessels is essential in order to obtain full benefit from the counter procedure.

Lack of appreciation by ships in convoy, of the vital importance of immediate indication of attack, no doubt contributed to the confusion that appears to have occurred after some attacks on convoys, such as the attack on HX83, but since the responsibility for destroying the enemy rests entirely upon the escorts, too much reliance should not be placed upon information from merchant ships. The importance of efficient lookout, particularly on bearings abaft the beam, cannot be over-emphasized. Good eyes and constant vigilance are the most likely qualifications to achieve success.

In order to improve the tactical efficiency of the destroyers, sloops, corvettes and trawlers, which now form escorts for convoys, these ships are being formed into groups to work under their own senior officers. As far as possible, ships of one group will always work together. [First mention of Escort Groups.]

In the night attacks by U-boats on our convoys we are faced with a straightforward, if difficult tactical problem, but with adequate numbers, maximum training, quick wits in appreciating the situation, good team work and inspired leadership, we shall succeed in mastering the enemy.

Chapter 4

The Major Turning-Point of the U-boat War – March 1941

:: JS ::
The U-boats' 'Happy Time' of autumn 1940 was brought to an end by atrocious weather in the Atlantic, but this had the positive spinoff that hardly any U-boats were seriously attacked. None were lost to enemy action in December 1940, nor in January and February 1941, but then suddenly, and without any prior warning, five went down in March and another one during the first days of April. This blow was far more shattering than might be imagined from reading this. One must bear in mind that despite the most intensive operations resulting in the U-boats' tremendous successes, only two of them were lost as a result of enemy action during the six months leading up that fateful March 1941. So six in the period of one month hit especially hard.

:: Hirschfeld ::
Perhaps the most poignant description of how this was perceived is in Wolfgang Hirschfeld's book *Feindfahrten*, where he mentions a meeting with an old friend who was a radio operator aboard the flotilla's escort ship. Hirschfeld's own boat, *U109* under Hans-Georg Fischer, had just come back from its final operational training and was due to head out into the Atlantic. The nature of their work assured that radio operators were usually better informed than anyone else and they often knew more about what was going on than officers. During this farewell drink Hirschfeld was told how his colleagues at flotilla headquarters had heard about the recent turmoil in the Atlantic; that several of the leading aces were no longer responding to calls to send their position and that Otto Kretschmer (*U99*) had broadcast a plain text message saying he was sinking. Hirschfeld wrote that the hearing of this news felt as if a cold shower was running down his back. Such a large number of boats with three famous aces among them was pretty difficult to digest and, to make matters worse, there were men on board whom Hirschfeld had seen and talked to only a few weeks earlier.

His immediate reaction was to ask, 'Have the Tommies got a new weapon?'

No one knew the answer.

Returning somewhat depressed to his own boat, Hirschfeld found the commander on his bunk opposite the radio room.

'Have we passed the final test?' asked Hirschfeld. 'Or do we have to repeat the training?'

'I suppose you would fancy another bout of training?' remarked the commander.

'Well, at the moment it seems as if it is pure hell out there in the Atlantic.'

Fischer jumped up and stuck his head into the radio room.

'So you have heard! You radio operators seem to know everything, but you must keep your mouth shut about this. You are not to mention this here. Is that clear?'

Hirschfeld promised. It wasn't easy. The news didn't provide a terribly comfortable feeling about going to war.

:: Dönitz ::

Dönitz reports the events more precisely but without any great emotion other than saying that the losses hit him and the U-boat Command staff especially hard. Following that, he goes on to exalt the men who had just been lost. Dönitz also explains that at the beginning of March he had moved the centre of operations further north, to the area just south of Iceland because he had the impression that Britain had diverted its convoys into colder waters. By the end of the month he revised these plans and evacuated that area again. After the war, Eberhard Godt (Head of the U-boat Operations Department) said in an interview that Dönitz was so shattered by the news that at one stage he withdrew into his office alone and only emerged a long time later with red eyes; suggesting he might have shed some tears.

:: JS ::

The U-boats lost during March 1941 were as follows:

U47 (Kptlt. Günther Prien), cause of sinking still unknown. No survivors. Last radio report sent at 04.54 hours on 7 March.

U70 (Kptlt. Joachim Matz), depth charged on 7 March 1941 by the corvettes *Arbutus* and *Camelia* while the boat was on its first operational patrol (25 survivors including the commander).

U99 (Kptlt. Otto Kretschmer), depth charged by HMS *Walker* on 17 March 1941 (40 survivors including the commander).

U100 (Kptlt. Joachim Schepke), rammed on 17 March by HMS *Vanoc* after having been attacked by HMS *Walker* very close to where *U99* was sunk (6 survivors).

U551 (Kptlt. Karl Schrott), depth charged by the converted trawler HMS *Visenda* during its first operational patrol on 23 March (no survivors).

In addition to these,

U76 (Oblt.z.S. Friedrich von Hippel), depth charged by HMS *Wolverine* and HMS *Scarborough* on 5 April while on its first operational patrol (40 survivors).

March 1941 also marks another significant turning point of the war at sea. During the autumn of 1940, each U-boat at sea was sinking almost six ships per month. When adding the general wartime over-estimation to this, people at the time could well have thought that the figure was as high as nine or more. There was a dramatic drop in these figures at the end of December and the statistics for March 1941 showed that less than two ships were sunk per month per U-boat at sea; as low as they had been a year earlier, when U-boats were still operating under the tight restrictions imposed on them by the Prize Regulations. It appears as if this turbulent and most significant phase of history has hardly been recognised and very little has been published about the causes and effects of that period. The overall successes of U-boats increased because larger numbers were appearing at the front, but the performance of each individual boat was getting worse.

:: The British Side ::

The Monthly U-boat Offensive Reviews offer a few explanations about this turn of events and suggest that the Germans had realised Britain had come to terms with the new attack method, therefore U-boats were now afraid of being counter-attacked while approaching convoys. It was also thought that the firing of star shells to illuminate the enemy at night had such a strong psychological effect upon U-boat men that they had abandoned the short-range surface attack at night. The Reviews go on to add that the evasive routing of convoys, introduced shortly before Christmas 1940 will have made it more difficult for U-boats to find targets. 'Evasive routing' seems to have been one of the most important countermeasures at this time. Masters of merchant ships usually met before the convoy sailed to be briefed as to the best route to avoid the majority of U-boats known to be at sea. At the same time they were given details of any drastic changes of course to be taken at sea if U-boats were reported to be in their path.

The Monthly Countermeasures Report state that operations against U-boats had been more successful in March 1941 than in any other month, but one has to look especially hard among masses of small print to find that *U100* might have escaped had she not been caught by HMS *Vanoc*'s radar. The word 'radar' had hardly been coined and the report uses to old name of ASV and RD/F. The first initials come from 'Air to Surface Vessel' because the equipment was used in aircraft before it was adapted for surface ships. The other stood for 'Radio Direction Finder'. Searching for contemporary information about this equipment is not easy. No one seems to have made a great song and dance about its introduction, perhaps because it did not produce any significant results at first. The report stated, in January 1941, that the introduction of ASV had been a disappointment. It produced reasonable results when conditions were good, but for most of the time the small escorts, with their receiver so close to the water, found that waves also reflected a mass of echoes, making it exceedingly difficult to distinguish between these and the tiny silhouette of a surfaced U-boat. The technical boffins were quick in finding a solution by merely making the device less sensitive and reducing its range from 10 to 5 miles.

The Monthly Anti-Submarine Report for February 1941 gives more specific details and says that Radio Direction Finders of Type 286M were fitted to 42 escorts and another two dozen were in the process of having the gear added. The ranges for these sets were as follows:

	Normal	*Maximum*
U-boat in surface trim	4,000 yds (3.6 km)	5,000 yds (4.5 km)
U-boat trimmed down	2,000 yds (1.8 km)	3,000 yds (2.7 km)
Aircraft at 2,000 ft	12 miles (19 km)	25 miles (40 km)
Destroyer	4 miles (6.5 km)	6 miles (9.7 km)
Large merchant ship	6 miles (9.7 km)	10 miles (16 km)

These figures are especially interesting because *U110* (Kptlt. Fritz-Julius Lemp) was close to the convoy (HX112) under attack by *U99* and *U100*. Had he been better informed about its exact position, he might have got there a little earlier. His attention during the calmness of the night was first taken by half a dozen torpedo detonations, some of them with such brilliance that it appeared as if a searchlight was illuminating one of the escorts. A little later Lemp saw destroyers dropping depth charges in the distance while sending wild Morse messages with lamps at the same time. Feeling the opposition was too alert and too determined, *U110* crept away quietly to return to port a few days later. Lemp almost certainly witnessed the sinking of *U99* or *U100* or both from a range of about five or so miles, just out of range of the radar then being used. Had he gone closer, he might have shared his colleagues' dramatic fate.

The big problem to have hit the Royal Navy so especially hard was that U-boats were not attacking from submerged positions, where they would have fired a salvo of torpedoes to get a hit. (For example, HM Submarine *Saracen* under Iwan Raikes attacked two small Italian ships of just over 1,000 tons each from ranges of 750 and 1,600 yards, shooting a salvo of three torpedoes on each occasion.) Instead of this U-boats approached on the surface at night, where Asdic could not detect them. The Germans called it 'short range attack at night'. U-boats closed in to about half a kilometre, often penetrating into the ranks of the convoy to choose the biggest and most valuable targets at point-blank range. The first person to use this technique was Kapitänleutnant Erich Topp on 24 August 1940 when he fired all three torpedoes from *U57*'s bow tubes, one after the other and sunk the British steamers *Saint Dunstan* 5,681 GRT) and *Cumberland* (10,939 GRT) and damaged SS *Havidar* (5,407 GRT) in Convoy OB202. Following this, such procedure became common practice, and it worked exceedingly well until the bad weather made operations too difficult and then, when the weather improved in spring of the following year, radar made it possible to 'see' surfaced submarines on the darkest of nights. The big handicap was that radar was going to take a while before it became really effective. So, although this new invention had its first major success in March 1941, some months were to pass before U-boat men at the receiving end were going to be worried by this new introduction.

Radar may have been used by Britain for the first time, but it was hardly a new invention. The Germans had been using it experimentally with considerable success since the early 1930s. The major handicap was that naval officers had to have had a leaving certificate from a grammar school to be accepted by the navy and to get this they had spent more time discussing literature and copying Latin texts than studying practical physics. Wolfgang Hirschfeld makes the comment that even high-powered officers like Heinrich ('Ajax') Bleichrodt relied blindly on their mechanical aids and cursed them like hell when they didn't work, without under-standing why things as simple as their sound detection gear wasn't producing the expected results in unfavourable conditions. The light cruiser *Königsberg* was fitted with an experimental radar set as early as 1938 or even a year or two earlier. It enabled the ship to negotiate the narrow channel leading from Wilhelmshaven to the deep water of the North Sea during the thickest of fogs by showing up the buoys on both sides at a time when other ships couldn't move. Despite this, the majority of officers were hostile to the new invention and research into radar was abandoned shortly after the start of the war.

U-boats were not the Royal Navy's only problem in March 1941. There had also been most worrying surface warship activity in the Atlantic and the first auxiliary or 'ghost' cruisers had set out in March–April 1940 to provide the Admiralty with a considerable headache. Despite the achievements of these ships being nowhere near as effective as the few U-boats, they had the potential to decimate entire convoys and also destroying the British makeshift auxiliary cruisers used to protect them. This furore is discussed exceedingly well by Patrick Beesly and by Dönitz and therefore does not need to be covered in this book, other than to emphasise that surface ship activity played a major role during this stage of the war.

The astonishing point about this fateful March of 1941 is that the serious losses of U-boats passed off without having created widespread alarm in the German Navy and also no one on the British side celebrated either. The U-boat war was becoming more intensive and everybody seemed to have been busy preparing for worse times ahead. Long after the war, while attempting to discuss the influence March 1941 had on U-boat men, one kept meeting the same answers, that the vast majority had not been unduly perturbed. One can only assume from such reactions that the propaganda system worked exceedingly well in softening the heavy blow and diverting people's thoughts into other spheres. So most people didn't even notice the downturn.

Chapter 5

Special Intelligence
Enters the War – May 1941

:: Dönitz on Radio ::

Dönitz states that the possibility of radio transmissions from U-boats being detected by direction finders had already played a part in his pre-war training schedules and the U-boat Command studied this with great care from the beginning of the war. He goes on to quote some results from this study as they were recorded in his logbook, as follows: the British were capable of detecting radio transmissions from U-boats, but the system incorporated considerable errors. The smallest of these occurred near the French coast where a difference of 30 nautical miles was recorded. Once further away from the coast, say a distance of more than 300 nautical miles, then the error was more likely to be between 60 and 80 nautical miles. The worst mistake was at a distance of 600 nautical miles where an error of 320 nautical miles was recorded.

It was obvious to the U-boat Command that these errors were likely to improve in favour of the opposition and that Britain would enlarge and improve its radio direction finder net; with stations as far apart as the north of Scotland, Land's End in the south, in the newly occupied Iceland and along the Canadian coast. This produced the great debate within the U-boat Command as to how far it was necessary to use radio in order to drive home attacks. This, in turn, resulted in standing orders that radio should be used in operations areas only to make tactically important reports or when asked to do by the U-boat Command or when the boat's position had been discovered by the opposition. During passage to and from operations areas U-boats were free to make greater use of their radios as long as they were not passing through areas occupied by other U-boats, so that their operations should not be compromised. There was also some technical advice to constantly change frequencies to make the tracking of signals more difficult.

:: JS ::

Dönitz goes on to explain how plans were conceived to lead the opposition astray by ordering U-boats to send fake messages from areas being evacuated. All this gives the impression that the U-boat Command hardly considered the possibility of anyone breaking the secret radio code. Yet this subject was also uppermost in Dönitz's mind, although he hardly mentions it in his memoirs. He discussed the secret U-boat code on several occasions with the Supreme Naval Command but on each occasion the 'experts' there found a set of good reasons why the opposition's reading of the radio code could not have been at the heart of any problem. The navy's coding machine, which can be referred to by its generic name of 'Enigma', was so complicated that cracking it was believed to be more than impossible and this belief persisted with stubborn strength until at least the late 1970s. Even if a machine was captured, it would become useless at the end of the period for which the owner carried documentation about the necessary settings.

Many U-boat commanders were far more paranoid about the use of radio than the small staff of the U-boat Command's Operations Room. Immediately after the war, when Günter Hessler compiled 'The U-boat War in the Atlantic', a team of German naval officers combed through logbooks and the sunk U-boat list to work out which ones had used their radio shortly before a serious attack. Otto Kretschmer didn't acquire the nickname 'Silent Otto' because he was less talkative than other officers but because he refused to transmit messages unless the opposition knew his position. Bleichrodt and many others even refused to answer urgent calls from the U-boat Command; as a result some were classified as sunk. This, incidentally, did not mean that their radio rooms were shut down. Only the transmitters were turned off. The receivers remained on and the radio crews were kept busy decoding messages from HQ and from other boats.

:: Radio from the British Side ::

Patrick Beesly states that the importance of capturing Enigma-related material from various weather trawlers and then from *U110* (Kptlt. Fritz-Julius Lemp) cannot be over-emphasised. The Royal Navy's boarding party under Sub-Lieutenant David Balme recovered the entire undisturbed contents of the radio room from *U110* and would have taken the transmitters and receivers as well, had these fitted through the hatches. They had already been unscrewed when the men discovered that the apparatus must have been assembled inside the U-boat and couldn't be taken out. The material from *U110* gave Bletchley Park more than just U-boat settings, it also provided the key for German supply ship operations around the time the battleship *Bismarck* was embarking on its one and only voyage.

Patrick Beesly goes into great detail, saying that the material from *U110* resulted in Bletchley Park being able to decipher some messages so that the Operational Intelligence Centre at the Admiralty could read them at about the same time as the people whom they were intended for. The boat was captured on 9 May 1941 and sank on the 11th while being towed by HMS *Bulldog*. It had set out from Lorient in France on 15 April. Being a long-range, ocean-going Type IXB meant it had documentation on board for up until the beginning of July and this arrived in Britain during the middle of June. Harry Hinsley adds more details, saying that the radio codebooks from *U110* provided a means of breaking 'officer only' messages for the rest of the war. He also makes the point that Bletchley Park, with its original name of GC and CS (Government Code and Cypher School), could read May's general naval traffic with a delay of three to seven days.

:: JS ::

Over the years there have been a number of bloodcurdling reports about David Balme shooting Fritz-Julius Lemp as he clambered back onto his U-boat to sink it, but all these stories have to be fabrications. Anyone examining the facts as they were recorded by Lemp's own crew must come to the conclusion that he almost certainly drowned in the cold Atlantic after having suffered serious concussion and having laid unconscious on the control room floor before his men helped him or almost carried him up to the top of the conning tower. It would appear that he was hardly capable of making the decision to abandon ship. He almost certainly never got back to his boat after he had abandoned it.

Moving on from this 'Secret Capture', the sinking of the *Bismarck* is well covered by Dönitz, Beesly and it is also mentioned by Constance Babington-Smith, but one important modification, which has only recently become available, needs to be added. That is that Flying Officer Michael Suckling was not responsible for detecting *Bismarck* and *Prinz Eugen* in the Norwegian fiords. At least one radio signal from *Bismarck* was decrypted and its approximate position confirmed by radio direction finders, but the Admiralty felt it was necessary to make visual contact by aircraft so as not to give away the fact that Bletchley Park was reading the signals. Therefore pilots were sent to Norway, despite appalling weather, and Suckling did spot the battleship and the heavy cruiser in Norway. The rest of the story is now well known. *Bismarck* was hunted to extinction and went down on 27 May 1941.

What is less well known and probably even more significant than the sinking of *Bismarck* is that there were also ten supply ships at sea during this period and only one of them returned to base. The rest were systematically hunted down and either captured, scuttled or sunk. Dönitz deals with the *Bismarck* operation in some depth, but does not mention this supply ship disaster, despite him having taken advantage of the situation to send U-boats a little further afield than they could have managed without replenishment at sea. Using that wonderful illuminator 'hindsight', one wonders why the sinking of such a large number of supply ships didn't ring any alarm bells in Germany. Several enquiries were held, but for some reason the possibility of Britain breaking the radio code was dismissed on each occasion.

Sinking such a large number of ships could easily compromise the Enigma secret and German Naval Intelligence was not Britain's only problem as far as this was concerned. Sooner or later British sea-going naval officers and members of Coastal Command were likely to ask why there had been such a sudden boost in successes. This led to the real problem that even some prisoner of war, perhaps a crashed airman, could give the Germans a clue that Britain might be reading their secret code. The Monthly Countermeasures Reports for May and June 1941 explain how the North Atlantic defences were strengthened by escorts from the Royal Canadian Navy and from additional ships handed over by the Americans. In addition to this, a refuelling base was made available in Hjalfjord (Iceland) to give escorts a longer endurance in the areas where U-boats were known to be operating. So, anyone reading the reports could be satisfied that nothing untoward or new had been introduced and the sudden surge in success was merely due to a double ration of what had been issued before. So, it was not difficult for people to imagine that ships sent out to deal with *Bismarck* ran into the German tankers in distant waters by chance.

There seems to be some dispute among reliable sources about the number of supply ships and tankers lost around the *Bismarck* operation. In view of this it may be worth adding a list of ships lost in June 1941. They were as follows:

Belchen, sunk 3 June
Esso Hamburg, scuttled 4 June
Gedania, captured 4 June
Gonzenheim, scuttled 4 June
Egerland, sunk 5 June
Friedrich Breme, sunk 12 June
Lothringen, sunk 15 June
Babitonga, scuttled 21 June
Altertor, scuttled 23 June
Spichern, returned to St. Nazaire

:: Anti-Submarine Reports Continued ::

U110 is not identified in contemporary accounts and HMS *Bulldog, Amazon* and *Rochester* get only a brief mention for having located U-boats attacking Convoy OB318 with the note that *Broadway* and *Aubretia* joined in the hunt, which might have resulted on at least one U-boat having been sunk. The report goes on to say that that there were even more U-boats at sea in June than in May and this gave rise to the following figures:

Type of attack in 1941	May	June
All attacks against U-boats:	64	82
Attacks by surface craft:	47	50
Attacks by aircraft:	15	32
Attacks by submarine:	2	?

The report then added that with Iceland having been occupied by British forces it was possible to escort convoys all the way across the Atlantic by the end of 1941 and the Countermeasures for June conclude by saying that the disappointment of the German Admiralty must have been very bitter, for, in addition to the comparative lack of success against merchant vessels, they suffered the severe loss of two or possibly three U-boats.

[There is another most interesting post-war postscript to add to the *U110* saga. Enigma machines remained in use by several nations during the Cold War era and therefore it was of paramount importance that the Bletchley Park secret didn't leak out. It would seem that the rumblings of Britain having cracked the code vibrated after the war. Thus one wonders whether the publishing of Stephen Roskill's book *The Secret Capture* was authorised by the Lords Commissioners of the Admiralty to suggest that Britain might have read the code for a few weeks after the capture of *U110*. In his official history, *The War at Sea*, Roskill mentions that *U110* had been sunk but then brought out this additional book in 1959, supposedly 'to put the record straight'. He describes the capture, but does not mention the breaking of the code.]

Chapter 6

Fragmentation of Strength – Summer 1941

:: Dönitz ::

Dönitz makes the point that investigations (definitely in the plural) within the U-boat Command into why it was so difficult to find convoys during the year 1941 always kept coming back to the same common denominator; that there were not enough eyes searching for them. This led him to call his Chapter Ten 'Shortages and Fragmentation'. It was going to be at least another year before the escalation of the submarine-building programme made any significant impact at sea and the shortage of boats was first reduced by accepting a group of Italian submarines to operate in the Atlantic from their own base in Bordeaux and to make use of reconnaissance aircraft.

Dönitz covers both Italian submarines in the Atlantic and reconnaissance aircraft in depth and both subjects are mentioned in British documents as well, but the happenings were very much on a tit for tat scale, requiring little comment. The fragmentation of forces, emphasised by Dönitz by using it in his chapter heading, is in many ways far more significant inasmuch that it resulted in more widespread consequences. Therefore it aroused notable comment on both sides, with Britain benefitting enormously from some of the defragmentation. Dönitz's doctrine was to send U-boats to operation areas as close to home ports as possible and he calculated his successes in the number of ships/tonnage sunk per U-boat at sea. In view of this he was against going further afield, even when higher authorities argued that this would help to draw the opposition's forces away from dangerous hotspots. Despite running his own show, there were times when Dönitz was ordered to employ U-boats away from the main convoy routes. For example, in June 1941 eight U-boats had to go into the Baltic for operations against Russian forces, although there were hardly any targets for them. Later, before there was any evidence of large scale shipping running to North Russia, other boats were dispatched to the Polar seas where they encountered meagre traffic consisting of such small ships that they were hardly worth a torpedo.

Some of this fragmentation of U-boat operations created noteworthy hazards for Britain and there were times when several African ports had to be closed until minesweeping units could be sent there to ensure the approaches were free from obstructions. In addition to this, the U-boat activity in far-off waters made it necessary to divert shipping along irritating detours, avoiding the troublesome areas. At first Britain did not know where long-distance U-boats were likely to strike and even if they did, the U-boats were so far ahead to make it pointless in sending any anti-submarine forces after them. So, it was very much a case of using the evasive routing techniques, which had stood Admiralty in good stead since the autumn of 1940. U-boats sent to southern waters, where there was hardly any opposition, reaped a magnificent harvest. In fact the most successful single wartime patrol took place during this time when *U107* under Kapitänleutnant Günter Hessler headed into the waters off Freetown.

:: Fragmentation from the British Side ::
Patrick Beesly deals with the second half of 1941 in great detail, under the heading 'Special Intelligence at Last'. This is most significant because 1941 was the time when the highly secret Submarine Tracking Room at the Admiralty's Operational Intelligence Centre in London started to bite with great force. Sadly much of this operation remained so highly secret for so long after the war that much of the information about how it worked has now been lost and the majority of people who knew how it was done have died without having left memoirs.

The supply ships lost after *Bismarck*'s cruise were not the only ones to suffer from the combined brilliance of the people at Bletchley Park and Rodger Winn's Submarine Tracking Room. Nobody has ever explained in detail how this enigmatic genius ended up tracking U-boats. The fact that he was a disabled civilian, unable to stand upright for any great length of time and that he probably became the first civilian ever to end up holding the rank of Royal Navy Captain goes some way to illustrate that no one contributed more to the outcome of the war at sea than Rodger Winn and his small staff. So Patrick Beesly's (Winn's deputy) comments are exceedingly valuable.

The loss of the supply ships around the *Bismarck* operation put long-range U-boat operations into such a dire predicament that some plans for going into distant waters had to be scrapped and, at the same time, auxiliary cruisers were called upon to supply U-boats. They used their radios so infrequently that the Operational Intelligence Centre never gained an insight into their activities and the only information available came from distress calls and from a few other scattered sources. Now, suddenly and without any warning, someone in the German Naval High

Command made that fateful decision to use *Atlantis* as a supply ship for the few U-boats in southern water and therefore the position of the raider was broadcast in U-boat code, which Bletchley Park had no problems in reading. The Operational Intelligence Centre in London reacted quickly and the Admiralty dispatched a heavy cruiser to the critical re-fuelling area. Consequently HMS *Devonshire* sank *Atlantis* on 22 November 1941 on her 622nd continuous day at sea. This story is now so well known that it should not be necessary to go into great detail. The dedicated submarine supply ship *Python* picked up survivors from *Atlantis*. Eight days later, on 30 November, another heavy cruiser, HMS *Dorsetshire*, sank the *Python* and survivors were then brought home by a number of German and Italian submarines. This made it quite plain to the U-boat Command that there was no longer any point in running long-distance operations with surface supply ships. This realisation came at about the same time as the United States joined in the war and this turn of events made it more than necessary to supply U-boats at sea if they were going to drive home their attacks in such far-off waters. Special supply submarines were already under construction, but it was going to be a while before these could put to sea.

By the summer of 1941, the secret Operational Intelligence Centre at the Admiralty in London was being broken by the weight of its own output and by the quantities of information being drawn in. This made it necessary to enlarge the outfit with more people, all of whom needed well above average intelligence. However, they were not magicians and for much of the time merely made use of whatever information Germany supplied and supplemented this with additional details from other sources. All this made the large number of successes of 1941 possible. Perhaps the most significant point of this input is that both Germany and Bletchley Park expected a captured Enigma machine to become useless once the documentation to operate it became out of date, but this didn't happen.

The Enigma machine had a plug board at the front with 26 double sockets. Wires with plugs at each end had to be inserted into these, to connect in the right order according to the settings of the day. This alone could produce more than 500,000,000,000 variations. The next step was to choose three wheels from a set of five to seven and place these in the correct order. Then each of these wheels had to be rotated to the correct starting position. This makes the number of variations almost endless and it was thought to be impossible to operate one of these machines without the documentation giving the daily settings. Yet astonishingly enough Bletchley Park was now so advanced that messages were still being read with a delay of only a few days. Dönitz himself made a significant contribution to the reading of the secret code by constantly bombarding commanders at sea with masses of information, thinking that the signals from his land-based transmitters were safe.

British Anti-Submarine Report, August 1941

During the month of August 1941, shipping casualties were comparatively light and so far as is known, fewer than thirty ships were torpedoed. More than thirty U-boats were operating in the Atlantic: it follows that some of them failed to sink even one ship during their August cruise.

A prominent feature of the enemy's strategy was the maintenance of a strong force of U-boats across the normal routes of convoys passing west of Ireland to and from Gibraltar and Freetown and the use of numerous Focke-Wulf Condor planes for almost daily reconnaissance of these routes. Attacks by such aircraft on convoys have become rarer, but their co-operation with U-boats as mobile reporting and directing stations increased markedly during August. It would seem that the enemy have a fairly shrewd estimate of the cycle of OG and OS convoys, and working from this as a datum, they appear to send the Condors to search out each day the area in which such a convoy is likely to be found, assuming it to have left home ports on a given day. Each day, even if no sighting has been affected, the search is moved further along the supposed route towards Gibraltar, and if contact is once made, very tenacious efforts are apparent thereafter to renew it on the following and subsequent days. The U-boats appear to depend on the aircraft's assistance in finding the convoy even more than was formerly the case and, in these circumstances, the role of the shadowing U-boat decreases in importance, leaving all U-boats more freedom to attack the convoy at night as soon as a favourable opportunity presents itself.

For the first time this month there were indications that U-boats made deliberate attacks on escorts, and it would seem that, in future, we must reckon an attack on our escort ships as an accepted U-boat policy.

There are also indications that U-boats are, at times, carrying out long range attacks on our convoys, probably firing a 'browning' salvo from a position on the bow or ahead. [A 'browning shot' was one directed at the middle of a group with the hope of hitting something.]

British Countermeasures Report – Summer of 1941

[*U110*'s 'Secret Capture', the sinking of battleship *Bismarck* and the loss of the nine supply ships took place in May – June 1941.] The British Counter-measure Reports state that many more U-boats were at sea in June than in May and the number of attacks on U-boats rose to 82. Of these 50 were made by surface vessel and 32 by aircraft. There were more accurate attacks in June than in any other month and the lack of successful U-boat activity was entirely due to the increased efficiency of British countermeasures.

Arrangements for escorting HX and SC convoys between Newfoundland and Iceland were completed and a force of RN and RCN destroyers, sloops and trawlers assembled at St. John's in Newfoundland. The first escorts sailed with Convoy HX129 on 31 May and Convoy OB331 was escorted from Iceland to the west. Later it was decided to escort convoys all the way from Halifax and this was made possible by Canada supplying a large force of corvettes, destroyers and other vessels.

The Germans hunted in vain for British transatlantic convoys until 23 June when Convoy HX133 was located. Then a large number of U-boats moved to the reported position to deliver the much overdue concentrated attack. However, early knowledge of the impending attack and fortunate disposition of anti-submarine forces enabled the escorts of this convoy to be reinforced.

Two ships from Convoy HX133 were damaged and five ships were sunk during surface attacks at night and another one went down later in daylight as a result of a submerged attack. In return, a number of U-boats received such incredible hammerings that it was assumed they had been sunk. Three boats, *U138*, *U147* and *U556*, were definitely sunk and the report for June ends with the comment the Germany's disappointment must have been bitter, for, in addition to the comparative lack of success against merchant vessels, the U-boats suffered the serious loss of three of their number. [Putting this a little more into statistical perspective, of the ships mentioned above, three were attacked by *U203* under Kptlt. Rolf Mützelburg, one by *U371* under Kptlt. Heinrich Driver, two by *U651* under Kptlt. Peter Lohmeyer, one by *U79* under Kptlt. Jost Metzler and three by *U564* under Kptlt. Teddy Suhren. This means there were another five U-boats in the group, which didn't damage or sink a target.]

July 1941 started out with even better results, without any U-boat attacks at all against convoys until the 26th. Five ships were lost after they had dispersed from the convoy and two independently sailing ships were sunk. This seemed to prove that evasive routing and well-protected convoys was working very well. The July report also made the point that improvements had been made in defensive arrangements and every effort was being made to press on with offensive weapons, which will ensure that a U-boat, once located, has only a slight chance of survival.

Chapter 7

New Weapons for Hunting Old U-boats – Summer 1941

:: JS ::

In addition to fine-tuning existing weapons, two significant new systems were introduced in 1941. One of these was an ahead-throwing mortar called Hedgehog and the other a High Frequency (Radio) Direction Finder originally abbreviated as H/F D/F and called 'Huff Duff'. The U-boat Command did not discover the existence of 'Huff Duff' until June 1944. Therefore this made a significant contribution to the Battle of the Atlantic and possibly played a greater role than the decoding of signals. It was introduced around the summer of 1941 and in use in fairly large numbers by the autumn. However, there were numerous teething troubles and several months were to pass before it really started to bite in earnest. 'Huff Duff' had the great advantage of being able to pinpoint the direction from which even brief radio signals were coming from. This specially-condensed code was too short for conventional radio direction finders.

The great advantage was that when this equipment was installed on both escorts and on some merchant ships it would indicate the start of an attack and give a fairly accurate indication of where it was going to come from. Once in their operation areas, U-boats maintained radio silence, but they sent a flock of signals the moment they started their run-in to attack. This was necessary to prevent two U-boats from attacking each other or colliding. This moment was also thought to have been an ideal time to transmit any waiting messages. Once the convoy commodore and the escorts were alerted that an attack was being launched, they could position a ship with radar in the U-boat's path and then after having detected it on the surface, force it under, to use Asdic to locate it for depth charging. In 1941 there were still not enough escorts to hunt U-boats to extinction, so boats had to be forced under and the hunter then returned to his position in the defensive screen around the convoy as quickly as possible to prevent another U-boat from slipping through the gap. H/F D/F made it exceedingly difficult for U-boats to get within firing range and most U-boats were driven away, frequently with serious damage.

:: The British Side ::

H/F D/F – Huff Duff

The information from a report about H/F D/F, released in 1941 is included in a later section on page 169.

Hedgehog – The Ahead Throwing Mortar

The other new introduction to hit U-boats was an ahead throwing mortar called Hedgehog. Depth charges had been the major weapon for dealing with submerged submarines before its introduction and these had several major disadvantages. First, the hunter lost Asdic contact once he got too close to his submerged target and then he had to go high speed so that the depth charges he dropped did not blow off his own stern. This interval gave the submerged submarine the opportunity of also increasing speed and hopefully evading the main thrust of the depth charges. The other difficulty was that it took 15–20 minutes before the disturbance created by the detonations subsided so that Asdic could be used again and therefore the search had to be started again from the very beginning.

Hedgehog had the advantage of throwing a large number of smaller charges forward and these exploded only if they hit a solid object, so there were no superfluous detonations to swamp Asdic. The device was described in the September 1941 issue of the Monthly Anti-Submarine Reports as follows:

A new A/S weapon, a multi-spigot mortar, commonly known as the *Hedgehog* has been developed. It throws twenty-four projectiles fitted with contact fuses so as to produce a pattern in the form of a ring whose centre is about 250 yards ahead of the ship. The fuse is armed after travelling about 10 ft through the water at high speed.

The *Hedgehog* has theoretically a greater chance of killing a submarine than a depth charge because it incorporates four important principles: – first the ahead throwing principle leads to a reduction of 'blind' time, secondly the multiple small charge principle, thirdly the contact principle and lastly training up to plus or minus 15 degrees.

The Ahead Throwing Principle
At present the position of the submarine can be determined with considerable accuracy but errors arise in a depth charge attack owing to the fact that a considerable time of 45 to 90 seconds must elapse between the loss of contact and the depth charges getting to the right place. In *Hedgehog* this 'dead' time is reduced to 15 – 20 seconds, with a consequent higher accuracy in placing the pattern.

The Multiple Small Charge Principle

A depth charge containing 300 lb of high explosives with a lethal range of 21 feet gives a target area, over which the explosion would be lethal, of 10,000 square feet for a 517-ton U-boat. A 30 lb charge with a lethal range of 6 feet, designed to explode only on contact, will have a lethal area of about 2,100 square feet for the same U-boat. Thus ten 30 lb charges of this kind will have about twice as good a chance of killing as a single 300 lb charge.

The Contact Principle

The contact fuse, like the proximity fuse, works at all depths. This is of particular importance in view of the fact that the present A/S detection gear does not determine the depth of the submarine.

Training up to Plus or Minus 15 degrees

The accuracy is improved since even if the ship is on an incorrect course, allowance could be made by tilting the mounting. The contact charge as, however, no anti-morale effect if it misses, as the submarine crew may well be unaware that they are being attacked.

Attacks were usually made by approaching at slow speed in such a way that the target was almost straight ahead and firing at the moment the correct range was reached.

Chapter 8

Fast-Moving Patrol Lines – September to December 1941

:: Dönitz ::

The results for July and August 1941 were very poor, amounting to the sinking of 45 ships totalling 174,519 GRT. Therefore, Dönitz decided to push the U-boats further west and, depending on the number available, set up two to four different groups. Instead of keeping these in an operational area, moving slowly backwards and forwards in the path of an anticipated convoy (moving towards the convoy during the day and going on the same heading at night), the commanders were told to head forwards all the time at a comparatively high cruising speed. They were also ordered to go further west than they had been before, this time all the way across the Atlantic as far as the coast of Greenland. This new technique of 'fast-moving patrol lines' produced immediate results inasmuch that Convoy SC42 was discovered on 11 September and the attacking U-boats immediately sank 11 ships. Unfortunately heavy fog made it impossible to attack again during the following night, thus saving the convoy from further carnage. Other convoys were found as well, one of them by German air reconnaissance, and a number of ships were sunk, despite considerable defences. This brought the total for September up to 53 ships of 202,820 GRT. (Actually, 61 ships were sunk. There is also a discrepancy as far as dates concerned with Dönitz being a day or two 'behind', possibly because his boats often didn't report details until after the action or he didn't have all the details at his disposal when writing his book.)

:: JS ::

The figures quoted here in relation to the tonnage sunk are somewhat meaningless without the numbers being put into some sort of perspective. The Third Department of the Naval War Staff in Berlin made every effort to collect such statistics for the Battle of the Atlantic and came to the conclusion that 700,000 tons of shipping had to be sunk to make any significant impression upon Britain's performance. Almost 600,000 tons of this accounted for new ships being brought into service.

The High Command also realised that the Battle of the Atlantic was 'the' dominating factor of whatever else might be happening on land or in the air. The American official history of the war at sea by Samuel Eliot Morison gives some interesting information as far as these statistical numbers are concerned and state that, according to the training manual, the sinking of a 6,000-ton ship and a 3,000-ton tanker adds up to the following: 42 tanks, 8 six-inch howitzers, 88 25-pounder guns, 40 two-pounder guns, 24 armoured cars, 50 Bren carriers, 5,210 tons of ammunition, 600 rifles, 428 tons of tank supplies, 2,000 tons of stores and 1,000 tanks of fuel. To knock out a similar quantity the air force would need to fly 3,000 bombing sorties.

:: The British Side ::

The following excerpt is from the Monthly Anti-Submarine Report:

After two months of good luck, the tide of fortune turned against us in September 1941, and our losses rose sharply. The enemy, reaping the fruits of the 1939 programme of U-boat construction, was able to maintain in operation perhaps five times as many U-boats as were at sea a year ago. Yet their achievements were by no means equal to the exertions. In September 1940, with an average of seven U-boats at sea, the enemy secured the destruction of 265,000 tons of shipping; a year later his far greater efforts were rewarded with a tonnage smaller by 50,000 tons. A year ago U-boats were attacking our convoys with impunity. Rarely was a U-boat sighted during her attack, even more rarely was the enemy counterattacked. Today it is a matter for the keenest disappointment if a convoy is attacked and the enemy escapes unpunished.

The first convoy attacked in September was SC42, which was sighted by U-boats when it was proceeding to the eastward of Greenland. Protected by a slender escort consisting of HMCS *Skeena* and three RCN corvettes, later reinforced by HMCS ships *Chambly* and *Moosejaw*, who were carrying out a 'shake-down' cruise in the neighbourhood, it was heavily attacked on the night of 9th/10th September, twice in daylight on the following day and again on the second night, fifteen out of sixty-seven ships being torpedoed. The enemy paid a fair price, for this success, since *Chambly* and *Moosejaw* celebrated their first appearance with a convoy by sinking a U-boat [*U501*, Kptlt. Hugo Förster] as they were closing SC42. [Note there is a discrepancy here with Dönitz's account.]

On 11th September, the escort was strongly reinforced by the arrival of the United Kingdom escort group and aircraft from Iceland. An encouraging feature of the episode was that, although the U-boats are believed to have been present in some force, the attacks carried out by the

45

Canadian escort on the 9th and 10th, and by HM ships *Veteran* and *Leamington* and the aircraft, after their joining on the 11th, were enough to discourage them from further efforts until the night of 16th/17th, when another ship was torpedoed.

It is possible that the summer of 1941 has seen a change, this time in our favour.

It is to be hoped that it is not extravagant to say that the offensive is passing from the enemy to ourselves. Last autumn an experienced U-boat captain could pick his victims – a large tanker here, a 7,000-ton freighter there. By March of this year U-boat 'aces' had started to pay the price of over-confidence, and within a few months the enemy had lost a number of star performers. Now, though still hard to combat due to the increase in the number of U-boats at sea, attacks seem to have lost some of their finesse, and our larger escorts and better A/S measures have started to compensate for this increase.

:: Hirschfeld ::

Wolfgang Hirschfeld gives a vivid, personal account of the events in the Greenland area as *U109*, with her new commander (Kptlt. Heinrich Bleichrodt), joined the 'Mordbrenner' group in those treacherous waters: 'The natural conditions men endured in that harsh weather must have been horrendous. U-boats had at least the great advantage over escorts inasmuch that they could dive below the raging waves and the bitterly cold spray for the men to at least enjoy a meal and a rest in the calm peace of the depths. There was no such letup for men in escorts and many didn't even get a hot meal when Atlantic waves got too rough and wet.'

Chapter 9

Audacity – Auxiliary Aircraft Carriers Step in – Christmas 1941

:: JS ::

The rescue operation to save the survivors from the auxiliary cruiser *Atlantis* and the submarine supply ship *Python* was underway when another group of U-boats were tackling convoys on the approaches to Gibraltar. There U-boats found themselves confronted with another new introduction, an auxiliary aircraft carrier, namely HMS *Audacity*. She had been converted from the captured German freighter *Hannover* by first removing the superstructure and then adding a flight deck to the top of the hull. Life aboard these early escort carriers, as they were also called, must have been exceedingly harsh and it is necessary to pay a special tribute to the 'ground crews' who maintained the aircraft on an open deck, without cover and without anything preventing them from slipping into the often raging waves of the cold Atlantic.

These carriers were not the only new aerial introduction, May 1941 saw the first CAM or Catapult Aircraft Merchantman, the *Empire Rainbow*, put to sea. CAM ships, with a fighter sitting prominently on a catapult mounted on the bows, were regarded by many sailors of the time as a bad thing because it was bound to be an attraction for U-boats. The fighters were old ones, no longer suitable for serious combat where they would encounter strong opposition, but ideal to end their days by ditching into the Atlantic close to a ship for the pilot to be picked up. The first of these CAM ships to be sunk, *Empire Hudson* went down on 10 September as part of Convoy SC42 as a result of an attack by *U82* (Kptlt. Siegfried Rollmann). By that time some fifty CAM conversions had been ordered and their prominent silhouette had become a startling new feature. (SC42 is the convoy mentioned in the previous chapter.)

:: Dönitz ::

Dönitz writes that the opposition knew that U-boats were poised near Gibraltar and therefore assured that their convoys were well protected, this time with the first auxiliary aircraft carrier *Audacity*. U-boats attacked

Convoy HG76 night and day with great tenacity until 22 December 1941, but the results were most depressing. The aircraft carrier was sunk on the 21st by *U751* [Kptlt. Gerhard Bigalk] and the destroyer *Stanley* was sunk two days earlier by *U574* [Kptlt. Dietrich Gengelbach]. Otherwise only two ships from Convoy HG76 were hit. In return Germany lost five U-boats. (*U574*, *U131*, Fregkpt. Arend Baumann, *U127*, Kptlt. Bruno Hansmann, *U434*, Kptlt. Wolfgang Heyda, and *U567*, Kptlt. Engelbert Endrass.) Among these was one of the best commanders, Engelbert Endrass, who had started the war as first watch officer of *U47* [Kptlt. Günther Prien]. He had aimed the torpedoes in the Royal Navy's anchorage at Scapa Flow, which sank the battleship *Royal Oak* on the night of 13/14 October 1939.

Following this failure and also considering the unsatisfactory results during the last two months, the small U-boat Command Staff took the view that Germany was no longer in a position to attack convoys. Dönitz did not share their opinion, saying the recent defeat came about as a one-off occurrence against a heavily guarded convoy, when conditions were most unfavourable for U-boats. There was almost no wind, at worst only a slight breeze and for most of the time the sea was as calm as a duckpond, making the detection of U-boats very easy for the opposition. Dönitz had expected the convoy to be well protected, but it was not until he was writing his book, after having read Stephen Roskill's official history *The War at Sea* that he knew more precisely what had happened with this battle. The merchant ships were kept in port for a couple of weeks until an especially strong escort force could be assembled. This then consisted of the auxiliary aircraft carrier, 3 destroyers, 7 corvettes and 2 sloops; a formidable force, especially as with excellent flying conditions, aircraft were providing round-the-clock cover. In addition to this, aircraft from the British base at Gibraltar also escorted the convoy and the escorts were under command of Britain's most successful anti-submarine commander, Johnnie Walker. The conditions may have been weighed against Germany and the year 1941 ended with the U-boat Command deeply worried and in great sorrow, but the higher officers were looking forward to better successes in the new year.

:: **The British Side** ::
The Monthly Submarine Report states:

> In the Atlantic during December the U-boat effort exerted was on a similar scale to that experienced in the latter part of November; no serious burden of shipping casualties was sustained. The outstanding feature of this chapter of U-boat history was the prolonged engagement between the escorts of Convoy HG76 and a pack of half a dozen U-boats. Ably led by HMS *Stork*, the escorts sank three of the original group of

about six or seven U-boats, which followed the convoy from the vicinity of Gibraltar; they may also have sunk another U-boat belonging to a second party which apparently joined in the attacks at a later stage. Only two merchant ships of the convoy were lost, but unfortunately HM Ships *Stanley* and *Audacity* were sunk, the latter after her fighters had rendered invaluable service.

The Monthly Countermeasures against U-boats go into greater detail, as follows:

December was a memorable month. Many effective attacks were made; seven U-boats are known to have been destroyed; for the first time aircraft successfully carried out night attacks on U-boats; most important of all, the naval and air escort of a convoy combined together to form a particularly successful anti-submarine striking force.

These successes are indeed notable, but even they must give pride of place to the passage of Convoy HG76. Its sailing, originally arranged for last month, was delayed for about a fortnight and, while it lay waiting in harbour, there was great activity in, and to the westward of, the Straits of Gibraltar. U-boats were frequently sighted in the Western Approaches to the Straits, and our forces made a strong effort to close the Straits themselves. The aircraft establishment at Gibraltar was strengthened by the arrival of Hudson aircraft of 233 Squadron and by Swordfish aircraft of the Fleet Air Arm. In the second week of December the patrol of the Straits was temporarily lifted and the escort group thus released was sent out to reinforce the group escorting an approaching outward-bound Gibraltar convoy. Hopes of offensive action inspired this decision but they were in vain; it was perhaps unfortunate for the campaign on U-boats that the enemy failed to locate this very strongly escorted convoy, which arrived safely in harbour on 13th December.

HG76 sailed during the afternoon of 14th December. It consisted of 32 ships and had, for the first two days a double escort, and thereafter two sloops, three destroyers and seven corvettes, with the auxiliary aircraft carrier *Audacity* in company. Of the destroyers, two left the convoy to return to Gibraltar on the morning of the 18th and the third (HMS *Stanley*) was sunk in the early hours of the 19th, when stationed right astern of the convoy on the outer screen. *Audacity* was sunk during the evening of 21st December in a position about ten miles from the convoy, which she was leaving in the hopes of obtaining greater safety from her speed whilst acting independently at some 30 miles range.

During the 22nd, Liberator aircraft, which had flown out some 750 miles, gave the convoy air cover; the aircraft escort during the afternoon attacked one U-boat with depth charges and sighted and put down two others. Thanks to this effective air cover, combined with drastic evasive action and a dummy starshell battle staged to take place in the position in which the convoy should have been, the U-boats were shaken off and the convoy, passing south of Ireland, came safely into harbour.

This convoy had to fight its way through the enemy. The casualties on our side were two merchant ships out of 32 leaving Gibraltar, *Stanley* and *Audacity*; the enemy lost three U-boats for certain and two Focke-Wulfs, a third being damaged. It provided a good example of the effective combination of aircraft with surface anti-submarine striking forces. The new auxiliary aircraft carriers will carry aircraft capable of detecting U-boats by ASV and attacking them with depth charges. It is hoped that these ships will commission at the rate of one a month during 1942'. [These last two sentences must be underlined and it is most important to emphasise that those simple little aircraft from auxiliary aircraft carriers carried both radar capable of detecting surfaced U-boats and depth charges for attacking them. The CAM fighters, on the other hand, were mere 'eyes in the sky' and often could do no more than perhaps shoot down German reconnaissance aircraft with their .303 machine guns; many of them had no means of attacking U-boats.]

U-boats have hitherto regarded the darkness as their best friend. Prisoners have spoken with feeling of Coastal Command's daylight sweeps, which have forced them continually to dive; at night they have been able to feel reasonably safe on the surface, relaxing strained nerves as well as charging batteries. Now, if night detection and night attacks by aircraft prove successful, U-boat crews may come, instead, to dread nightfall. Attacks by day and attacks by night should have a cumulative effect upon their morale.

Though we know that we destroyed seven U-boats during the month, the enemy is building them faster than we can sink them. Every new U-boat at sea proportionately reduces the value of evasive routeing, which, though it has been carried out with success, is essentially defensive. The German Navy is again maintaining a large number of U-boats in the North Atlantic, and is also carrying out an offensive against us in the Mediterranean. It may be thought that the enemy will have difficulty in manning the U-boats now coming from the yards, but the problem is not beyond his solution, as long as he can find a keen and experienced officer to act as Captain and half a dozen officers and petty officers of average efficiency. As for the rest of the crew, a little training and a good deal of propaganda will provide him with a number of obedient ratings. This is the stuff of which successful U-boat crews can be made. [It is strange that the building yards were not bombed until the end of the war and even then some of the most significant destruction was carried out by ground troops after the ceasefire.]

Propaganda may be found a poor substitute for thorough training when it comes to action with a well-drilled team but it may well succeed when a U-boat crew realize that they have escaped from an awkward position because the attacking ship has been unready or inefficient. Thus the failure to set a pattern of depth charges correctly, the loss of Asdic contact when it should have been maintained, or some other mistake boosts the morale of propaganda-fed and inadequately trained Germans and transforms them into a confident and dangerous crew. The proof of the above fact can be found in the high percentage of U-boats that are sunk on their maiden war cruise. Furthermore, though we have sunk a satisfactory number of U-boats in the past few months we have mostly destroyed those commanded by the less distinguished captains. Too many 'aces' still remain at large.

Chapter 10

America Joins the War
Operation 'Paukenschlag' (The First
Thrust) – January 1942

:: JS ::

After more than half a century of being bombarded with intensive propaganda, many people do not know that the United States was hankering to join in the war from the very beginning and weighed its neutrality exceedingly heavily in Britain's favour. Right from the autumn of 1939 German ships were pursued by American warships broadcasting their position in plain language so that comparatively few Royal Navy units could take charge of valuable German ships. Later neutral United States warships escorted shipping into combat zones and then cried pitifully when they were attacked during the darkest of nights by U-boats, which couldn't identify their nationality. So in many ways the German admirals felt some relief when Hitler finally declared war on this peaceful, caring and badly done-by nation. Yet, at the same time, the move filled the majority of Germans with the deepest trepidation of having to face another powerful opponent.

:: Dönitz ::

Dönitz goes into some detail, explaining the belligerence of the United States before the 'official' outbreak of war with Germany on 11 December 1941. This happened less than six months after Germany found itself forced to invade the Soviet Union. Once again, the propaganda systems have assured that this was presented as Hitler's move to spread his powerbase further east, where in reality he was responding to intensive Russian preparations being made for an invasion of the west and the Germans felt it was necessary to nip this offensive in the bud before it was ready to strike. All this dives deeply into serious political history and the aim of writing this here is merely to put into perspective the feelings of German officers as they prepared to cross the Atlantic, to launch a submarine thrust against the most powerful nation on earth and one which was also a terribly long way from German bases.

While considering the American entry into the war, Dönitz makes the point that the International Tribunal at Nuremberg did recognise that, despite Germany having declared war against the United States, the attack by U-boats was not a 'War of Aggression'.

The Japanese attack against Pearl Harbor came on 7 December 1941 and it was two days later, on the 9th, that the German Naval War Staff informed the U-boat Command that all restrictions of operating in the western Atlantic against American forces had been lifted. There were no U-boats anywhere near those waters at the time, so the question of diverting units already at sea did not arise. Instead, shortly after this declaration, Dönitz asked for permission to send twelve U-boats across the Atlantic. In his book he also goes into considerable details of the general situation and the constraints he was working under at the time. Much of this has been written, re-written and chewed over by historians that the story of this first thrust, Operation 'Paukenschlag', is now well known. However, it does not, as so many have claimed, mean a 'roll on the drums', despite this still being the best translation. A 'Pauke' is the largest drum and a 'Paukenschlag' means something far more significant and much more impressive than a mere roll on the drums. It is pity that there is no equivalent English word. (The first pack to go to American waters was made up of *U66*, *U109*, *U123*, *U125* and *U130*.)

:: The British Side ::
The Monthly Reviews of the U-boat Offensive reported in January 1942 as follows:-

The month of January 1942 was a gloomy chapter in the history of the Battle of the Atlantic. A large force of U-boats, perhaps 20 in all, began simultaneously to operate off the Atlantic seaboard of the United States and in coastal areas of Nova Scotia and Newfoundland. Between 12th January, when the first casualty west of 60°W occurred, and the end of the month over 225,000 tons of shipping were sunk.

The westward movement of the U-boats had been foreseen as a probable development, but it did not prove possible to provide any anti-submarine protection for shipping passing such focal points as Cape Hatteras, North Carolina, or the entrance to Hampton Roads, Virginia, and a large proportion of the losses occurred in these localities. The U-boats operating in the far west have shown themselves to be very selective in their choice of targets, many tankers have been picked out and most of the ships attacked have been of substantial displacement. No escorted convoy was attacked or, apparently, reported. Logically enough, where worthwhile targets abounded in the form of single ships, the U-boats kept clear of escorts, whose attacks, even if only moderate damage had been inflicted, might well have prevented their return to their distant bases.

Very few details have so far been received in the Admiralty of the attacks carried out on the enemy. There was one promising attack by a Catalina on 21st January in a position to the south-west of Argentia [Newfoundland on Placentia Bay, near St. John's] and the Commander-in-Chief of the United States Fleet has reported that there is credible evidence of the sinking or seriously damaging of some six or seven U-boats up to the 7th February. [None were sunk.]

In other areas comparatively little occurred which is noteworthy. The total number of U-boats at sea in all areas, including the Mediterranean, is considered to have reached a new high peak of approximately 60 in the last week of the month, a substantial proportion of them were on passage to and from the American area.

The Countermeasures Report for January 1942 states:

An extraordinary change in the Battle of the Atlantic has occurred in the latter part of January. The enemy suddenly increased his effort and concentrated his forces in the West Atlantic area. With one exception, the convoys in this area have passed unassailed through waters in which many unescorted ships have been sunk. This policy of avoiding possibly expensive contact with our escort vessels has paid the enemy well. He has taken a very heavy toll of shipping in North American waters.

Unfortunately only scanty information is at present available of the Allied countermeasures in this area. It is, however, known that the Royal Canadian Navy, the Royal Canadian Air Force and the United States Navy have taken all possible countermeasures with the forces at their disposal. United States aircraft are making use of a 350-lb. anti-submarine bomb. A Catalina aircraft of 116 Squadron of the RCAF made a promising attack off Sydney, Cape Breton, on the 21st January, and the United States Naval Authorities announce that there is credible evidence of the sinking, or severely damaging, of a number of U-boats. [This is an interesting statement and one wonders whether the authors of the reports knew that it took a while before the Americans made any effort to combat U-boats in their waters.]

On the 26th January, the Free French corvette *Roselys* lightly rammed a U-boat, which was also attacked with depth charges, but unfortunately these were set to 100 ft and not to 50 ft; it is probable that the U-boat reached home. SS *Aagtekerk* is also reported to have made a promising attack. [No U-boats were lost.]

Only four convoys, in addition to the one attacked in West Atlantic area, were in contact with the enemy. In two cases, escort vessels were sunk – HMS *Culver* to the westward of Ushant, and HMS *Belmont* in a position 300 miles to the southward of Newfoundland – without attacks being made on merchant ships. Convoy SL97G was passing through the area in which *U93* [Oblt.z.S. Horst Elfe] was sunk and, although prisoners from her stated that there were other U-boats in the vicinity, the convoy was not attacked. [Forty men were saved.]

The night anti-submarine patrols initiated last month have been continued with some measure of success by the ASV-fitted Swordfish operating in the Mediterranean, but in the Bay of Biscay there were no night attacks during January.

The events in the West Atlantic are not only serious by reason of the loss of tonnage. Of even greater importance is the fact that the U-boat crews are gaining not only successes against shipping but also experience and confidence. Some of the ratings who return from these operations will form a valuable nucleus for the manning of the U-boats now coming from the yards in such numbers. Although there are a few new weapons with which to help defeat the U-boats, our main business is to perfect our tactics, training and tools, and to visualise beforehand opportunities which may arise, so that when they come and excitement is high, drill is perfect and nothing left to chance.

::JS::
Patrick Beesly adds only a few useful and unexpected comments to this chapter of the war, but he does give a good overview of the general situation at the time. He states that Rodger Winn had forecast a move into American waters as early as 29 December, but this could have hardly have come as a surprise to anyone, considering that Germany had declared war on 11 December, almost three weeks earlier.

Beesly also makes the point that it is now almost beyond belief that the United States was taken so much by surprise by the German onslaught. Exactly the same happened in Britain at the start of the war. After one year of fighting Britain had still not supplied its merchant ships with basic lifesaving equipment. Possibly the good reason for both nations sacrificing such a large number of sailors was to get greater support from their own considerable anti-war lobby by showing them that Germany was ruthlessly slaughtering the innocent. Another pointer showing in this direction was that many of the early British defences against an invasion were placed in places where they could be well seen, even when much better protected and better-concealed locations were on hand. So it seems as if inadequate defences were built to impress the local population, rather than to deter an invader.

Chapter 11

The U-boat Command's Biggest Blunder?

:: JS ::

When considering the war at sea in 1942, it is necessary to remember two important points, which often tend to be forgotten.

First, preparations had been ongoing since the autumn of 1941 to improve the security of the secret U-boat radio code and this was achieved by adding a fourth wheel to the original three in the Enigma machine. Each wheel was made slightly thinner to fit into the same slot. The switchover to the new code was made in February 1942 and at once made it impossible for Bletchley Park to decrypt the Atlantic signals. This state of affairs lasted until the end of the year, when one of these new machines was captured from *U559* under Kapitänleutnant Hans Heidtmann. So, for almost all of 1942 Britain was unable to read the Atlantic U-boat code. However, many other units such as the meteorological flights and coastal flotillas, continued to use the old system and in some cases their base stations decoded these signals and then coded them again with the new system before forwarding the data to Berlin. This gave the cryptanalysts at Bletchley Park the great advantage of knowing exactly what the 'unreadable' messages were saying and therefore helped them in cracking the new code.

This switch couldn't have been made at a more inappropriate time, however, because all the other parameters of the war at sea changed to such an extent that no one in Germany noticed the black out in Britain.

The other important point concerns the number of U-boats at sea. In 1940 and 1941 the number of U-boats at sea each day crept up to a maximum of thirty-eight. One third of these were usually on their way out, another third on their way back and the other third would have been spread over the various operational areas. This number also dropped down as low as eight and for much of the time was around a dozen rather than at the maximum.

In 1942 and early 1943 there was a dramatic increase, so that the number of boats at sea each day was as follows:

1942	Jan:	42
	Feb:	50
	Mar:	48
	Apr:	49
	May:	61
	Jun:	59
	Jul:	70
	Aug:	86
	Sep:	100
	Oct:	105
	Nov:	95
	Dec:	97
1943	Jan:	92
	Feb:	116
	Mar:	116
	Apr:	111
	May:	118
	Jun:	86

This shows that there were an incredibly large number of U-boats at sea for much of 1942, but the first large-scale convoy battle, the 'clash of the titans' when a large wolf pack attacked a convoy, didn't take place until March 1943. So, despite Britain being unable to understand the U-boat radio code, the Operational Intelligence Centre at the Admiralty in London was managing to route the majority of ships away from most of the U-boats.

:: Dönitz ::
Dönitz goes into considerable detail about U-boat production problems and explains how plans were frustrated by the weather. Early wartime plans had allowed for about twenty boats being commissioned every month, but the 1941/42 winter was so exceptionally cold that much of the southern Baltic froze solid meaning it was impossible to continue with training. In addition, the weather caused a considerable slow-down in the building programme. This reduced the number of boats coming to the front to an average of thirteen per month and at times this dropped as low as ten. The interesting point with this was that the building programmes were slowed down by the weather, but not stopped altogether. This resulted in a build-up of boats ready to go through their training and thus brought that considerable number to the front towards the end of 1942.

Chapter 12

War in American Waters. The Second and Later Thrusts – February 1942

:: Dönitz ::

Two things happened as a result of Operation 'Paukenschlag', the initial attack against the United States. First, long-range ocean-going boats were prepared to make for the Caribbean and, at the same time, smaller Type VIIC boats headed towards the more northerly waters on the western side of the Atlantic, where the distances involved were considerably shorter. These medium-sized sea-going types were initially sent to the area south of Halifax and from there individual boats penetrated further south, some of them going as far as New York. In many cases this unforeseen move hadn't been part of the operational plan, but to avoid the dreadful weather in the northern latitudes. (The first offensive against America was made up of long-range, ocean-going Types IX with double hulls, which could carry enough fuel for such long voyages, but they didn't stand up all that well to depth charging and were therefore not so suited to take the punishment being meted out by British escorts. Despite their size and extra range, they still needed supply tankers to make such long journeys really effective.)

Sending comparatively small submarines so far from home introduced a totally new dimension to U-boat warfare and created a situation not experienced before. For the first time since they had first been commissioned during the autumn of 1940, sea-going Type VIIC boats undertook voyages at the most economical speed for several days on end. This had never happened before because earlier conditions made it necessary for them to also travel at fast cruising speed or even increase to a higher fuel-guzzling speed while making for their operations areas nearer the British Isles. This crossing of the Atlantic established the fact that the machinery was considerably more economical than had previously been thought and there was no problem with medium-sized sea-going boats making such long voyages.

Dönitz goes on to say, 'It is noteworthy that the crews themselves made every effort to increase the time they could stay at sea and, without having been told, made considerable sacrifices to take on board more fuel and provisions.' This worried Dönitz because he knew that German U-boats were far more uncomfortable than submarines from other nations. They had been designed by the Supreme Naval Command to make use of as much tonnage as possible for creating the most powerful fighting weapon, without regard to the comfort of the crew or the requirements of provisions they had to carry. He was astonished that crews were prepared to give up what little comfort they had in order to improve their fighting efficiency. They even sacrificed their sleeping spaces so that they could be used to store more provisions. This went so far that he felt it was necessary to step in and give orders that they did not go too far and thus put their own safety at risk. (It might be thought likely that a callous commanding officer, who did not himself have to experience the miseries at sea, might come up with such a statement to justify his own heavy-handed actions. Yet, after the war, enough U-boat men confirmed that this was true.)

Towards the end of January 1942 U-boats in Germany were ordered to make for the French Biscay ports at high cruising speed so that they could be kitted out and refuelled there for crossing the Atlantic. This practice had just about been established when, suddenly, there came new orders from the Naval War Staff. Eight U-boats were to be diverted immediately to the area between Iceland, the Faeroes and Scotland against a possible invasion of Norway. Dönitz explains the arguments between him and the Naval War Staff about this unexpected diversion, but nothing could be done because Hitler had a hunch that the Allies were likely to invade Scandinavia and his direct orders had to be obeyed. Later the situation was made worse, when a dozen or so boats were ordered to be especially modified so that they could act as transports for non-naval operations and by the middle of February some twenty boats were ready to take positions off Norway. Some of these were sent far north into the Polar Seas, where they achieved very little in terms of tonnage sunk. Dönitz was still arguing that much more would be achieved if they operated in the richer hunting grounds of the western Atlantic.

Although he doesn't mention it, because U-boats were not involved, one must remember that this was also the time of the now famous 'Channel Dash', when the battleship *Scharnhorst* and *Gneisenau* and the heavy cruiser *Prinz Eugen* left Brest to sail through the English Channel to reach Germany before going on to Norway. This incredibly well planned undertaking took place from 11–13 February 1942. On arriving in the Elbe Estuary the naval officer and war correspondent, Walter Schöppe, captioned a photo of the sunrise with the words 'When we left France none of thought that we would ever see this.' Bearing in mind that much of the route taken by the German naval squadron had to be cleared by minesweepers, that a number of destroyers and many coastal craft were required as escorts and almost constant air cover was necessary, shows that valuable resources were diverted as a result of Hitler's hunch.

:: The British Side ::

[It took a while before the British latched on to this massive undertaking in northern waters. Most of the information about this unexpected move came from Special Intelligence and great care was taken to disguise the source, so it is likely that it was not mentioned publicly at all. Roskill mentions the event in his official history, *The War at Sea*, by saying that one of Hitler's hunches luckily took great pressure of the struggling Allied forces in the western Atlantic.]

The U-boat Offensive Review for February doesn't mention it all. This states:

On the 16th February the long expected campaign against shipping in the Caribbean Sea was opened by three U-boat attacks, carried out almost simultaneously at Aruba and Curaçao and in the Gulf of Venezuela. Thereafter events crowded fast and heavy upon the extremely slender anti-submarine forces available in the area. An attack was made probably by two U-boats on Port of Spain, Trinidad, and a force totalling five or six German U-boats, supported first by two and later by four Italians, operated to the eastward of Trinidad during the rest of the month.

Except for the region of the Panama Canal, the whole of the Caribbean Sea was patrolled by the U-boats, and at least two settled down for two or three days between the 19th and the 23rd February in the strait between Florida and the Bahamas; they had substantial successes against coastwise shipping and tankers bound from the Gulf of Mexico.

Tanker losses in American waters during the latter part of January, and during February, have been severe and, as regards this class of shipping, the German claims, although exaggerated, have not been fantastically out of relation to the truth.

Off Cape Hatteras there have been several U-boats on patrol and a few encounters took place to the southward of Newfoundland and Nova Scotia. No escorted convoy, however, was attacked in the area west of 50°W.

In the area east of 30°W, pressure by the U-boats was comparatively light; two convoys only were attacked, an escort vessel being sunk in each case.

One outward-bound convoy was attacked about 450 miles south-east of Cape Race on the 21st/22nd February and again on the 23rd/24th. In the interval between the two attacks several U-boats, probably five in all, had apparently gathered into a group, but the United States escort was successful in warding off any disastrous attack and only four merchant-men were lost; the enemy claimed seven ships sunk and six damaged.

The scale of the German and Italian U-boat effort during the month was slightly lower than in January, but it is estimated that on the average over 40 U-boats were at sea in the Atlantic. In the Mediterranean no great activity was apparent; in the South Atlantic and Arctic increasing activity was foreshadowed, rather than realised, by the end of the month.

Chapter 13

Back to Freetown (Africa) – March 1942

:: Dönitz ::

In October 1941 the U-boat Command came to the conclusion that the British traffic running along the African coast to and from the Middle and Far East was probably being diverted through the Pan-American Neutrality Zone to avoid U-boats on the eastern side of the Atlantic. This made the journey considerably longer, but was probably a better option for the opposition. The traffic through the Suez Canal and the Mediterranean had been brought to a standstill by Italy's entry into the war in 1940 so British shipping had been sailing around South Africa ever since then.

In February 1942, reports from the German radio monitoring service and from other sources suggested that these long routes along the American coastline were no longer being used and much of the traffic had reverted to run along the shorter route on the eastern edge of the Atlantic. In view of this, Dönitz immediately made preparations to use these possible opportunities nearer home, but he could send only two U-boats further south, into the waters off Freetown. Eleven ships were sunk in quick succession, proving quite conclusively that the diversion had been worth it. Yet, despite these successes, the area off American's eastern seaboard remained as Germany's main operations area.

The Americans were most reluctant to take precautions against U-boats and often went as far as helping them by broadcasting sailing schedules in plain language. All this resulted in such a terrific bonanza for Germany that another generation of U-boat 'aces' was being created and the fervour the nation displayed towards the heroes of autumn 1940 was now being re-kindled as new celebrities stepped into the limelight. The successful results in American waters lasted until April 1942, when it was noticed that the traffic was being diverted away from known U-boat positions and, at the same time, there was a marked increase in anti-submarine activity. Dönitz refers to this period having been most economic. Large quantities of shipping were sunk by a few U-boats without hardly any loss or damage to themselves. Convoys or determined opposition was hardly encountered and the supply operations, which made much of this possible, ran without a hitch. (With the British unable to read the new four-wheel Enigma code, designated 'Shark' by them, the Operational Intelligence Centre in London could not find out the re-fuelling positions and even the combined Allies did not have the resources to search for these vital spots.)

Dönitz's operation rooms with their adjacent 'museum' (a room containing visual displays of all available data – similar to the operations in British headquarters), contained constantly updated displays for comparing vital statistics of the daily goings-on. So the U-boat Command knew exactly what was being achieved at sea and the officers could see that the overall results were not anywhere near as good as the figures had been during the autumn of 1940. The time-consuming voyage to America meant that each U-boat at sea was sinking no more than two ships per month and the combined Allies were building ships at a considerably faster rate. During the autumn of 1940 each U-boat at sea was sinking up to six ships per month.

Dönitz mentions concerns about the sinking of three boats. This came about after a successful attack off Cape Race (Canada) against Convoy ONS67, which was sighted and the tracked by U155 (Kptlt. Adolf Cornelius Piening) towards the end of February. This showed that not much had changed in the intensive convoy war. Yet, a short time later U82 (Oblt.z.S. Siegfried Rollmann), U587 (Korvkpt. Ulrich Borcherdt) and U252 (Kptlt. Kai Lerchen) were lost in the same area, all three under strange circumstances, despite U252 having been warned to take extra care. It appeared as if the opposition was now sending out special submarine trap convoys, but there was no positive evidence of this. There was just a deep-down suspicion that the incident where Schepke (U100) and Kretschmer (U99) were lost seemed to be repeating itself. By the time Dönitz was writing his book, he had already known that these losses were attributed directly to the enemy having made use of new 'short wave' radar. This equipment was capable of detecting a submarine's conning tower the moment it appeared on the horizon.

Another weak link with successes off America was that such long-distance operations could not have been conducted without U-boats refuelling at sea and the reason this was so successful was that Bletchley Park could not read the U-boat code, to work out the meeting points in time for hunters to disrupt proceedings. Dönitz describes these refuelling operations in detail and explains how effective they were in helping to achieve the high sinking figures in United States waters. The period of high successes without any significant opposition lasted just over four months and by May things were becoming noticeably more difficult, with convoys and anti-submarine forces bringing an end to the 'Second Happy Time'.

:: The British Side ::

The Monthly U-boat Offensive Reviews for April 1942 do not add a great deal to what Dönitz must have known at the time and merely reinforce what has already been mentioned, as follows:

For the third month in succession the enemy concentrated his effort against independent shipping, especially tankers, to the westward of 45°00'W. The resulting losses to Allied shipping were not quite as heavy as in March, but this may in part have been due to a temporary suspension of sailings in certain areas.

About four U-boats arrived in the Caribbean Sea at the beginning of the month and a number of ships were sunk; restrictions on sailings undoubtedly prevented the losses being heavier. By the end of the month there were indications that as many as twelve U-boats were operating south of 30°N and west of 55°W, and the number of sinkings began to increase.

Activity close to the North American coast from Jacksonville, Florida, to New York continued but on a somewhat reduced scale. This doubtless was due to more effective countermeasures, an example of which was the sinking on 14th April of *U85* [Kptlt. Eberhard Greger], a 500-ton U-boat, by USS *Roper* off Cape Hatteras. Towards the end of the month there was considerable activity in the area 400 miles west to northwest of Bermuda and a number of ships were sunk. There was evidence of the presence of U-boats in the area south of Newfoundland and Nova Scotia but, as in March, they achieved little and were probably only passing through the area on passage to and from the United States coast. The average number of U-boats in the area to the northward of 30°N and to the westward of 45°W, including U-boats on passage, was about eighteen.

Except for a few attacks at the beginning of the month the Freetown area was quiet, but an attack by a Sunderland aircraft on 18th April showed that at least one U-boat was still in the area. After that date there was no further activity.

Several ships were sunk off the north coast of Brazil during the first half of the month. It is probable that two or three Italian U-boats were responsible. As five Italian U-boats were operating off the West Indies in March, it is apparent that the Italians are making a greater effort than in 1941 to assist their allies, possibly in return for the twenty or twenty-five 500-ton U-boats, which the Germans sent to the Mediterranean.

On 19th April a transit aircraft sighted a 'supply ship' and three U-boats some 500 miles to the eastward of St. Paul's Rocks. It is probable that the U-boats were those operating off the north coast of Brazil and that they subsequently returned to France, as they were not again located.

Despite several reports of 'suspicious' ships, there was no other reliable evidence that U-boats in the Western Atlantic or Caribbean Sea were being refuelled. 500-ton U-boats are quite capable of operating as far south and west as Cape Hatteras for from two to three weeks, and 740-ton U-boats can operate in the Caribbean Sea for a similar period without refuelling. The limiting factor on the length of their cruises is more probably the number of torpedoes carried and the endurance of the crews, rather than any shortage of fuel.

The Western Approaches remained quiet, though a number of sightings of and attacks on U-boats were made. It is probable that these U-boats were on passage from Germany to French ports and there was no evidence of the establishment of a patrol in this area. The victim of HM Ships *Vetch* and *Stork* may have been such a U-boat, but the position of the sinking makes it more likely that it was a U-boat homeward bound from America. [This was *U252* under Kptlt. Kai Lerchen, which had landed agents in Iceland and was then on her way to a new base in France, having come from Kiel via Heligoland.]

The Monthly Countermeasures Report states;

The general policy of the enemy remained the same in March as it had been in February and it continued to pay him a handsome dividend. He inflicted severe losses on British and Allied shipping in North and Central American waters, to say nothing of an occasional attack on a genuine South American neutral. During the latter half of the month an increasing number of attacks were carried out by the forces of the United Nations operating in these waters. The United States Naval Authorities report two attacks by surface craft and three by aircraft, all of which may have destroyed or damaged a U-boat, and there has been some surface evidence that damage was caused by an attack by a ship of the Royal Canadian Navy and by two attacks by aircraft of the Royal Canadian Air Force. Detailed accounts of these attacks by units of the Canadian and United States Forces are not available.

Plans have been prepared for the establishment of Caribbean convoys and of convoys for coastwise Atlantic shipping. They will be put into force as soon as adequate escorts are available.

The month has also seen a renewal of U-boat activity in the North-Western Approaches and in the Rockall area. Up to the present date this renewal of activity has been a great encouragement to us and, it must be presumed, a great disappointment to Admiral Dönitz. It has produced no attack on any of our convoys but has resulted in several attacks by our surface forces on the U-boats. Unhappily in no case has the attack given the ship the deep satisfaction of seeing a U-boat come to the surface, with her crew tumbling on deck to surrender, but the evidence shows that several attacks were extremely promising and it is to be hoped that some resulted in 'clean kills'. Attacks carried out in this area included a hunt by United States Ships *Rabbit* and *Badger*, who were escorting Convoy SCL71, on 6th March in a position 59°00'N 25°53'W.

The anticipated attack upon our convoys between Iceland and Russia has come to pass. There were indications that U-boats were in the neighbourhood of the homeward bound Convoy QP9, but no attack developed; in the case of the outward Convoy PQ13, however, U-boats were sighted and several signals, evidently U-boat transmissions, were made in the area. PQ13 sailed on Friday the 13th March. With the exception of bad luck in meeting with heavy weather, which appears to have partially scattered the Convoy, it seems to have survived ill omens in a remarkable way, considering the scale of the effort made by the enemy. Not only did the convoy meet a heavy concentration of U-boats, but it was attacked by aircraft and destroyers into the bargain. Nevertheless, out of the nineteen ships, which sailed, fourteen reached harbour; four are known to have been sunk, and one is still missing and is presumed lost. There was at least one promising attack on a U-boat in the course of the convoy's passage.

It is interesting to note that the U-boats operating in the Rockall – North-Western Approaches area appear to have been working more often as single units, rather than in 'wolf-pack' formation. It may be that this is more apparent than real, and has been due to the quick action of surface forces in locating and counterattacking the first U-boat to make contact.

A feature of the month was the unusual number of sightings by surface craft of U-boats on the surface; cruisers and destroyers sighted ten, and corvettes and trawlers three. The U-boat, at one time regarded as an almost entirely underwater craft, has tended, during this war, to become more arid more a surface craft endowed with the power of submerging but, nevertheless, no specific reason can be given to account for this large number of sightings. It may be due to a better lookout kept by our ships; alternatively, it may indicate that U-boat crews are less highly trained and more careless than they used to be. If this is so, there should be some good opportunities for successful attacks.

The Monthly Anti-Submarine Report for May 1942 makes the following comments:

During April two U-boats are known to have been sunk. On the 14th USS *Roper* sank *U85* off Cape Hatteras and about midnight on the same day

HM Ships *Vetch* and *Stork*, escorting Convoy OG82, sank another, whose number is not known. [This was *U252* under Kptlt. Kai Lerchen.]

A full report of *Roper's* success has not yet been received but it is believed that she detected the U-boat by RDF and attacked it first with gunfire and then with depth charges. No survivors were picked up but 29 bodies were recovered. [There were a good number of survivors swimming in the water, but it would appear that *Roper* deliberately killed them by throwing a depth charge into the group before picking up the corpses and dumping them in a huge untidy heap on her deck.]

The action with the other U-boat also began with an RDF contact, obtained by *Vetch*, who was some five miles ahead of the convoy.

The enemy has continued to make his main effort in the Western Atlantic and our losses have again been heavy, though there has been a slight reduction as compared with March. It is also satisfactory to record that ships have escaped attack, in some cases after opening fire. It is hoped that the coming month will see the introduction of convoy and escort in United States coastal waters, but it appears that more time must elapse before convoy can be instituted in the Caribbean Sea. With the coming of convoy and the commissioning of newly built anti-submarine craft, we can look for an improvement in the situation and a reduction in the serious losses, which have occurred in the early months of the year.

Aircraft of the Royal Canadian Air Force have made an increased number of attacks: in some of them, at least, it can be said with assurance that damage must have been inflicted.

The reappearance of U-boat activity in the North-Western Approaches and in the Rockall area, mentioned in the last Report, has not been continued, perhaps as a result of the rough handling which the enemy then received. An occasional U-boat was sighted from the air and attacked but these were probably boats on passage; no attempts to make contact with our convoys seem to have been made.

Outside the Western Atlantic and the Caribbean Sea, the main U-boat operations of the month have been in Arctic waters, where a considerable force of U-boats has co-operated with both air and surface craft to interfere with our convoys to and from Russia.

Confined to a comparatively narrow sea-lane off the coast by the ice and within easy distance of enemy air bases, there has been no possibility of evasion and the Russian convoys have had to fight their way through.

In the event we have suffered losses both by U-boat and air attack, but considering the scale of the effort made by the enemy, these losses cannot be considered heavy. We have been able to reinforce our anti-submarine escorts and have given the convoys generous anti-submarine, protection, judged by Atlantic standards. As a result, there have been several encounters between our anti-submarine forces and the U-boats and, although no definite case of a 'Known Sunk' can be claimed, there can be little doubt that some U-boats have been damaged in varying degree and that a large number have been thoroughly well shaken up, to the detriment, it is hoped, of their morale.

Chapter 14

After the American Excursion – After May 1942

:: Dönitz ::

Early in May Dönitz started making preparations for a withdrawal from American waters, but was loath to give up the still comparatively good results being achieved there. These thoughts came as a result of convoys having being introduced in the western Atlantic as far south as the Caribbean, making it considerably more difficult to sink shipping. As a compromise he changed tactics and sent boats westward along known convoy routes, with the hope that they might encounter good targets on the way and therefore save themselves some time in reaching a lucrative area of operations. This produced early results when *U569* (Oblt.z.S. Hans-Peter Hinsch) spotted a convoy (ONS92) after only a few days at sea and managed to call in four boats to sink seven ships during their first combined attack. The convoy then slipped through a gap in the patrol line and escaped without being relocated for another attack.

The German Radio Monitoring Service was still working well during this period and produced evidence that other convoys were using this same great circle route between Britain and Canada as a main highway. In view of view of this, Dönitz cancelled the plans to allow these U-boats to continue to America and ordered them back onto the convoy routes of mid-Atlantic. This was not without reward, but the expected major successes didn't come either. Things had definitely changed in those wild waters.

At their debriefings, several U-boat commanders reported that they were repeatedly attacked at night by destroyers bearing down at them at fast speed, but apparently without having detected the U-boat. Today we know that reason for this was that the surfaced submarine had been detected on radar but this contact was lost at around the same time as the escort was spotted by the lookouts atop the conning tower. So, the escort continued running 'blind' at high speed but was unable to make out its target in the darkness. The German enquiry looking into the question whether Britain had introduced new techniques or new weapons came to the conclusion that there were neither new countermeasures nor new apparatus for detecting surfaced submarines.

The situation nearer home, especially in the Bay of Biscay, was also getting noticeably worse and this became far more worrying than the goings-on in mid-ocean. Since the beginning of 1942, U-boats reported meeting more modern, faster and bigger planes than before, but these did not make any significant impact until June 1942, when the air war intensified quite rapidly. For some time before this month, U-boats had been expecting air attacks on nights with moderate to good moonlight. This was new inasmuch that early in 1942, U-boats still considered themselves safe at night and immune from air attack during the hours of darkness. During most encounters with aircraft, the lookouts on the conning tower saw what was happening in good time and took evasive action before running into trouble.

Now it was different. In June U-boats were suddenly illuminated with a searchlight during the blackest of nights and attacked at almost the same time. So far, evasive action by U-boats had been possible due to the same electronic problem as mentioned earlier; that of radar losing contact once the distance to the target became too short. Now aircraft had overcome this by the introducing the so-called Leigh Light. This made it quite plain to the Germans that the aircraft must have detected the U-boat before switching on the light at a range of 1–2 kilometres and left them in no doubt that radar must have played a role.

The immediate answer was to order U-boats to cross the Bay of Biscay submerged and, at the same time to make provisions for providing them with a radar detector and to supply them temporarily with machine guns until additional anti-aircraft armament could be fitted. At this period of time, the majority of U-boats were fitted with a large 88mm or 105mm quick-firing deck gun for use against surface targets and a single 20mm anti-aircraft gun on a small platform on the conning tower. Dönitz emphasised that all these German countermeasures were 'defensive' and did not change the fact that Britain had introduced a far-reaching and highly-accurate detection aid, which made the situation for U-boats considerably more dangerous.

He also made the point that this marked the beginning of a new phase in the war between U-boats and escorts, but the final decision as to who would win had not yet been made. It must be remembered that U-boats were now appearing in increasing numbers and it would not be long before 100 of them were at sea at the same time. Dönitz said that there were many occasions where Britain could be content that bad weather had prevented a significant number of attacks and subsequent sinkings of merchant ships. Indeed, the gloomy outlook in the German high command stretched as far as the Admiralty in London, where several Royal Navy officers remarked after the war that they were most depressed by the U-boats' achievements in 1942. So for many this indicated the beginning of a new phase, but it was not yet looked upon as a turning point and the battle continued with great gusto, heavy losses on both sides and some hard-earned but great achievements.

The fact that this combination of radar and new, improved aircraft with Leigh Lights worked was driven home to the Germans very quickly when three outward-bound boats were so seriously damaged that they had to return to base. This was made even more frustrating because the U-boat Command could not provide protection or any other support for bringing these seriously crippled boats back to base. Condor reconnaissance aircraft were sent out at once, but these had been developed from pre-war long-range passenger aircraft and were unsuited for aerial combat. Dönitz goes on to describe the internal battles with the Luftwaffe and after some while was allowed to have more suitable aircraft on standby to help stricken U-boats. However, the problem of escorting damaged U-boats back to port was never satisfactorily solved, despite Germany having spent a fortune on building the immense U-boat bunkers along the French Atlantic coast. The route through the Bay of Biscay remained so dangerous that the Germans nicknamed it the 'Black Pit'.

The three damaged U-boats mentioned above, although not identified by Dönitz were: *U71* under Kapitänleutnant Walter Flachsenberg, *U105* under Kapitänleutnant Heinrich Schuch and *U753* under Korvkpt. Alfred Manhardt von Mannstein.

:: The British Side ::

Once again, in view of the deepest doom and gloom from the German side, it is surprising that British documents were not laced with more self-congratulatory passages. Instead they give the impression that only little of significance went on.

The U-boat Offensive Report states:

During June the number of U-boats operating in the Atlantic is estimated to have risen gradually to a total of 60–65 and there were further indications that the cruises of individual U-boats were of even greater length than it has hitherto been supposed possible to sustain. There is still no concrete evidence establishing that in actual fact any U-boat has, or must have, fuelled or obtained torpedoes in American waters or from any place on the American Continent. It has long been thought that fuel, at any rate, could be obtained over there in quantities sufficient to extend cruising endurance for a week or two and it may, in fact, have happened in one or two instances that a U-boat has availed itself of some pre-arranged cache of supplies; it is, however, in the highest degree improbable that torpedoes could have been secured.

Mines were laid in the Chesapeake, which caused several casualties in the third week of the month, but sweeping has probably disposed of the whole crop sown. It may be that this mine laying represented the first effort of one of the new 1,600-ton mine-laying U-boats, which the enemy are thought to be now producing.

Convoy HG84 was very heavily and persistently shadowed and attacked between the 14th and 16th June but was defended with great skill and energy by the escorts, depleted though these had been by the despatch of a destroyer and a corvette to hunt a U-boat, which had been damaged by air attack and was making for Ferrol [*U105*, mentioned above]. The losses sustained were not unduly heavy in these circumstances and it is hoped that some damage may have been inflicted on the U-boats, of which probably seven or eight had gathered before the chase was abandoned.

The U-boat Countermeasures Review adds:

The enemy's main strategy has remained substantially the same and he has found it worth his while to continue to concentrate his primary effort off the American coast and in the Caribbean Sea, accepting the long distance on passage thus involved. There is no conclusive evidence that U-boats are being fuelled or given fresh torpedoes except when they return to French ports.

There has been a great increase in anti-submarine attacks, particularly to the westward of 40° W. On some days up to four, or even more, aircraft attacks have been made.

There is no doubt that the most striking development of the month has been the great increase in effective air attacks on U-boats. In addition to the attacks on U-boats mentioned above, one German and one Italian were forced to take refuge in Spanish ports as a result of damage caused by Torpex depth charges. The episode of the Italian U-boat is of particular interest in that the first damaging attack was made by a Wellington aircraft fitted with a Leigh searchlight.

The attack, which caused the German U-boat to seek shelter in Spain was made in daylight and is typical of the attacks, which are being made with increasing frequency by aircraft of Coastal Command. There have been five other attacks, which sound most promising, but of which we have no corroborative details; one of these was the first to be carried out by a Lancaster, the aircraft being on passage to escort Convoy HG84.

In fact, we now face a possible change in U-boat strategy. A renewal at the present time of the attacks on the convoys in mid-Atlantic and Eastern Atlantic waters would come at a time when the strength of our escorts with individual convoys has been reduced by the transfer of some of our anti-submarine forces to meet the danger in the Western Atlantic and to reinforce our convoys to and from Russia in fighting their way through U-boat and aircraft attack.

The weakness of our escorts cannot be denied, but against this there are some solid advantages. There is a steadily growing feeling of confidence amongst our escort groups that they can compete with and defeat the U-boat attacking at night; many of them have worked together for some time now and have acquired a team spirit and mutual self-confidence. Moreover, there is the steadily increasing efficiency of Radio Direction Finders, which brings with it an ever-growing confidence in this method of U-boat detection; very good results have also been recently achieved by intelligent and efficient use of High and Medium Frequency Direction Finders.

It is to be hoped that we may be able to add to these advantages an increase in the deadliness of our anti-submarine attack resulting from the advent of the ahead-thrown weapon. The Hedgehog, however, still awaits adequate opportunities to prove itself and remains an untried development; perhaps the Mark X (one ton) depth charge may yet be the first new weapon to claim a U-boat victim.

Whatever the outcome, we can confidently expect that, if the onslaught on our Atlantic convoys is renewed, the U-boats will find themselves given a far more difficult task than they had in the past. We shall, inevitably, suffer losses, but we should also be able to inflict heavy losses on the enemy.

It is significant that U-boats have been sighted or D/F'd in the vicinity of our convoys and that there have been a certain number of attacks on convoys in mid-ocean; perhaps of even greater-significance is the re-appearance of German U-boats in the Freetown area. Finally, we are in the unusual position of having been given a tip straight from the horse's mouth; Admiral Dönitz has given one of his rare interviews to the German Press and has broadcast to the German nation.

Leigh Lights: A Night Attack in the Bay of Biscay by a Wellington Aircraft Fitted with a Searchlight and its Sequel

The following passage was first released in the Monthly Anti-Submarine Report for June 1942:

In the early hours of 4th June 1942, a Wellington aircraft of 172 Squadron RAF was carrying out an anti-submarine patrol at a height of 2,000 feet. She was painted with black camouflage. At 0144 hours she obtained an ASV contact at a range of 6.5 miles on the starboard bow. This disappeared after 15 seconds, but the aircraft switched on her beam aerials and regained contact, the range then being 5 miles. Having circled and picked up the contact, she closed and, when the range was one mile, switched on her searchlight. The beam illuminated a U-boat, dead ahead, three-quarters of a mile away.

The Wellington had dropped down to 450 feet and continued down to attack but, owing to the steepness of her dive, the searchlight beam was obscured by the fuselage and the U-boat was lost from sight.

The Wellington circled to port and climbing to a height of 600 feet regained contact on the beam aerial at a range of 3.5 miles. She was turning to port to home on the U-boat when the latter gave away her position by firing a two-star red flare. Thus assisted and with ASV contact regained, the aircraft closed to within a mile before switching on her searchlight, the beam of which again picked up the U-boat from a range of three-quarters of a mile.

The Wellington came down to 50 feet and dropped four 250 lb Torpex-filled depth charges, set to 25 feet and spaced 35 feet apart. Three of them were seen to explode, straddling the U-boat, which was making about 10 knots.

After making this attack the aircraft circled to regain ASV contact, but it was not until she had made a wide circle six miles from the scene of the attack and had, after turning through 360°, approached again with her homing aerials switched on, that she re-established contact. The range was 3.5 miles. When this had been reduced to one mile, the searchlight was switched on again. This illuminated another U-boat, smaller than the one previously attacked and steering on the same course of 200°. The vessel fired a rocket, which exploded at 400 feet into five or six stars. The Wellington, by putting the searchlight to extreme deflection, was able to illuminate the U-boat sufficiently for the rear-gunner to see the target and fire 200 rounds, many of which hit the conning tower and hull along the water line. The aircraft was then flying at 150 feet.

The conning tower opened and about ten men appeared with their hands raised in surrender. As they made no attempt to man the gun, the aircraft did not feel justified in opening fire on them, though the proper course would have been to have machine-gunned the men on the conning tower and any others who might have come up after this had been done. [One wonders what would have happened if such an order to shoot men with their hands raised in surrender would have been given by a German and the details discovered by the Allies after the war.]

Owing to lack of fuel Hudson had to leave the scene within half an hour of the attack and the U-boat. Though seriously damaged, managed to get into Cartagena. It has been laid down that there is no duty to cease fire on a mere showing of the white flag or holding up of hands on token of surrender by some members of a force. Capitulation is a surrender of a whole force and one who is called upon to accept capitulation is entitled to be satisfied that the whole force is agreeing to surrender before he orders the 'cease fire'.

Similarly, the pilot of an aircraft is entitled to be satisfied that all resistance is ceasing in a U-boat before he ceases offensive action himself. It must almost always be impossible for a pilot to be so satisfied and an aircraft is, therefore, fully justified in continuing action until surrender is either complete or at any rate assured.

On 24 June 1942 the Admiralty made a signal from which the following is an extract: 'Aircraft are in no position to differentiate between genuine surrender and ruse de guerre. Offensive action with all available weapons is therefore to continue unless capture by close co-operation with surface craft is practically certain. Even then, the machine-gunning of the decks of the U-boat is necessary to keep the crew below and prevent scuttling. In no other case should offensive action be in any way relaxed against a U-boat.'

[First, to add a timescale to these events: *U570* (Kptlt. Hans-Joachim Rahmlow) was captured by Hudson (S) piloted by J. H. Thompson on 27 August 1941, ten months before this incident. Secondly, the U-boat mentioned in the above passage was *U105* under command of Korvkpt. Heinrich Schuch. Another boat to have surrendered to an aircraft was *U573* (Kptlt. Heinrich Heinsohn), on 1 May 1942. The damage done by the aircraft was repaired and *U573* then made for neutral Spain. In view of the signal made by the Admiralty, it may be of interest to add that an Allied court tried Kpt.z.S. Hellmuth von Ruckteschell after the war for having attacked too aggressively.]

Chapter 15

The Mid-Atlantic Shock – July 1942

:: Dönitz ::

On 17 July 1942, *U202* (Kptlt. Hans-Heinz Linder), while on the way home from American waters, ran into a convoy (OS34) in Mid-Atlantic. This unexpected meeting took place some 800 nautical miles (almost 1,500 km) from the nearest land base, but the lookouts also spotted a four-engine, land-based aircraft flying over the merchant ships and its movements suggested that it was equipped with some type of detection gear. Dönitz said that this news of aircraft flying so far from their nearest base was a most unpleasant surprise. After the war it became apparent that this was an isolated case of an American Liberator having attempted such a long flight as an experiment and another six months were to pass before such aircraft became a regular feature in the so-called 'Mid-Atlantic Air Gap'.

U-boats had now been out of mid-Atlantic operational areas for six months and during that time there had been such an enormous number of changes that the U-boat Command in France had the greatest of problems in working out what was going on. Urgent clarification was called for and there was no time to wait until boats came home for de-briefings. So, at this stage of the proceedings Dönitz introduced a new technique of holding 'live' conversations with commanders at sea. Live voice transmissions were still in the future and as a stop-gap measure the U-boat Command made contact with a boat and Dönitz asked a question; an Enigma operator typed this text into the machine as fast as he could and the radio operator sent the message by Morse code the moment the code letter illuminated above the keyboard. Wolfgang Hirschfeld describes how this was first done experimentally while *U109* was lying in port and how the process ran quite smoothly and easily. Such a conversation lasted about half an hour and was, of course, only carried out with boats whose position was known to the enemy, usually immediately after an attack. This was tried for the first time for real around 22 July 1942 after a convoy had been sighted and had been expected to run into a tight pack of nine U-boats, but none of them came

76

close enough to attack. Using this radiotelephone technique with *U552* under Kapitänleutnant Erich Topp, Dönitz discovered that the most appalling weather had prevented everyone from launching torpedoes. In view of these terrible conditions, he realised that further attacks would be futile and therefore called off the patrol line.

Something similar happened a few days later with Convoy ON115. This time fog prevented any significant action. Dönitz took the view that if two convoy battles had been messed up by the weather, then the third might just strike lucky and he continued with the tactics he had established. Although Convoy SC94 was spotted by *U593* (Kptlt. Gerd Kelbing) on 5 August, the prospects didn't look terribly promising for two main reasons. First, many of the boats making up this patrol line were on their first or second mission with comparatively inexperienced commanders and, secondly, a good number of the boats were 'behind' the convoy and therefore needed to chase it at relatively high speeds. Yet, despite early trepidation, the plan worked and seven success reports came flooding in but the final costs added up to two U-boats lost. After the war it was established that in fact 11 ships totalling 52,461 GRT had been sunk. The two U-boats that were lost, *U210* (Kptlt. Rudolf Lemcke) and *U379* (Korvkpt. Paul-Hugo Kettner) were both on their first operational mission; having set out from Kiel on 19 July and 25 June respectively.

Dönitz said that the real credit for this operation had got to go to the men of *U593*, who kept in close contact with the convoy for three days despite escorts depth charging the boat on several occasions. The British Monthly Anti-Submarine Report add considerable praise by saying, 'It is noteworthy that the U-boat commander who attacked Convoy SC94 at 13.25 on 8th August showed a skill which was much in excess of that displayed by the commanders of the other U-boats engaged. The efficient handling of certain U-boats was likewise noticed by the escorts of Convoy ON115'.

All this produced more than a mere glimmer of hope in the U-boat Command, it resulted more in a sparkle that the established methods were still working and even inexperienced crews could make some significant impression on the convoy war. Of course, the point one tends to forget when reading this is that by this time there were some 70 – 80 at sea each day. So, there must have been a great deal of other action as well. The most famous alternative battle in July 1942 was one in the Arctic for Convoy PQ17, which has dominated history books ever since.

:: The British Side ::

The Monthly U-boat Offensive Reviews does not even mention the events in mid-Atlantic and concentrates on other matters as follows:

With the exception of Convoy PQ17, which was seriously cut up by U-boats operating east of Bear Island, shipping casualties inflicted by U-boat attacks have not been very heavy during July.

The anti-submarine escorts of PQ17 protected the convoy magnificently throughout a long stretch between Jan Mayen and Bear Island and drove off the shadowing U-boat repeatedly but, after the convoy had been ordered to scatter when south-east of Spitzbergen, to reduce losses from the surface ship attack then apparently pending, and the destroyers had been withdrawn, it became vulnerable to attacks by the U-boat pack then operating. The corresponding QP Convoy fortunately escaped the U-boats entirely. It is apparent from various indications that the enemy must now be maintaining at least twenty U-boats in Norwegian bases, primarily for the purpose of attacking North Russian convoys.

It would seem that the enemy may have decided to put a time limit to his intense campaign in American waters, counting the mounting dangers no longer justified by the diminishing gains. But before withdrawing, as apparently he now has done, from the Central Caribbean and to a lesser but fairly complete extent from the Gulf of Mexico and the Florida coast, he sent several U-boats to the Western Caribbean, including the Colon area, and at least three into Mexican coastal waters near Tampico and Corpus Christi. Near Cape Hatteras a coastal convoy was attacked but this focal point was far less dangerous than in the previous month.

One outward convoy [ON113] was shadowed for four days when northeast of Virgin Rocks and had five ships torpedoed but one of the escorts, HMCS *St Croix*, sank a U-boat [*U90* under Kapitänleutnant Hans-Jürgen Oldörp]. Another bold commander took his U-boat well up the St Lawrence River and sank three ships in convoy there [*U132* under Kptlt. Ernst Vogelsang sank the 3,382 GRT *Anastassios Pateras*, the 4,312 GRT *Hainaut* and the 2,555 GRT *Dinaric* on 6 July 1942.]

There is little doubt that a new phase of the U-boat offensive began during July. Increasing attention is being given to intercepting and attacking convoys on the supply routes between the United States and Great Britain and between Great Britain and the Middle East. There will be heavier losses of ships engaged on these routes and on journeys from Sierra Leone to Great Britain but our escorts will have ampler opportunity to come to grips with the U-boats. Already the frequency with which really promising attacks are reported is increasing and an appreciable effect on U-boat morale may soon be manifested.

The Countermeasures Review for August 1942 states:

Admiral Dönitz has also shown himself to be a good prophet and, although this comparatively large number of ships has been sunk in convoy, the lot of the German U-boat has undoubtedly been hard. Four out of the six German U-boats known to have been destroyed were sunk while attacking a convoy and many other U-boats were very severely harassed and probably damaged.

Numerically our escorts are weak, but there is little doubt that technical improvements, leading to a greater reliability in such aids as H/F D/F and RDF, combined with lack of experience on the part of the U-boats, are telling, heavily in our favour; the numbers, range and anti-submarine weapons of our aircraft are also considerably more formidable than they were. There can, however, be no time for complacency. During the last two months, very large numbers of U-boats are thought to have come into operational service, and in the same period the number of U-boats operating in the Atlantic is estimated to have increased by fifty per cent.

When the ships are so fitted for reception, the first indications of the presence of U-boats have been in every case H/F D/F bearings, and these have also been of great assistance to Escort Commanders in appreciating the subsequent situations. Type 271 RDF has proved a most efficient detector by night and the quick action taken by escort vessels has, in many cases, thwarted the night attack.

This has apparently forced the U-boats to abandon their usual tactics and to attack submerged in daylight, accepting lack of mobility and a low speed against an escort weakened by members searching on D/F bearings. These day attacks have resulted in as many as five ships being torpedoed by one salvo; to lessen the chance of such success recurring, instructions were issued in the third week of August to open out the distance between the columns of a convoy to five cables by day as well as by night.

Escort Group No. 42, escorting Convoy SL118, is worthy of special mention. The H/F D/F fitted in HM Ships *Gorleston*, *Wellington* and *Folkestone*, enabled the Senior Officer to deduce the movements and indications of the U-boat with considerable accuracy, the correctness of his deductions being proved on several occasions by subsequent sightings and attacks. He was unfortunately, unable to obtain decisive results in his engagement with the enemy, owing to the number of escorts available and their slow speed. Again and again, encounters, which might otherwise have been pursued to a successful conclusion had to be prematurely broken off in order to maintain safe minimum escort with the convoy.

With the incidence of day attacks on convoys, some discretion is necessary in coming to a decision as to whether it is profitable to search for the enemy on an H/F D/F bearing. What certainly is worthwhile is to take every possible step to attack the first U-boat to report a convoy, as this may at least cause her to lose touch and cease making shadowing reports.

On the night of 16th August *Folkestone* obtained an RDF contact ahead of Convoy SL118 at 6,000 yards range and moving rapidly away towards the port bow. This U-boat was forced to dive by starshell and six attacks were carried out on it. Within an hour of making contact, *Folkestone* and *Gorleston* chased an RDF contact away to the northward, but it is not clear whether this was the same U-boat resurfaced, or another.

H/F D/F bearings continued to show that the convoy was still being shadowed by about three U-boats and at 0706 *Gorleston* sighted two of them 12 miles on the port quarter. One dived but the other may have followed the cutter back to the convoy when she rejoined later in the day, since one U-boat carried out a daylight attack on the convoy when only three escorts were in company. One merchant ship was hit and sunk.

After dark on the 17th HM Ships *Pentstemon* and *Wellington* chased a U-boat away to the westward, and an hour later *Folkestone* intercepted a U-boat with the aid of RDF and attacked it four times, repeating the success on another U-boat early in the morning on the 18th when she carried out two depth-charge attacks.

During the morning of the 18th the persistence of the enemy was revealed by H/F D/F bearings, which indicated the presence of about three U-boats. Searches by *Wellington, Pentstemon, Folkestone* and *Gorleston* were, however, unsuccessful, and in the afternoon a U-boat carried out another daylight attack and obtained hits on two merchant ships, one of which was sunk, and on HMS *Cheshire*.

That night *Folkestone* intercepted a U-boat broad on the port bow of the convoy and by gunfire forced it to dive. Nevertheless, the H/F D/F bearings continued to tell the same tale of about three shadowing U-boats, and a Liberator aircraft attacked one of them on the port beam of the convoy at daylight on the 19th. That afternoon the final attack was made and one ship was torpedoed and sunk. The U-boats then ceased action, having followed the convoy for three days.

Convoy ON115 was attacked on the night of 1st/2nd August and had three ships torpedoed. The escort, which already had the sinking of a German U-boat to its credit, drove off U-boats on the 2nd and 3rd August and brought the convoy into harbour without further loss.

The passage then continues with the following highly significant passage:

Convoy ON122 was attacked by a pack of U-boats from the night of 23rd

1. There are two types of leader, one who leads because men will follow him or one who pushes his troops forward from behind. Commanders of the first type have several points in common; they often wear their badges differently to how their men are supposed to display them. In this case the Iron Cross should be worn at the top and only one U-boat badge was usually pinned on, but Dönitz has the Second World War version above and the First World War one below it. Field Marshal Montgomery wore two hat badges instead of one, so good leaders displayed some quirks for people to distinguish them from the ordinary men.

2. Leaders who push their men into battle need them to stand at rigid attention or perhaps at ease when addressing them. Dynamic leaders like Montgomery, Dönitz and many others preferred the men to gather around them naturally. In this case Dönitz is holding his admiral's baton, indicating he is the Supreme Commander-in-Chief of the Navy, but he has no hang-ups when talking to his men. He had an excellent memory for personal details and would often remember private matters for many months on end. Many U-boat men said that he always had a personal word for everyone and it was not unusual for him to listen to family stories from the lowest ranks.

3. At the beginning of the Second World War, Germany had three different types of U-boat. A small coastal version (Type II) of about 300 tons, a sea-going boat of 600 tons (Types I and VII) and a long-range, ocean-going Type IX of 900 tons. A few small Type II boats did make it out into the Atlantic, but the larger versions bore the brunt of the battle, especially the Type VIIC, which became the largest

submarine class ever to have been built. This Type VIIC with the emblem of the 7th U-boat Flotilla shows how conning towers were later modified to cope with waves and spray. The pressure hulls of later boats were also strengthened, enabling them to dive a little deeper and stand up better to depth-charging.

4. The bows of a Type VIIC with the stalk-like head of a sound detector close to the hydraulic capstan. Note that the 88mm gun has the optical sight mounted.

5. The layout of an early type of conning tower of a Type IX with single 20mm anti-aircraft gun and the housing for the all-important radio direction finder in the front casing. The stalks in the middle are supports for periscopes. The rear one, on the left, has a magnetic sighting compass attached and the huge torpedo aimer, slightly off-centre, automatically transmitted data to the torpedo calculator in the commander's control room inside the conning tower. Special binoculars were clipped onto the top when it was in use. Although slightly bigger than and with almost identical armament to the Type VII, the Type IX did not stand up so well to depth-charging, but it had two stern torpedo tubes instead of one.

6. Victor Oehrn, who was born in Russia, made a deep impression on the German Navy with his highly methodical brain. He masterminded the incredible attack on Scapa Flow, which was executed so brilliantly by *U47* under Günther Prien, and it was he who devised the format for the U-boat Command's war diary. During the summer of 1940, he was serving as a staff officer, but he was also a fully-qualified U-boat commander, having served in *U14* for almost two years until 1937. The dire shortage of officers created by the unexpected outbreak of war then directed him back to sea. In May 1940 he took the ocean-going *U37* into the North Atlantic and despite several disappointing torpedo failures, kick-started the German U-boat offensive again after its depressing failures earlier in the year.

7. Dönitz greeting the survivors from the supply ship *Belchen*, who were brought home by *U93* under Käpitanleutnant Claus Korth. The *Belchen* was one of eight ships sunk around the time of the *Bismarck* breakout and should have set off alarm bells in Germany, telling the naval staff that Britain was reading the secret radio code. The High Command ignored the warning, however, and thus allowed Germany to slip further down the slippery road of serious losses.

8. The mansion at Bletchley Park was one of the most significant lynchpins of Britain's success, but the majority of code breakers there did not spend their days in such elaborate surroundings. The brains of the Park worked in small wooden huts. These were hot in summer and unpleasantly cold in winter. Yet the geniuses who endured these conditions worked well and made a most significant contribution to the outcome of the war.

9. The British Western Approaches had its headquarters in Liverpool and after the war many years passed before it became known that the Admiralty also had a highly significant Operational Intelligence Centre with a secret Submarine Tracking Room inside this bunker close to Admiralty Arch in London. It was this setup which translated the intelligence flooding in from numerous sources into meaningful information. This was so secret that even the First Sea Lord was not told about all the goings-on in this most crucial centre.

10. U-boats often maintained radio silence until their position had been discovered or until shortly before starting an attack. Then messages accumulated during the previous days would be transmitted with great gusto. A number of Allied radio operators remarked that once this happened the massive volume of Morse in the ether surprised them. This does not mean that submarine radio rooms were idle for much of the time. The radio operator was not allowed to remove his headset, even when doing something not connected with his receiver, so that he would not miss incoming messages. U-boats submerged off the eastern seaboard of America could still pick up signals from their massive *Goliath* transmitter near Kalbe, but often they went too deep to receive them. Then the radio operator would change positions to occupy the sound detection room where he listened for the noises being picked up by the sensitive hydrophones on the outside of the hull.

11. Operators eavesdropping on German radio had a most frustrating job inasmuch that many of them could not transmit signals and spent all their working day writing down long chains of meaningless letters. Yet, without this massive army of well-trained men and women, the codebreakers could not have been able to make such a massive contribution to the outcome of the war. To make this procedure even more exasperating, it was often necessary to concentrate on one of several Morse messages being picked up at the same time. The skill, effort, determination and perseverance of the people at the listening stations were never fully acknowledged and many of these made a far greater contribution to the outcome of the war than some of the highly decorated heroes at the front.

12. The three-dimensional spiderweb-like aerial on the top of this mast is the High Frequency Radio Direction Finder or H/F D/F and there is a Type 276 Surface Warning (Radar) aerial below it. It is strange that these most distinctive features in such prominent positions, high up on masts or control towers, were not spotted and that no one on the German side seemed to have investigated their possible influence on the war at sea.

13. During heavy storms men in escorts were far worse off than their counterparts in U-boats. Submariners could dive below the turbulence, to enjoy a rest and a meal in peace and quiet, while the small escorts were tossed about more fiercely than any imaginable fairground ride. What is more, corvettes and the like were built for agility to outmanoeuvre their opponents, not for comfort.

14. A CAM or Catapult Aircraft Merchant Ship with an old and almost obsolete fighter sitting high up on the bows, ready for take-off. Although cumbersome and only capable of making its last flight before ditching in the sea, these fighters did make a significant contribution to the war. The pilot's life must have been most precarious and one wonders how many of these brave men survived.

15. HMS *Biter* and HMS *Avenger* pitching through the ferocity of the North Atlantic. Many of these hastily-converted escort carriers had no means of accommodating aircraft in below-deck hangars. Thus the flimsy machines were always exposed to the elements and 'ground crews' worked in these inhospitable conditions to keep them airborne.

16. A Swordfish aboard the escort carrier HMS *Chaser*, has found the 450-foot long flight deck a little short and has almost overshot to go tumbling into the water. At the beginning of the war such flimsy aircraft as these found that their anti-submarine bombs bounced and sometimes exploded in mid-air, bringing an abrupt end to operations.

17. *U123*, one of the fourteen ocean-going Type IXB boats. Although capable of crossing the Atlantic and coming home again, fuel was so limited that these boats could not have operated in American waters for any length of time, if they had not had a supply tanker supporting them.

18. Although classified as ocean-going, accommodation aboard the larger Type IX boats was still so cramped that many of the lower ranks slept on hammocks or on the floor.

19. Both Types VII and IX had space for four torpedoes below the deck of the bow compartment and two more could be placed on top. These had some flat boards placed over them to provide some floor and table space. U-boat men were provided with the best rations, but it was not until much later in the war that proper storage, such as freezers, was installed. It seems strange that the German Navy designed and built such a vast U-boat fleet without regard to basic necessities as keeping food fresh or providing means for men to wash properly or even supplying a ventilation system.

20. One wonders how photographers managed to take pictures like this in such horrendous conditions without their cameras flooding. The autumn of 1941 was especially bad for U-boats and shipping, with an unusual number of heavy storms sweeping across the North Atlantic.

21. Operations against the United States had only just begun when on 1 February 1942 Germany changed the coding system for Atlantic U-boats and blacked out Bletchley Park in England until the end of the year. The change was quite straightforward; a fourth wheel was added to the Enigma machine, making it impossible for anyone with a three-wheel machine to understand the new code.

22. The change in the Atlantic U-boat code coincided with an exceptionally harsh winter in Eastern Europe. Much of the Baltic froze solid, meaning U-boat training was severely disrupted. The extreme cold also slowed down production, but didn't bring it to a total standstill. Congestion starting building up and this resulted in an unusually high number of U-boats appearing later in 1942.

23. The immediate response to the ever-increasing number of aircraft in the Atlantic was to fit additional anti-aircraft armament to U-boats, but it took a while before effective weapons could be produced and as a stop-gap measure Germany provided light machine guns as can be see here on *U132* under Käpitanleutnant Ernst Vogelsang. The attack periscope, with the small lens, is visible behind the commander's flagpole. The sighting compass, attached to the periscope mount, can also be seen.

24. Once Germany realised that radar was responsible for finding U-boats at night, a French radio receiver, named Metox, was installed to pick up the radar signals. These sets were at first supplied with a rough wooden aerial, which had to be turned by hand and taken below when the boat dived. Since the danger area was at first in French coastal waters, these aerials became known as 'Biscay Crosses'. The stamp, saying 'Gesperrt!' (Closed), was added by the censor.

25. The rough-and-ready wooden 'Biscay Crosses' were quickly replaced by more durable circular aerials as can be seen here. Some of these were merely welded to the conning tower but later models were retractable so that they could be lowered into the fairing when the boat dived. Part of the censor's stamp, Gesperrt! (Closed) is just visible towards the right by the inked cross.

26. Photographs showing naval headquarters and conferences are extremely rare, so it is difficult to illustrate what such important decision-making moments looked like. This shows a meeting of the Naval War Staff for the Baltic Command with Admiral Rolf Carls presiding. Sitting on the far right-hand corner of the table is Claus Korth, who won the Knight's Cross while commanding *U93*.

27. HMS *Pevensey* Castle, a 'Castle' class corvette of just over 1000 tons, with her H/F D/F aerial set clearly against the lighter sky.

28. Life aboard convoy escorts must have been exceedingly harsh. There was no let-up from the natural conditions, the wet and the turbulent waves. Work on the lower deck was hard and keeping watch on an open bridge not a great deal of fun in such appalling conditions. Firing depth charges might have been exciting, but for most of the time these small ships were faced with vast open seas and cruel elements and none of their weapons were capable of calming the discomfort these caused the ships and men.

29. The gunner of a 20mm anti-aircraft gun wearing naval issue sunglasses because attacking aircraft often burst upon U-boats from out of the sun. The gun was perfectly balanced and all he had to do was to point it at his target and press the trigger when it came within range. Although this sounds simple, the pitching and rolling of the boat made such shooting very difficult.

30. Two U-boats showing the improved anti-aircraft armament, introduced for the latter part of the war. The upper platform generally held two twin 20mm and the lower platform either one single (later a twin) 37mm or a quadruple 20mm gun.

31. A drawing of the ahead-throwing mortar, Squid, as it appeared in the Monthly Anti-Submarine Reports during the war.

32. USS *Donnell* with her stern blown off. The German anti-destroyer torpedo, the sound-sensitive *Zaunkönig*, had a major fault that it exploded some distance before reaching its target. This made life in escorts most uncomfortable because propellers and engines were damaged and a few had their stern blown off, but unknown to the U-boat Command, the vast majority of ships attacked with this weapon survived.

August to the night of the 25th. The escort, making full use of H/F D/F and RDF – 14 contacts were obtained between 2215 on 23rd August and 1231 on the 25th, and there was only one occasion when the sighting of a U-boat was not preceded by a contact – carried out a number of most persistent and spirited attacks. A Hedgehog attack was made by HMS *Viscount*, who reported that within two seconds of the charges hitting the water there was a tremendous rippling explosion, followed three seconds later by a small explosion.

Excellent work was done by the other ships of the escort, HNoM Ships *Potentilla*, *Eglantine*, *Acanthus* and *Montbretia*. *Potentilla* specially distinguished herself, using all her depth charges in a number of well-delivered attacks, and at one time holding off two U-boats simultaneously. The convoy had three ships sunk but on only one occasion was the escort forced by superior numbers to yield the initiative and the enemy did not gain his objectives cheaply. It was thought that the U-boats attacked all endeavoured to surface as soon as they considered that they had the smallest chance of escaping.

:: Dönitz ::

Dönitz mentions the same convoy, saying that during the attack on ON122 towards the end of August 1942, during the building-up of fog, U-boats were repeatedly surprised by gunfire attacks from destroyers without having received any indication on their warning devices that they had been detected on radar. Therefore it was obvious that the opposition was using a radar wavelength beyond those capable of being picked up by the German detector. The depressing point about this discovery was that the radar detector had only been introduced a few weeks earlier. Initially, radar detectors produced such impressive results that U-boats managed to avoid so many attacks and Roskill remarked that the war against U-boats came to a standstill as a result.

Chapter 16

Postscript to the Summer's Battles – September 1942

:: Dönitz ::

Dönitz briefly mentions the attack by the 'Vorwärts Two' Pack against Convoy ON127, which, when he was writing his book, presented an excellent opportunity of comparing combat performances because he knew from Stephen Roskill's *War at Sea* that none of the escorts had been fitted with radar. However, when comparing his notes with the Secret Anti-Submarine Reports one sees that these mention H/F D/F rather than radar and this makes one wonder whether he had grasped the fundamental differences between these two aids when writing his book. According to Dönitz, parameters for the action in September 1942 should have been similar to how they had been two years earlier, except that many of the U-boats were then on their first operation with new crews and it could well be that they were pitched against more experienced escorts. The result of a four day long battle added up to the sinking of seven ships of 50,205 GRT from a total of eleven ships of 86,346 GRT having been torpedoed. None of the U-boats were lost. Dönitz was delighted. Indeed the figures might look most impressive, but one must also consider that on average every boat of this wolf pack was at sea for over forty days. Had they achieved the same as during the autumn of 1940, then they would hit well over a hundred merchant ships. [The 'Vorwärts Two' Group was made up of twelve U-boats.]

:: The British Side ::

The Monthly U-boat Offensive Report states:

> The operational strength of the available Atlantic U-boat force is more considerable than ever. Sinkings during the month may have reduced it by 5 per cent, but new boats becoming operational probably amounted to 15 per cent. In a broad sense it may be approximately true to say that at present 45 per cent, of the total effort is devoted to operations in the North Atlantic, mainly between 20°W and 45°W but including the Nova Scotia and United States areas, 20 per cent to the Trinidad and Caribbean

areas, 10 per cent to the South Atlantic, 5 per cent to Freetown, 10 per cent to the Arctic and 10 per cent to the Mediterranean.

The only convoy attack during September resulting in heavy loss was on ON127, which was shadowed and intermittently attacked by five or six U-boats and had seven ships sunk. The relevant enemy broadcast claimed nineteen ships and gave credit to several new crews for having achieved so much on their first war cruise. In comparison, the PQ and QP convoys to and from North Russia ran without excessive losses from U-boat attack.

The Monthly U-boat Countermeasures Report adds to this:

U-boats have continued to pay considerable attention to convoys and ON127 suffered particularly heavily, losing seven merchant ships and one of the escorts, HMCS *Ottawa*. Unfortunately none of the escorts were fitted with H/F D/F. The first attack took place during the afternoon of the 10th September, another daylight attack was delivered that evening and a third attack was made during the night; three more night attacks were carried out twenty-four hours later. *Ottawa* was sunk in the early hours of the 14th. The convoy consisted of nine columns and the positions of the sunken ships suggest that the attacks were made from outside the convoy. Reports of the attacks made by the escorts have not yet been received.

It was noticeable that the main weight of attack on Atlantic convoys was delivered in the areas outside full shore-based air cover. An example of what can be achieved by intelligent disposition of the surface escort – now largely a matter of correct use of information derived from H/F D/F – and by good co-operation with aircraft, is given by Convoy HX206, which without loss reached the United Kingdom on 16th September. The surface escort was able to deal with those U-boats, which were not put down by the air escort.

A new development in our countermeasures has been the establishment in mid-Atlantic of a temporary reinforcing group, whose primary object was the destruction of U-boats rather than the immediate defence of trade. HMS *Stork* was Senior Officer of the group, which was designated the 20th Escort Group, and other ships taking part in its operations were HM Ships *Deptford, Spey, Rother, Exe, Tay, Sabre, Sardonyx, Saladin* and *Scimitar*. The oiler *Laurelwood* was sailed in Convoy ONS132 with 1,500 tons of furnace oil and a supply of depth charges but unfortunately the inexperience of her crew made refuelling at sea extremely difficult. [Reinforcing Group was an early term for Support Group.]

The operations, which began on the 22nd September with the sailing from Londonderry of *Stork, Deptford, Spey, Rother* and *Exe* with orders to reinforce the escort of Convoy ONS132, were hampered by bad weather and by the fact that, owing to vessels having to be detached for a variety of reasons, the ships of the Escort Group were never all in company. The operations lasted until the 3rd October.

At 1730 on the 24th the ships were ordered to support Convoy SC100, which had been attacked on the two preceding days but it was not met as expected and they were only in company for a few hours on the 25th. The escort of ONS132 was reinforced from the 26th to the 29th September and that of SC102 from the 1st to 3rd October. Shortage of fuel made it necessary for *Scimitar* and *Saladin* to leave ONS132 at 1800 on the 25th September and for the same reason *Sabre* had to part company at 1000 on the 27th. These destroyers were, however, instructed to give support to Convoy RB1, which was being attacked.

The weather, too, was unfavourable for the first week but nevertheless the Group achieved its essential purpose, that of catching U-boats unawares between the convoy's close escort and the Reinforcing Group. At 1331 on the 26th an R/T report from HNoMS *Eglantine* to HMS *Fame*, Senior Officer of the close escort of ON132 was intercepted; this stated that a U-boat was believed to have dived four miles ahead of the convoy. About half an hour later *Fame* was heard reporting that a U-boat was passing between the fifth and sixth columns of the convoy. The Group, which had been disposed with ships in line abreast eight miles apart, thereupon closed in to form an anti-submarine sweep. At 1520 the convoy was sighted ten miles ahead.

Twenty minutes later a U-boat – probably that referred to by *Eglantine* and *Fame* – surfaced a mile ahead of *Stork*. The discovery of the latter must have been an unpleasant surprise for the U-boat captain, intent on the convoy, which he was following, and he dived in fifty seconds. Contact was at once gained and held almost continuously for an hour and twenty minutes under most difficult Asdic conditions. A counterattack and four deliberate attacks were made by *Stork* between 1548 and 1702 and *Spey* also made a depth charge and a Hedgehog attack. A large quantity of oil was seen and it is thought that the U-boat was at least severely damaged. After the attacks the ships of the Group took up positions on the outer screen of the convoy.

At 1443 on the following day *Rother* reported a U-boat surfacing 1,000 yards on her beam – that is to say seven miles on the starboard bow of the convoy. It was blowing a full gale but *Rother* attacked, possibly with some success; *Stork* closed her but in the prevailing conditions did not endeavour to hunt. It is thought that this U-boat had dived well ahead of the convoy in order to obtain some respite from the unpleasant weather and had surfaced in a good shadowing position, quite unaware of the reinforcement of the escort.

On the 28th, after an aircraft had reported attacking a U-boat thirty miles astern of the convoy, *Stork* and *Rother* in company with HMS *Viscount* made a sweep astern but without result.

The Group's operations may have resulted in at least severely damaging two U-boats, and Convoy ONS132, which the enemy had had time to reconnoitre, was probably saved from attack. An indication of the value of a freelance Escort Group may be gauged from the fact that the U-boats, which surfaced so imprudently more or less alongside *Stork* and *Rother* were, in fact, reconnoitring the convoy in the safest position normally available to them.

:: Dönitz ::

Dönitz does not refer to the new Reinforcing or Support Group mentioned above, possibly because no one noticed it as a separate unit. However, he was fully aware of another such group supporting Convoy SC104 and this is mentioned in the next but one chapter. He wrote that on 14 October the U-boats noticed that the security ring around the convoy had been reinforced to such an extent that it was impossible to approach the merchant ships during calm weather.

Chapter 17

New Weapons for Outdated Boats – September 1942

:: Dönitz ::

Dönitz writes that during the second half of 1942, 'There was no longer any doubt that, despite our considerable successes, the opposition had gained the upper hand in the convoy war.' He explains in detail how this was discussed with the Supreme Naval Command on 28 September and how this was considered to have been so important that the matter was brought to Hitler's attention on the same day. After this he lists the improvements necessary to regain the upper hand in the important all-out battles in the Atlantic.

Considerable importance was attached to the high underwater speed submarines being developed by Hellmuth Walter, and Dönitz made the point that they should be put into production as soon as possible. Walter's new submarines with incredibly high underwater speeds used extremely dangerous concentrated hydrogen peroxide as fuel. After the war, the Allies were eager to get their hands on this new technology but no one seemed to be able to make it work properly and these propulsion systems were never adopted for operational submarines, so one must conclude that the principle didn't work terribly well.

Some time was going to be required before these new proposals would appear at the front and as stopgap measure it was going to be necessary to modify existing boats so that they could cope with the advances being made against them. Dönitz describes the details of what went on at this most significant meeting in September 1942 and they are also recorded in *Führer Conferences on Naval Affairs*. One can perhaps sum up the events by quoting an admiral who said, 'Dönitz had been asking for Type VIIC U-boats since the beginning of the war and now where these are in full production, he changes his mind and asks for something totally different.' This makes it quite obvious that the war had changed far beyond the parameters envisaged at the beginning in 1939.

Chapter 18

Action in the Mid-Atlantic Air Gap – October 1942

:: Dönitz ::

With somewhere in region of 100 U-boats at sea every day it was possible to assemble two large packs, one on each side of the so-called Air Gap, the area in the Mid-Atlantic which could not be reached by land-based aircraft. The plan was to station each pack on the 'departure' side, locate a convoy and chase it across the air gap. This was done using the earlier technique of sailing at an economical slow speed towards the expected convoy during daylight and then turning on the same heading and at the same expected speed as the convoy for the hours of darkness. The positions of the convoy were provided by the Radio Monitoring Service, the B-Dienst under Heinz Bonatz, from decrypted radio signals and Dönitz added what he called 'Fingerspitzengefühl' (fingertip feeling), but the appalling weather made operations impossible and at least two convoys slipped through the patrol lines.

However, on 11 October the experienced commander of *U221*, Kapitänleutnant Hans-Hartwig Trojer, sighted a corvette. The weather was rough enough for him to lose it again, but following his intuition he spotted it again the following day and then it led him directly to Convoy SC104. The weather, still too rough for day-trippers, produced masses of white wave tops of intermittent height, ideal for concealing a U-boat on radar screens. As a result Trojer launched somewhere in the region of nine attacks, sinking six ships, including the tanker refuelling the escorts at sea. Other U-boats closed in as well, but managed only one ship each, to bring the total up to eight merchant ships.

Two weeks later, Dönitz tried the same trick when *U606* (Oblt.z.S. Hans-Heinrich Döhler) spotted an escort and followed it northwards. The entire pack was set to follow but this time no one found a convoy. Instead the merchant ships circumnavigated the obstruction and arrived home safely. Dönitz remarked that this showed how unreliable the basic information was.

:: The British Side ::

The Monthly U-boat Offensive Review states:

The figure of losses for the month of October 1942 compares unfavourably with September and it is a consideration enjoining moderation upon the optimistic that two homeward-bound convoys in the central North Atlantic were attacked heavily and with considerable success by U-boat packs.

Despite some progress in utilising long-range aircraft from Iceland, there is still a black pit of excessive danger in the main traffic area north-east of Newfoundland and it seems clear that the German U-boat Command is making strategic dispositions to intercept SC and HX convoys so near as may be to Cape Race – in some cases actually well within potential air cover from Canadian bases – and to develop against any convoys thus intercepted a rapid concentration of half-a-dozen U-boats, which will hang on so long as the convoy is not receiving effective air protection.

Experience is repeatedly affirming that a convoy, not protected by aircraft, may be so disorganised by a concentrated attack and the resultant breaks in formation for rescue work and other adjustment that the escorts may become comparatively ineffective for either protection or offence, whereas the presence, even for a few hours, of one or two aircraft has again and again prevented a concentrated attack from developing.

The Countermeasures Report adds:

Admiral Dönitz found his new 'soft spot' off the Cape of Good Hope and, though the blow had been anticipated, his U-boats sank 14 independently routed ships within four days. Fortunately losses did not continue at this rate and, though more attacks were made in an, area, which extended to Durban, the sinkings after the first outbreak were not heavy. A number of aircraft attacks were made on these U-boats and on the 3rd October HMS *Active* gave one of them the full benefit of a ten-charge pattern, which resulted in an oil patch three miles long and half a mile wide.

On the Transatlantic trade routes, although the Germans may claim successful attacks on four convoys, it is significant that 16 others were shadowed without any visible signs of attacks on the merchantmen in convoy. Another 18 evaded the U-boats altogether. The four convoys attacked were SC104, ON139, SL125 and HX212, which lost a total of 28 ships in the course of 15 attacks.

In selecting convoy routes the advantage of the northerly route within the range of air cover from Iceland has to be balanced against the increased time on voyage, due to greater distance and worse weather, and the advantage which is restored to the U-boat at night when Type 271 [RDF – radar] in the escorts is not functioning at full efficiency.

This month the U-boats made all their assaults by night and most of them in rough weather. It is probably safe to assume that the enemy still prefers to attack by night but that competent U-boat commanders, if frustrated night after night by well-handled escorts taking full advantage of their RDF, Type 271, will occasionally manage to gain bearing on the convoy sufficient for a submerged attack by day. The rough weather during the month, by reducing the efficiency of RDF, was, to that extent at least, in favour of U-boats attacking by night, but it may interest the escort vessels to know that, according to broadcast reports, the weather has also been a severe strain on the Germans.

U-boats have been sighted or attacked off the United States eastern seaboard and in the Gulf of Mexico but, thanks to the effectiveness of the United States Navy's countermeasures, there have been no losses in North or Central American waters, except in the busy Trinidad area. Thus, in just over nine months from their entry into the war, the United States, by the institution of escorted convoys and the provision of air cover and air patrols, have achieved a high degree of immunity from U-boat attack.

Two reinforcing groups, similar to the 20th Escort Group, have been operating in the Western Approaches but both had to be diverted to rescue work.

During the attacks on Convoy SC104, HM Ships *Viscount* and *Fame* each rammed a U-boat. *Fame* got prisoners from *U353* – the captain was caught asleep in his bunk – but her boarding party had to withdraw quickly from the sinking U-boat.

An incomplete report of a 'Mousetrap' [US rocket-propelled bomb thrower – see Chapter 19] attack by a United States patrol craft has been received, stating that three hits were made.

New U-boats continue to make the passage north or south of the Faeroes, and it is probable that between 20 and 30 passed into the Atlantic during the month. Aircraft patrols are now being reinforced by three destroyers working from Sullum Voe under the orders of Commander-in-Chief, Rosyth.

Operations against Shadowing U-boats.
Report by an Escort Commander October 1942.
Bearing in mind that this was a period when Bletchley Park could not read the U-boat code, Convoy ONS138 provides a good example of how Britain coped with attacking U-boats under such conditions when evasive routing was not on the menu of operations. The convoy assembled in North

Channel on 12 October where the lightly ballasted ships were immediately scattered by a moderate south-westerly gale, meaning they made very little westward progress until this abated a few days later. ONS138 was then pitched against the Leopard Patrol Line, consisting of eight U-boats. During the night of 23/24 October, when the high frequency direction finder (H/F D/F) indicated enemy activity astern, it became evident to the escort commander that the convoy had been sighted. Following this, bearings were taken on at least four U-boats and the escorts were kept busy dealing with the shadowers. Several attacks were made against U-boats, but none of them produced any evidence of a 'kill'.

The escort commander later reported that the main feature of the operations was the astonishing number of enemy signals intercepted, which the use of H/F D/F enabled him to plot the movements of U-boats for a period of 24 hours, at the end of which the U-boats were finally driven off without any attack being delivered on the convoy.

Daylight arrived without any contact having been made with U-boats and the last escort chasing them rejoined the convoy's protective screen in anticipation of a dawn attack. Radio transmission indicated one U-boat ahead of the convoy and another on the starboard bow. Escorts were sent out at 25 knots to search for both contacts, but no contact was made. *U443* (Kptlt. Konstantin von Puttkamer) launched an attack late on 22 October, sinking two ships, but none of the other managed to get close enough for firing torpedoes. The escorts were continuously heading towards positions indicated by their H/F D/F and at one stage lookouts in a crow's nest spotted something which could have been a submarine and a periscope was reported as well, but it looks as if this most valuable radio aid and the U-boats' insistence on using their radios prevented a clash.

The report by the escort commander stated that the intelligent use of excellent H/F D/F information and the lucky Asdic detection of a U-boat about to attack saved the convoy. He also added that only one of the escorts, HMS *Hesperus*, had been fitted with this equipment. The fact that frequencies had to be changed induced the Admiralty to not only provide more escorts with such sets but also provide each ship with more than one set so that they could watch on more than one wave band.

Chapter 19

Hedgehog, Mousetrap and Depth Charge Attacks – July/September 1942 with Additions from Autumn 1941 Reports

The projectiles for the Hedgehog ahead-throwing mortar were launched by an explosive charge which meant that it could not be used on some of the lightly-constructed escorts because there was a danger of the recoil damaging the deck. In view of this the Americans developed an alternative with rocket-propelled bombs called Mousetrap.

Having mentioned Mousetrap above it might be appropriate to add the following account first released in the Monthly Anti-Submarine Reports in July and August 1942.

The Mousetrap is a projector, firing a number of relatively small, fast sinking charges equipped with contact fuses that has been developed suitable for installation on small anti-submarine warfare vessels. As the light construction of these vessels will not permit any great amount of deck thrust, the projector utilizes the rocket principle for launching the projectile in flight.

The projector as adopted consists of two groups of rails, each accommodating four projectiles; this permits a salvo of eight projectiles, each carrying a charge of 32 lb of TNT, to be fired with a range of 300 yards and spread in a line perpendicular to the line of fire about 50 yards wide.

The projectiles now in use are copies of the Hedgehog projectiles fitted with suitable rocket motors in the tail. Tests have determined that, except under extreme conditions of weather, a fixed elevation of 48 degrees on the projectile rails gives very little range due to the pitching of the launching vessel. As no provision exists for training the projector, the anti-submarine warfare vessel must be headed in the direction of the contact with a proper lead angle for the tactical situation existing. Modifications have been made to the American type Chemical Recorder to permit accurate determination of the proper firing range as the contact is approached. While it is recognized that considerable dispersion will result from the rolling of the anti-submarine warfare vessel, tests indicate that it is possible to obtain acceptable accuracy by firing when the ship is on an approximately even keel.

These Mousetrap projectors are now being produced in limited numbers but arrangements have been made for quantity production to commence in the near future. Live ammunition is not available at present in more than limited quantities but, as 'Hedgehog' ammunition is adaptable for use with the Mousetrap, an ample supply will be available at an early date.

While no actual attacks on enemy submarines have yet been made by Mousetrap installations, the number of patrol craft equipped with this new weapon is increasing daily and it is hoped that we will have reports of service trials very shortly.

Experimental Mousetrap Attacks

Attacks upon friendly submarines at sea were carried out in April, June and July by two patrol boats. The boat made hits in two attacks on a submarine travelling at 3 knots and 100 feet down by approaching it at 6 knots from the quarter and assuming that the sound range was 50 yards short of the conning tower range. This assumption was confirmed later by one of the patrol boats, which made three hits in a similar attack at 10 knots. Attacks by a patrol boat on June 26 were on the whole unsatisfactory, owing to poor sound conditions.

On the basis of the satisfactory results obtained by the patrol boat on July 28 and 29, it is now possible to set up a definite plan of attack with confidence that, in the hands of a skilful conning officer, it will succeed. It is probably worthwhile to report these attacks in some detail. A standard attacking speed of 10 knots was decided upon as being sufficient to catch any submarine eventually. An officer of the sound school staff personally conned all attacks. The same range rates were given by the recorder and by a stopwatch.

Developments in Depth Charges and Equipment

The Mark IV depth-charge thrower, which retains its depth charge carrier and has quick-loading stowage rack adjacent, is fitted in all twin-screw corvettes, 'R' class and later fleet destroyers, new construction sloops, etc.

A depth-charge firing clock system has been evolved. This comprises a small box on the bridge on which is set the type of pattern desired and the ship's attacking speed. The single pressing of a knob on the box or the making of contacts on the new Type 144/5 A/S recorder automatically fires the pattern of five, ten or fourteen charges, at the correct intervals. Allowance is also made on the clock for firing single depth charges. With this clock the hydraulic pump of the release system is located aft between decks and the link from the bridge is electrical.

Depth-charge firing clock equipment is now being fitted in HMS *Scimitar* for trial.

A modification to the existing pistol has been produced, enabling depths to be preset on Mark VII (light) depth charges at safe in the rails, ready for counterattacks. A more positive position for each depth setting is also obtained. This modification, which is within the capabilities of base staffs depends on the 'back flooding principle' – the admission of pressure to both sides of the pistol diaphragm when at safe. Fifty modified pistols will shortly be available for extensive sea trials in the Western Approaches.

Mark X Depth Charges

Some doubts as to the safety of this weapon have been expressed by commanding officers of ships carrying it. It is, in fact, perfectly safe while on board, as the detonator, should it go off, will not explode the charge until the primer safety gear has operated; this occurs at a depth of 30 feet, provided that the depth charge is clear of the tube.

The danger from fire is no different from warheads or other depth charges; great heat melts the Amatol and, whether melted or not, it would burn fiercely but there have been practically no cases of warheads or depth charges burning to detonation. There have been a number of warheads burnt during air raids at Malta, so that experience on this point is considerable.

The danger from sympathetic detonation is the same as for other depth charges and warheads – among the numerous cases of these being damaged by rifle or cannon fire and the like, there have been practically no instances of detonation – and the primer, should be withdrawn if action with enemy surface craft or aircraft is probable.

Eight or ten ships have now been issued with the Mark X charges. A considerable number of escorts have had the necessary modification to their torpedo tubes completed and stocks of charges are held at the home bases awaiting supply to the ships at the next opportunity.

Aircraft Depth Charges

The Mark XI depth charge, with Mark XIII and Mark XVI pistol (the latter being not yet in production), is Torpex-filled and, provided with a nose spoiler (nose pressing reversed) and a tail, it has achieved the requirement of firing at 20 feet when dropped from aircraft. It is being produced at the rate of 3,000 a month, the majority being supplied to Coastal Command of RAF.

Accuracy of Firing Depth Charge Patterns

A number of recorder traces forwarded by A/S vessels that have hunted U-boats have been analysed to determine the accuracy of the time of release of depth charges. The attacks have been reconstructed, using the settings that the A/S control officer should have had on the recorder, but it should be noted that reports do not provide evidence for deducing the distance that the charges exploded from the U-boat.

The analysis of 26 attacks has shown that: –

Charges were fired early in 16 per cent of the attacks.
Charges were fired accurately in 42 per cent of the attacks.
Charges were fired late in 42 per cent of the attacks.
Charges were badly spaced in 31 per cent of the attacks.

The worst feature of the analysis is the number of patterns that were fired late. The average error in time to fire over all 26 attacks was 4 seconds late, giving a range error of 30 yards at 12 knots. In eleven cases the average error was 15 seconds late, or 100 yards. This distance of itself is enough to allow the escape of a U-boat, however accurate the other factors of the attack.

The charges badly spaced in 31 per cent of the attacks would have resulted in irregular patterns, with spaces between charges in which a U-boat could escape lethal damage. The errors are due to either a firing error on the part of the A/S control officer, or bad drill by the depth charge crews, or a combination of both, and show that there is still room for considerable improvement in this important side of an A/S vessel's offensive role.

The possibility of supplying concrete filled dummy depth charges to escort bases for the use of drilling crews and for exercising release arrangements is being investigated. These were carried by destroyers in peace time and their use was found to be very beneficial for correcting errors in drill and spacing.

Hedgehogs

There are now over 60 Hedgehogs at sea and fitting has been extended to anti-submarine escorts of the approved classes employed anywhere in the Atlantic. Supply of all items of the equipment, including Torpex-filled ammunition, is now reasonably satisfactory, though one component of the control gear is still in short supply.

Remarks on Anti-Submarine Weapons

Various weapons are under development with a view to improving the methods of dealing with U-boats. The following gives a brief summary of the present state of these weapons:

Heavy Depth Charge. – Mark X, 2,000 lbs of TNT fired from a torpedo tube. Slow sinking 5 to 6 feet per second, 20 charges ordered. Speed of sinking is too fast at present, thus possibly endangering the firing ship. This will be remedied. Trials completed from British tubes, trials from American tubes in hand. No date for sea trials can yet be given but it is hoped they will take place in one month's time.

Mark IX Depth Charge. – This is a Mark VII heavy charge with a magnetic pistol. This should operate 30ft from the centre line of a submarine, and can be fired from a thrower. Trials have not been satisfactory and a redesign has been found necessary. No date can be given for completion, but it is not expected for at least four months.

Charges Thrown Ahead. – Various methods of throwing charges ahead are under investigation and it is hoped to make a decision shortly as to which weapon will be adopted.

Mark VII Depth Charge. – Thrown 300 yards ahead in the form of a five-charge pattern. Full scale trials have been carried out in HMS *Whitehall*.

Multi-Spigot Electric Firing. – Weapon consists of a number of small contact projectiles. Trials have taken place in HMS *Westcott* and more are pending. Development of fuse projectile and control is almost complete.

Multi-Spigot Percussion Firing. – Similar to Mark VII, but not quite so far advanced.

Fairlie Multi-Mortar. – One mounting in HMS *Kingfisher* about to commence sea trials. Preliminary fuse and projectile trials carried out.

Holman A/S Projector. – Operates similarly to a mortar. Preliminary trials progressing.

A/S multi-projector. – Rocket impulse. Preliminary trials progressing.

Chapter 20

Luck as Vital Ingredient – October to November 1942

:: Dönitz ::

Despite shipping moving at the excruciatingly slow speed of a pedal cyclist, there are times when things appear to suddenly speed up and one must act instantly or miss a brilliant opportunity. This happened on 30 October 1942 when lookouts on *U381* (Kptlt. Wilhelm-Heinrich Count von Pückler und Limpurg) reported Convoy SC107 close to the Newfoundland Bank. At more or less the same time, the B-Dienst supplied a decrypted British signal giving its course. Dönitz states that the U-boat Command took advantage of this by setting up Group 'Veilchen' as a tight patrol line in its path. The problem was that all of the thirteen boats available had been at sea for some time and were running desperately low on fuel. That meant this lucky strike was going to be wasted unless they got in without further ado. This timing was so critical that the U-boat Command was expecting total failure if the boats could not find the convoy in the immediate future. They were lucky. The ensuing battle lasted for two nights and resulted in fifteen ships totalling 87,818 GRT being sunk. In return one U-boat was thought to have been lost to an aircraft and another went down when it got too close to an exploding munitions ship. After the war, Dönitz learned from British sources that both *U520* (Kptlt. Volkmar Schwarzkopf) and *U132* (Kptlt. Ernst Vogelsang) had been sunk by aircraft, but this would appear to be untrue. Latest research by Axel Niestlé suggests *U132* did indeed go down as a result of the British SS *Hatimura* blowing up.

The other piece of luck for this period of time befell to the opposition, but cost them dearly. Eight U-boats of Group 'Streitaxt' searched for and attacked Convoy SL125 to the west of Gibraltar, sinking thirteen ships with 85,686 GRT. In doing so, the U-boats' attention was turned on this one convoy and the Germans missed the brilliant opportunity of hitting the very much bigger Operation 'Torch' – the landings in North Africa. As a result, the invasion flotilla reached its objective unscathed and without the Germans even being even aware that this momentous step was taking place.

Dönitz goes into great detail about why Germany missed this vital target and what it meant to the war in general. The significant point is that this time luck played more than just an important role in the war; this time it played a vital part in allowing Britain and the United States to establish a powerful base on the African continent.

:: The British Side ::
The U-boat Offensive Reports for October and November 1942 state:

The operation against French North Africa which opened early in November naturally involved the diversion of a great deal of merchant shipping and many escorts from their normal use. Its success should really be taken into the account of credits and debits for October, in which month the foundations were firmly laid for the achievement of the safe arrival of the first operational convoys.

In a very real sense these coming events cast their shadow over October's events, for the enemy disposed an abnormally large proportion of his Atlantic U-boat force to the east and south-east of the Azores and to the south-east of Madeira. This suggests that, in a broad – but fortunately inaccurate – sense, the German command had appreciated the likelihood of an Allied attack on Africa, but that probably Dakar and possibly, at a later stage, Benghazi or Tripoli were thought to be the most likely objectives.

The number of U-boats sighted or fixed by wireless telegraphy evidence early in November to the eastward of Gibraltar corroborates the Admiralty estimates during the last ten days of October that a growing force was being collected in the western approaches to Gibraltar and to the eastward of the Azores.

One consequence directly resulting from this re-disposition of U-boat forces was that Convoy SL125 was severely mauled during a four-day pursuit by a pack of U-boats which grew by accumulation to six or seven in number. This pursuit was abruptly dropped before it drew the U-boats away from the area south-west of Portugal; it may have been regarded as of greater importance that they should stay there and reconnoitre than that they should further pursue an ordinary trade convoy.

Shipping casualties were severe, particularly in the early days of the month. Well over half a million tons of shipping were sunk by U-boats in the Atlantic alone and a new 'soft spot' was exploited by two groups, each of half-a-dozen U-boats, which reached the Cape Town area and eventually passed Cape Agulhas to operate to the eastward in the southern part of the Indian Ocean.

Whilst the main brunt of attack has been borne by convoys in the

North Atlantic, the Trinidad campaign has by no means petered out and losses in that area have been fairly serious. A continuation of trouble in the Caribbean, particularly in the south-eastern section, is to be anticipated. On the other hand, activity has for some time past been wholly negligible off Florida and the eastern seaboard of the United States.

The enemy's effort against the North African operations was only achieved by drawing U-boats away from trade convoys, and proved very costly to him. By the end of the month he had, at any rate temporarily, abandoned this policy, and over 30 U-boats were again operating on the North Atlantic convoy routes. Considering the force of U-boats concentrated east and west of Gibraltar, shipping losses were not unduly heavy, thanks in no small measure to the scale of air cover provided.

By the second week in November two or three of the U-boats, which had been operating south-west of Cape Town had proceeded to the Mozambique Channel. A number of independent ships were sunk in this area. These U-boats were probably refuelled either by a supply U-boat or by a tanker.

Losses in the Trinidad area were rather lighter, and, though by the end of the month several U-boats were patrolling in the St. Paul Rocks area, they had not achieved much success.

The figure of about 650,000 tons sunk by U-boats during November is a heavy one, but in view of the North African operations it might have been much worse.

The Countermeasures Review for November 1942 states:

For the first time for many months it can be said with fair certainty that the number of operational U-boats has decreased. Apparently only about 12 U-boats made the westerly passage north of Scotland. Our best estimate is a decrease of 10 during the month. In connection with the North African operations there is certain evidence of the killing of seven U-boats and, as far as can be judged from preliminary reports from surface craft, another dozen attacks will eventually be assessed as 'Sunk' or 'Probably Sunk'; aircraft made 110 sightings and carried out 64 attacks, some 20 of which resulted in claims for the destruction or serious damaging of U-boats.

It seems incredible that no U-boat success was achieved against the convoys of the expeditionary force until after the assault troops had landed, for they appeared to pass through concentrations aggregating 30 to 40 U-boats before reaching Gibraltar. Even after the 8th November, our losses were not severe though, despite casualties, the number of U-boats operating in the Western Mediterranean rose from about 10 on the 8th to about 20 on the 11th.

The North African operations have not interrupted the Battle of the Atlantic, which has continued in much the same fashion as before. Between 70 and 80 U-boats were operating against the 16 regular convoys which were at sea in the course of the month. U-boats were in contact with 12 of these 16 but only five of them suffered loss. The main attack was on Convoy SC107; an analysis of the U-boat operations has not yet been completed.

:: Dönitz ::

Dönitz was informed of the North African landings by telephone at 0630 hours on 8 November and immediately ordered all boats between the Bay of Biscay and the Cape Verde Islands with enough fuel to the Moroccan coast. Later, when the situation became clearer, boats from Atlantic operations were diverted to this critical area as well. Yet, despite this instant response, there was no one close enough for any action before at least the end of the following day. *U173* (Oblt.z.S. Hans-Adolf Schweichel), one of the first to arrive, found the defences to be especially strong with every target surrounded by what looked like a mass of escorts, yet despite this, three ships were hit. The next boat, *U130* (not *U150* as reported by Dönitz) under the more experienced Korvettenkapitän Ernst Kals was illuminated by strong radar impulses from land, sea and air but still managed to drive home an attack against a mass of twenty ships within sight. Dönitz remarks that the shallow water was especially unfavourable for U-boats and the defences too strong to tackle the more attractive targets, such as aircraft carriers. Again both U-boats were comparatively lucky inasmuch that they succeeded in finding holes in the defences. Later boats found the defences far more alert and much more active, making it exceedingly difficult to hit at supply ships close to the coast. The Allies were obviously not taking any chances and a protective mine barrage around the landing area damaged *U509* (Kptlt. Karl-Heinz Wolff) during her approach, forcing a return to France for repairs, without there having been an opportunity for firing torpedoes.

Dönitz emphasises that the sinking of supply ships was going to be of paramount importance. Every effort had to be made to disrupt the Allied activities in North Africa, even if this was to the detriment of trade convoys elsewhere. On the other hand, the opposition was fully aware of its shaky predicament and did not have resources for allowing such a massive undertaking to fail. The precariousness of this undertaking can be illustrated by a German study of the time. Just a few months earlier the Supreme Naval Command considered Allied landings in North Africa as a possibility, but eventually rejected the idea because everybody thought that even the combined resources of Britain and the United States would not be sufficient to mount such a large invasion. So, it was a case of Britain and the United States making every effort to ensure that the operation succeeded.

Chapter 21

Another Bout of Luck? The Tanker Convoy TM1 – January 1943

:: Dönitz ::

Dönitz describes the battle for Convoy TM1 in some detail and this incredible success has featured in many post-war accounts. The question one needs to ask is whether this was also due to luck or calculation combined with vigorous action. Therefore it is of greater interest to look into the reasons as to why it happened, rather than how the battle unfolded. The basic facts are straightforward. Nine tankers left Trinidad with two more a short distance behind, making an effort to catch up in order to make maximum use of the combined escorts. The two ships were sighted on 29 December by *U124* (Kptlt. Johann Mohr), but not reported as a convoy until five days later when *U514* caught a glimpse of all the tankers heading north-east towards Gibraltar. No special ability was required to guess that they were making for North Africa and were going to be of utmost importance to the recent landings there. This was so important that Dönitz immediately cancelled the plans he had made for Group 'Delphin' and ordered all ten boats to head towards this convoy at high speed. This was no easy decision. First, his staff did not agree with the change of plans and, secondly, there were still some 900 nautical miles (1,600 kilometres) between the two, with ample opportunities for the opposition to circumnavigate the patrol line. Or, as had happened so often in the past, for some other outside influence to prevent U-boats from finding and attacking the target. This time the gamble paid off and only two of the tankers reached Gibraltar on 14 January 1943. Generaloberst Sixt von Armin, Erwin Rommel's successor as Commander-in-Chief in North Africa, knew exactly what this was going to mean to his forces and sent a special 'thank-you' telegram to Dönitz. Roskill summed up the results by saying that the convoy was hacked to pieces. Bearing in mind that there were several occasions when it was thought the U-boats would never meet the tankers, this was indeed an outstanding performance.

:: The British Side ::

The background as to why this happened could well have its roots inside the Submarine Tracking Room at Admiralty's Operational Intelligence Centre and is explained most admirably by Patrick Beesly. Rodger Winn collapsed towards the beginning of December 1942, having suffered such mental and physical exhaustion that his doctor told him he would never work again unless he took a serious rest. As a result, Winn was absent from the nerve centre he had created until early in January and during this time the Submarine Tracking Room was also suffering from an acute shortage of staff. Although individual U-boats may not have been achieving very much to keep up with the pace of the war, there were now large numbers of them; a hundred U-boat at sea every day and many of the most able officers had been transferred to seagoing commands to combat this massive threat. The Admiralty, although operational, was manned largely by civilians and the unions objected ardently to female graduate WRENS being employed instead of civil servants, making the acute shortage of personnel even more frustrating. Of course, being highly secret meant that some branches like this suffered because hardly anyone knew they existed. Patrick Beesly poses the question whether the battle for Convoy TM1 might have ended differently if Winn had been present for all of the operation and makes the flattering remark that Winn had an uncanny flair for that type of guesswork.

The new Atlantic U-boat radio code, called 'Triton' in Germany and 'Shark' in England, was introduced eleven months earlier, on 1 February 1942 and resulted in a blackout at Bletchley Park. This made it impossible to read the messages being sent, but land-based and coastal units continued using the old system. The blackout lasted until the end of the year. One of these new, four-wheel machines was captured from *U559* (Kptlt. Hans Heidtmann) on 30 October 1942 by Anthony Fasson, Colin Grazier and Tommy Brown from HMS *Petard* and the news that this had made it possible for Bletchley Park to break the Triton code came at about the same time as Rodger Winn was taken ill.

The short sighting report from *U514* was intercepted in Britain, but could not be decrypted. The decryption process was not running smoothly and on this occasion there was a seven-day delay between receiving signals and being able to read them. However, by this time the secret Submarine Tracking Room had become proficient enough to identify this as a sighting report and radio direction finders indicated that these few short jumbled letters of radio code could result in the most serious consequences for Convoy TM1. On this occasion the Submarine Tracking Room was up against ten cautious U-boat commanders who did not make a great deal of use of their radios and, at the same time, the U-boat Command in France did not know exactly what was going on at sea and therefore didn't transmit a great deal of directions to the pack. As a result the Special Information from Bletchley Park was rather sparse. The cipher settings, necessary to fully understand what the U-boats were saying, didn't become known until shortly after this event.

Men at sea would have known nothing of what Beesly has written in his book and the British reports of the period obviously excludes any references to Special Intelligence. The Monthly U-boat Offensive Report for January 1943 states:

During January the strategic dispositions of U-boats appeared, so far as could be estimated, to be designed primarily to cut the main artery from the United States to Great Britain. Of the hundred or more U-boats which on any one day were probably at sea, over fifty are thought to have operated north of 50°N, most of them between Newfoundland and the longitude of Central Iceland.

The weather was almost consistently unfavourable to U-boat operations and, whilst the high seas and violent winds inflicted considerable marine losses upon our shipping, it cannot be denied that more convoys and other ships would have been attacked, had U-boats been able to move more freely and remain more on the surface.

The lesson was again learnt that VLR aircraft are a vital need for convoy protection.

An HX convoy was intercepted a few hours before it reached the extreme range of aircraft based in Iceland and Ireland, but cover was provided at the earliest possible moment and the development of an effective mass attack was greatly impeded.

Evasive alterations of route were employed tactically with success, but it should be appreciated that, with the growth of the operational U-boat force and the consequently greater areas covered by their patrols – which sometimes appear to approach ubiquity [i.e. being in all places at the same time] – the use of this method is limited and may soon be outworn. Several convoys came through with an immunity, which owed more to good luck than good judgment.

The actual losses during the month were so low as to give an entirely false impression of the gravity of the threat to our shipping and supplies, and of the modern scale of U-boat operations. The potentially annihilating superiority which the enemy, given a favourable strategic situation, might bring to bear on a convoy unlucky enough to be caught early in a homeward journey and far away from effective air cover, cannot be appreciated by reference to any past experience, still less to the fortunate phase which we have recently enjoyed.

The fate of a tanker convoy [TM1] bound from Trinidad to Gibraltar is a truer index of the strength of a U-boat pack operating in favourable conditions. Out of nine tankers, with an escort of one destroyer and three corvettes, only two survived.

Concentration against shipping of immediate importance for military operations and a bolder and more reckless strategy are the keynotes of the enemy's present policy. The tempo is quickening, and the critical phase of the U-boat war in the Atlantic cannot be long postponed.

The Monthly U-boat Countermeasures Report for January 1943 states:

As regards merchant shipping losses, which were lower than in any month of 1942, the new year started well, but it also saw the Germans for the first time operating a hundred U-boats in the Atlantic. [The 'magic' number of 100 had been reached already in September 1942, without the Allies being aware of this.] In spite of this large concentration on our northern trade routes it is astonishing that the U-boats did not succeed in massing and attacking any of our convoys, though they did manage to pick off a few stragglers. Unfortunately no U-boats were sunk in this area.

In the southern part of the North Atlantic they had considerable success in their attacks on Convoy TM1 bound from the Dutch West Indies to Gibraltar, and sank seven out of nine tankers. The first attack was made at 2145 on the 3rd January when the convoy was about 1,100 miles north-east of Trinidad and may well have been the result of a chance encounter but, once sighted, the identity and probable destination of the convoy was evidently correctly appreciated. For five nights the tankers proceeded unmolested but on the night of the 9th/10th, when they were about 600 miles west of the Canary Islands, a series of heavy attacks resulted in the loss of five ships. At least one of these might have been able to reach harbour but the size of the escort – one destroyer and three corvettes – was insufficient to permit leaving anyone behind to stand by the damaged ships, nor were the escort able to hunt the U-boats to destruction. There were indications that U-boats were damaged by the escorts but no proofs of kills.

Twenty-four hours after this attack, one of the three ships then remaining was torpedoed and burst into flames, revealing four U-boats between the convoy and its escorts.

All four escort vessels were fitted with RDF, Type 271, and the destroyer had H/F D/F, but during the critical period the RDF in two out of the three corvettes was broken down. Some of the U-boats were probably able to reach favourable positions and then to get past the escort

– the protection that is afforded to the normal trade convoy cannot rightly be called 'a screen' – submerged and undetected. All the attacks on the convoy took place well out of range of shore-based aircraft.

The only other convoy to suffer serious loss was TB 1 (Trinidad to Baja), which had four out of twelve ships torpedoed and sunk. The U-boats, operating in comparatively shallow water to the northward of Guiana, took advantage of a gap in the air cover to make their attacks.

To meet to some extent the need for shore-based air cover for transatlantic convoys, Coastal Command should, by the end of February, have forty VLR aircraft, with an endurance of 2,000 to 2,500 miles. Action has been taken to increase considerably the number of VLR aircraft on both sides of the Atlantic. Four Hudson aircraft of Coastal Command have operated as an experiment from Bluie West I Airfield in Greenland; it is hoped that soon there will be long-range aircraft at this airfield but their operations will be restricted by weather and other conditions.

It is now possible to provide continuous shore-based air cover on the coastal route between Gibraltar and Freetown.

Chapter 22

New Developments – End of 1942

:: Dönitz ::

The earlier chapter 'New Weapons for Old Boats' mentions how matters reached such a point in the Atlantic that the latest developments were discussed with the Supreme Naval Command on 28 September 1942 and that the admirals considered this to have been so important that the situation was also presented to Hitler later that same day. One of the ramifications from these meetings was to find out exactly what type of equipment was being used by the Allies. To do this Germany built a special VHF (Very High Frequency) radio receiver to track radar impulses. The only place to try this out was at sea, so the apparatus was fitted aboard *U524* (Kptlt. Freiherr Walter von Steinaecker). Surprisingly, in mid-November this also picked up British voice messages, but the set was so new that no one on board knew its range and therefore could not determine whether this VHF voice traffic was nearby or far away. On hearing this news, the U-boat Command in France assumed the voices had to be fairly close to the U-boat and set up a patrol line to intercept the anticipated convoy. This worked reasonably well and did result in a good contact, but this had hardly been made when radio stations in Germany also picked up radio signals from aircraft in the same area of what was still regarded as the 'Mid-Atlantic Air Gap'. The ensuing battle was bitter and decisive. The opposition frustrated most of the attacks and only a few ships were sunk.

:: The British Side ::

Despite obviously having statistically gained the upper hand at sea, there was still a long way to go before the Allies could relax and consider themselves to have won the war and several technical projects had come to fruition, where new technology was making a noteworthy impression. (Losses due to U-boats were exceedingly high throughout 1942 but that was due to there having been an exceptionally large number of U-boats at sea, but each individual U-boat was sinking very little. In 1940 each U-boat at sea was sinking up to about six ships per month. In 1942 this figure had dropped dramatically to never more than two and for much of the time was not much higher than one.)

Towards the end of 1942, the British Anti-Submarine Reports mention the following:

Asdic Type 144

Some experience has now been gained with the new Asdic set, Type 144 as an experimental model and various modifications have been made and the advantages, which are summarized below, amply warrant the increased complications.

The Advantages of the New Type 144 Asdic Set

1.

Automatic training gives accurate gyro step angles and enables the operator to watch range recorder as well as listen; it therefore provides greater certainty of initial detection.

2.

With automatic training, bearings are obtained more quickly and more easily.

3.

The bearing recorder provides a memory of the bearings. There is, therefore, less chance of losing contact. In addition, the mean of several bearings can be found and the bearing rate obtained with greater precision.

4.

The bearing recorder gives the bearing on which to aim ahead-thrown weapons and the course to steer for ahead-thrown attacks.

5.

The bearing recorder assists in obtaining the correct course to steer for attacks with depth charges dropped from the stern.

6.

An improved range recorder gives greater accuracy in obtaining the range and time to fire for both ahead-thrown attacks and depth-charge attacks.

7.

The Asdic information is obtained and the course to steer transmitted to the helmsman with the minimum of delay.

8

The automatic volume control receiver (which is also being incorporated in existing sets) provides general improvements in detection, including better recording of echoes on the range recorder.

9.

The Captain is free to attend to the general fighting of his ship.

Mark 29 (625 pounds) Aircraft Depth Bombs

During the past month a number of operating units have been supplied with Mark 29 depth bomb for service use. These bombs contain 464 pounds of TNT. The number of bombs which can be carried by each type of airplane is reduced in proportion to the additional weight of the new type depth bomb.

To date, nine attacks have been reported where Mark 29 bombs have been dropped.

On 28th August an attack was made on a diving submarine with four Mark 29 bombs with 50-feet depth settings. Centre charges were estimated to have landed close aboard on either side of the submarine. It appeared as if the force of the explosions so disabled the submarine that it was unable to submerge. The aircraft called up a surface anti-submarine vessel, which was in the area, and in the ensuing action HMCS *Oakville* finished off the U-boat. It is believed that if 25-foot settings had been used the initial attack would have been lethal and the aircraft would have been credited with a sinking rather than an assist. However, it is encouraging to note that the Mark 29 bomb is apparently capable of doing crippling damage to a surfaced submarine, even when set at 50 feet depth. [The U-boat was *U94* commanded by Kapitänleutnant Otto Ites, one-time watch officer aboard *U48*, the most successful U-boat of the Second World War. The initial attack was made by an aircraft from US Navy Squadron VP-92 and *U94* was sunk as a result of being rammed by HMCS *Oakville*.]

In a second attack, three Mark 29 bombs were dropped across a surfaced submarine, about 40 feet forward of the conning tower. From dispatch reports it appears that this submarine was severely damaged.

In the third attack, the aircraft dropped three Mark 29 bombs, which apparently landed too far from the target to give any evidence of damage.

The fourth attack, aircraft dropped three Mark 17 bombs close aboard which apparently caused submarine to lose control. On second attack plane dropped one Mark 29 bomb close alongside as submarine was diving. After 20 minutes large swirls and turbulence in the vicinity indicated that submarine was probably seriously damaged.

In the fifth attack, aircraft dropped a combination of two Mark 17's and two Mark 29's. One Mark 29 landed close aboard as submarine was diving. In first three minutes after attack oil and air spouted to the surface in large quantities. One survivor was observed to surface about five minutes after the attack. Oil and bubbles continued to rise for 30 minutes. Aircraft dropped raft for survivor, on which to date no further information is available. After three hours oil slick covered an area of approximately six square miles.

Detection of Mines by Asdics

It has always been considered possible for moored mines to be detected by Asdics and the 'short transmission unit' was originally fitted to Asdic sets to increase the efficiency in this detection. Peacetime results showed that the most favorable direction of Asdic transmission is along the line of the lay, so that a ripple of small echoes is received which is easily noticeable. Such a condition may not often obtain and war-time experience has proved that a surface craft Asdic set can by no means be relied upon in all circumstances for certain detection of moored mines. Successful detection has, however, been reported on several occasions and, in particular, HMAS *Stuart,* off Alexandria, initially detected one minefield by Asdic and delineated another to the minesweepers that successfully cleared it.

As regards submarines, a greater success in detection has been obtained, probably due to the reduction in extraneous water noises while submerged, making the small echoes more noticeable.

Ground Mines

Echoes were obtained from ground mines at ranges between 200 and 1,000 yards but on this occasion the state of the mines – whether they were deeply embedded or not – was not known. The results were however very inconsistent and unreliable and it is apparent that there is no possibility of obtaining results unless weather and Asdic conditions are extremely good. The tide did not appear to have any effect one-way or the other.

No opportunity occurred to attempt detection of ground mines laid in depths greater than 60 feet but the possibility of doing so is not regarded with optimism.

Moored Mines

Echoes were obtained from mines 30 feet below the surface at ranges from 100 to 700 yards and from mines 8 feet below the surface at ranges from 100 to 1,500 yards. Attempts were made without success to obtain echoes from an enemy moored mine whose horns could just be seen on the surface.

The conclusion is that the detection of moored mines between 8 feet and 30 feet deep is fairly reliable under good Asdic conditions but occasions may arise when, although a good contact has been obtained, it will not again be located when approaching on a different course a short time later.

It is probable that no difference exists in the character or echo strength of the contact from shallow or deep mines and, therefore, it is impossible to estimate their depth.

Conclusions

These wartime experiences bear out the opinions already expressed. Although some success has been obtained in detecting moored mines by Asdic, it is not safe to assume that, because no results are obtained, an area is free of mines, especially if the mines are shallow or sparsely laid. The Asdic might be of great assistance for the initial detection of evenly laid fields of moored mines, such as our own on the east coast, and for directing the minesweepers towards them. It is essential that Asdic fitted vessels should be worked up on our own minefields, so that they obtain practice in this form of sweeping and the use of the short transmission unit, before attempting operational sweeping.

Hedgehog Ammunition

Two modifications to the fuse have been introduced to obviate any chance of premature detonations. One is the straightening of the vanes of the propeller to increase the arming depth, and the other is the incorporation of a modified spring and striker. The former has been universally introduced by signal and modified components for the latter have already been issued to the home escort ports and will be supplied to bases abroad shortly. Ships have been instructed to exchange their outfits for modified ammunition at the first opportunity. Satisfactory sea trials of the modified ammunition have been carried out by HMY *Shemara*.

Anti-Submarine Bombs

100 lb anti-submarine bomb trials have shown that the bomb must have 5 feet of water over it to ensure safety of aircraft at 250 feet, that the present bomb is liable to arm and ricochet, and that drops cannot be permitted below 450 feet. For the present there is no requirement for this bomb as, even if modifications prove successful, the minimum dropping height would be 250 feet; at this height the trajectory of the bomb is such that it does not compare favorably with the depth charges.

The 600 lb Minol-filled anti-submarine bomb is liable to counter-mining and mutual damage restriction radius. Provisionally it is cleared for 90 feet spacing and sticks of two bombs but it is expected that this will be improved by screening fittings.

Chapter 23

The Hardest Convoy Battle: The Buildup to the Climax – January and February 1943

:: Dönitz ::

Dönitz made the point that the effectiveness of each individual submarine had declined dramatically and Germany now needed three times as many U-boats at sea to achieve the same results as at the beginning of the war. His big bone of contention was still the activity in cold northern waters, where the majority of boats were achieving very little. Therefore, once again, he asked for permission to divert at least some of them to more productive areas further south. Grand Admiral Erich Raeder, the Commander-in-Chief of the Navy, agreed to this only a short time before telling Dönitz that he was going to retire and would like to nominate him as one of his possible successors.

One of the most significant reasons for the U-boats' low performance in the Atlantic was thought to have been the weather. Appalling storms had been blowing more or less continuously since early autumn, making the finding, tracking and attacking of convoys incredibly difficult. Yet, despite this, Dönitz had a deep down feeling that there had also been some significant changes out at sea. Wolf packs were failing miserably, especially when it came to finding convoys. When writing his book, he thought that the cause for this could have been the new leader on the British side. Admiral Percy Noble had been replaced by Max Horton, who had been a submarine commander during the First World War and commanded the Silent Service before moving to Liverpool to become Commander-in-Chief for the British Western Approaches. Several other historians have fallen into a similar seemingly obvious trap, but one must remember that Percy Noble managed to keep the majority of Allied forces away from the teeth of the wolf packs at a time when Bletchley Park could not read the U-boat code and many reviewers do not seem to have taken the massive build-up of U-boats into account. So, the contribution made by Percy Noble was enormous, far greater than what many reviewers have assumed.

The first weeks of 1943 were taken up by that most dramatic battle against the tanker Convoy TM1, which has been mentioned earlier, but there were many more boats further north. The climax up there came towards the end of the month, when *U456* (Kptlt. Max-Martin Teichert) spotted Convoy HX224 and despite the most appalling weather followed it for three days, sinking three ships in the process. The other five boats directed towards it were some distance behind the merchant ships and were unable to catch up, so the rest of the wolf pack did not achieve a great deal.

Shortly after this, luck played once more into German hands. First, the B-Dienst decrypted details of Convoy SC118 carrying valuable war supplies from America bound for Murmansk (Russia) and at about the same time *U632* (Kptlt. Hans Karpf) rescued a British officer, who had been shipwrecked a few days earlier and who told Karpf about the other convoy. This time the German 'Fingerspitzengefühl' (Finger Tip Feeling) paid off and the convoy ran right into the middle of Group 'Pfeil', consisting of thirteen U-boats, but knowing what was at stake, the Allies supplied strong escorts and intensive air cover. Dönitz recorded the sinking of 13 ships with 59,765 GRT, but he also had to mourn the loss of three U-boats (*U187*, Kptlt. Ralph Münnich, *U609*, Kptlt. Klaus Rudloff and *U624*, Kptlt. Graf Ulrich von Soden-Fraunhofen). Four more boats were so heavily damaged that they were lucky to get back to base. Three-quarters of this group fell foul to attacks and those that were not depth charged were hit hard by bad weather. Dönitz said that this must have been the most difficult convoy battle of the whole war, where some of the commanders did not leave the bridge for a period of four days because the survival of each boat depended on their quick reaction. He said that what these commanders achieved was the greatest feat in the history of submarine warfare in both world wars.

Dönitz was somewhat astonished by the large number of ships sunk, despite such a mass of escorts frustrating many attacks and he came to the conclusion that many of these did not have terribly well-experienced crews. What is more, they tossed about so many depth charges that normal escorts could not have carried all of them at the same time and must, therefore, have been replenished from supply ships within the convoy.

:: The British Side ::
The U-boat Offensive Report for February 1943 states:

> The outstanding characteristic of U-boat operations in February was concentration of effort in the North Atlantic. Never before has the enemy displayed such singleness of purpose in utilizing his strength against one objective – the interruption of supplies from America to Great Britain. As a result, engagements were embittered and successes against U-boats

reached a record peak; it was probably the best month ever known in respect of U-boats sunk.

Only two convoys were heavily attacked – one SC and one ON [SC118 was attacked by thirteen U-boats and ON166 by four]. In each case severe losses were sustained, but the escorts of both convoys gave a very good account of themselves. The air cover for the SC convoy was a dominant factor in the successful solution of an originally adverse situation, but in the case of the ON convoy such assistance was unfortunately precluded by the distance from shore bases at which the attack developed. In both actions about twenty U-boats were concentrated to operate and, although it is probable that less than half this number were at any time in contact, it cannot be denied that in such conditions a purely surface escort is bound eventually to be overwhelmed by sheer weight of numbers.

Bad weather and the practice of evasive routeing contributed to the favourable outcome of the month's experiences, but both of these factors are played out and will supply little help in the next months. What is needed – and is being supplied – is the assistance of an increased force of VLR aircraft.

The Countermeasure Report for February 1943 states:

It is evident that the U-boats are trying hard to get ahead of convoys and to attack submerged in order to avoid detection by RDF or visual sighting. With broad fronted convoys it is not possible for the few escort vessels available to give much of a screen against such a maneuver, and, where the defence has been successful, the U-boats have almost invariably been detected on the surface while trying to get into an attacking position.

On the whole it is considered that the U-boats are willing to get inside the convoy by day or on moonlight nights but that they are unlikely to accept such a situation voluntarily on a dark night.

It is estimated that over twenty U-boats made contact with Convoy SC118, which lost its rescue ship and eight merchantmen, one of these being a straggler. The convoy was first sighted on 4th February but it was not until the night of the 6th/7th that the U-boats really developed their attack and sank seven ships. An attack made on the following night cost the convoy only one ship. U187, who probably made the first sighting, was sunk on the 4th by HMS *Vimy* after a sweep along an H/F D/F bearing ahead of the convoy. The U-boat probably first sighted a Snowflake which was fired by mistake about dawn on 4 February.

The escort on the night of the 6th/7th consisted of 12 ships, three being United States' destroyers. Air cover was provided on and after 6th February, despite the fact that the Iceland aircraft were grounded on the

7th. Co-operation between the air and surface escort was good – the 'Air Patrol Table' worked well – and there were a number of promising attacks by both ships and aircraft, resulting, it is thought, in two U-boats being sunk, in addition to *U187* [Kptlt. Ralph Münnich], and seven or eight being damaged. [The two boats sunk were *U559* under Korvkpt. Karl Thurmann and *U265* under Oblt.z.S. Leonhard Aufhammer.]

A meeting was held at Liverpool after the arrival of the convoy and the following points were brought out. First, the Escort Commander, who was ahead of the convoy, was not fully apprised of the situation and would undoubtedly have been better placed astern – the nights were dark and the wind quarterly, force 5; secondly, escorts must keep their Senior Officer fully informed of important incidents and of any deviation from his last instructions; thirdly, it is most necessary to take prompt offensive action when a convoy is attacked; and fourthly, it is extremely important for the Senior Officer to control firmly the number of escort vessels engaged in rescue work or screening other ships engaged in rescue work.

The only other eastbound convoy to be attacked was HX224. After proceeding uneventfully for five days, it was attacked on the 2nd and 3rd February; on both nights the time chosen was during the middle watch and the rear ship of a column was hit. Another attack was attempted and frustrated at 2037 on the 2nd. The U-boats remained in contact until the convoy was within 36 hours of Barra Head but made no more attacks.

The convoy was a big one, consisting of 58 ships in 14 columns, and it was estimated that at one time during its passage it covered an area of no less than 52 square miles. Weather conditions were bad and on the night of 30th/31st January, the wind, which was blowing from the south-west, increased from Force 6–7 to 8, causing a dozen ships on the port wing to heave to and eventually to leave the convoy. Presumably the U-boats also found these conditions difficult.

The escort consisted of HMS *Highlander* as Senior Officer, HMC Ships *Restigouche, Collingwood, Amherst* and *Sherbrooke* and HMS *Asphodel*, who were reinforced by HM Ships *Clare* and *Londonderry* on 2nd February. It was unfortunate that circumstances made it necessary to deprive *Highlander* of the ships to which six months group training and preparation had been devoted. Loyal and intelligent as was the co-operation shown by the ships allotted to her, it could not make up for the group training and mutual understanding which had been achieved and which lie at the very root of successful convoy escort. Despite these difficulties, operations which lasted from about noon on 1st February to about midnight on the 3rd were carried out with a minimum of loss and possibly resulted in the sinking of a U-boat. [No losses have been recorded.] At 1452 on 1st February, *Amherst*, on the port quarter, reported sighting a suspicious object bearing 234° distant 7 miles but, though *Amherst* and *Sherbrooke* investigated, they found nothing, nor was a Fortress aircraft any more successful.

At 2000 *Highlander's* appreciation was that there were two U-boats in the vicinity but there was nothing to show that either of them was actually in contact with the convoy, though the stragglers might have been reported. It was a moonless night with a high sea and the wind blowing strongly from the convoy's port quarter, and *Highlander* did not anticipate attack that night. It developed, none the less, at about 0115/2nd, the U-boat firing from the port quarter to sink the rear ship of the port wing column. No white rockets were fired – the convoy was at the time enveloped in a heavy sleet shower – and there was unfortunately a delay of about five minutes in reporting the attack to *Highlander*. She at once ordered *Sherbrooke* and *Amherst* to carry out 'Observant' round the wreck, but nothing was sighted. It is thought that the U-boat escaped to leeward in the rain.

From then onwards H/F D/F bearings indicated that the convoy was being shadowed and that other U-boats were closing it. Two fixes were obtained about noon but, though *Amherst*, *Asphodel* and *Restigouche* were sent off to sweep, neither U-boat could be located. At 2000 it was considered that the convoy was being shadowed from the starboard quarter, with a U-boat on each bow, one on the port quarter and possibly two more in the neighbourhood. The U-boat on the starboard bow apparently closed for an attack – there was a light horizon in the north-west and the convoy's course was 086° – but her enterprise was foiled by *Restigouche*, who returned from her sweep just in time to force her to dive, and perhaps also by *Collingwood*, who carried out an attack on a doubtful contact at 2037.

At 2200/2nd the H/F D/F plot indicated that the procedure of the enemy was to shadow from the windward quarter but to close in astern at frequent intervals to check the convoy's course. Having done this and made a report, the U-boat would quickly move out to the quarter again. *Highlander* determined to take advantage of this deduction and, calculating that the U-boat would make its next dart in astern at 2300, despatched *Clare* and *Londonderry*, who had joined during the afternoon, together with *Asphodel*, on an RDF sweep to a depth of 5 miles astern of the convoy. They started at 2239 and punctually at 2300 the shadower was heard making her report but, owing to a misunderstanding, the ships did not find her.

Two hours later, at 0102 on the 3rd, the enemy attacked again. As before, the attack coincided with a heavy shower and caught the rear ship of a column – this time the centre. On this occasion a rocket was sighted and a search was carried out, but there was a delay of 10 minutes in the firing of snowflake by the merchantmen; the U-boat apparently passed close to the wreck about 10 minutes after the torpedoing and then made off at high speed on a westerly course to leeward, as in the first attack.

A fine batch of H/F D/F bearings showed that the illumination of the convoy had not been wasted upon the U-boats in contact and enabled *Highlander* to place one on the port bow, one on the port quarter and a third on the starboard quarter, at ranges estimated to be between 20 and 25 miles. There appeared to be no U-boats ahead or on the starboard bow. To forestall the attack which, it was thought, might be made at about 0300, a starshell search was carried out a quarter of an hour before that time. Nothing was sighted and no attack developed.

The enemy was still in contact on the afternoon of the 3rd and *Highlander* devised a mild stratagem, which both secured the convoy's safety and possibly destroyed the industrious shadower astern. The Commodore was requested to alter course from 080° to 100° at 1700 – the time at which the air escort were due to leave – as if making for Malin Head, and to alter back at 2200. *Clare* and *Londonderry* were ordered to make a RDF sweep astern, starting at 2145, so as to prevent the shadower from observing the alteration back. *Restigouche* was to go six miles ahead to put down the U-boats shadowing from this direction.

Just before 2200, *Highlander* heard the shadower astern making her first report and then, almost simultaneously, received *Londonderry's* report that she was investigating an RDF contact four miles astern in the anticipated position. Asdic contact was obtained and the two ships carried out five depth-charge attacks, the results of which are regarded as promising. During the action *Londonderry* was damaged by a torpedo explosion from a non-contact torpedo, but she was able to reach harbour in tow on the 6th. The convoy arrived off Barra Head without further incident at 1000 on 5th February.

The H/F D/F plot was the hinge of the whole operation and it was gratifying that *Highlander* was able to test her deduction of the shadowing U-boat's procedure in such a satisfactory manner.

The outward bound convoys suffered more severely than the homeward bound. Convoy ON166 was first attacked at 1600 on 21st February, when about 750 miles west-south-west of Cape Clear, and the fight went on until 0725 on the 25th, by which time 12 ships had been sunk, one other being torpedoed but getting in, thanks to the devotion of her master and 15 of her crew. Of these 13 ships, a total of six were torpedoed during attacks made between 0630 and 0730 on three consecutive mornings; on the nights of both the 21st and 22nd attacks were made at about 2130, causing the loss of four ships. The Senior

Officer of the escort was USS *Campbell,* but early on the second night of the battle she was 'in collision with a U-boat' from which she obtained 13 prisoners [*U606* under Oblt.z.S. Hans Dohler]. Her engine room was flooded, but she was able to make St. John's in tow. HMS *Dianthus* also attacked a U-boat and claims to have sunk it. [It escaped.]

Convoy ON167, which like ON166 was given a southerly route and had air cover until it was a thousand miles from the United Kingdom, was attacked on the night of the 21st/22nd and lost Nos. 11 and 13. No H/F D/F bearings were obtained before the torpedoings but a U-boat was detected by RDF as it was attempting to escape on the surface after the attack and depth-charged by FS *Aconit.* Four hours later H/F D/F bearings were obtained and at 0410/22nd HMS *Harvester* (Senior Officer) established RDF contact with a U-boat after running down a ground wave bearing given by her FH4 attachment; the U-boat was then sighted and attacked with three patterns of depth-charges. It is perhaps significant that the convoy was not reported again.

A third outward-bound convoy to suffer loss was UC1 [UK – Caribbean] which consisted of 32 tankers, bound from the United Kingdom to the Dutch West Indies. The convoy was apparently first reported by a U-boat during the afternoon of the 22nd, when it was about 450 miles west of Lisbon. The U-boats attacked next day, first sinking a straggler and then torpedoing four in the convoy, two being sunk. The following day the escort, which consisted of four sloops, four USN destroyers and two frigates, attacked six U-boats so successfully that, although one U-boat seems to have shadowed the convoy for another three days, no more attacks developed.

Chapter 24

The Largest Convoy Battle of All Time – March 1943

:: Dönitz ::

In February the U-boat Command came to the conclusion that the patrol lines were not finding anticipated convoys and the few, which were sighted always ran into one end of the wolf pack rather than into its middle. What is more, a considerable number of convoys were discovered after they had passed the patrol line. The first mentioned resulted in many U-boats not being able to reach the merchant ships in time and the other caused them to use too much fuel in chasing after merchant ships and the weather was often so bad that they could not catch up at all. All this posed the question as to how Britain was managing these brilliant evading manoeuvres. Dönitz explains the thought processes within the U-boat Command. The fact that the opposition was reading his secret radio code occurred to him again, but, once more, the experts in the Supreme Naval Command suggested a number of alternatives, saying it was absolutely impossible to crack the radio code. Dönitz also explains how the German Radio Monitoring Service was reading British signals with considerable ease and speed and therefore knew that Britain was fully aware of what the U-boats were doing. In the end, the blame was pegged onto air reconnaissance, with high-quality radar being the main method used to track U-boats. It was thought that spies in French bases also contributed vital details of sailing times. Dönitz laments the absence of effective air reconnaissance for U-boats, saying how much easier it would be if he had more sighting reports.

Following this insight into radio, Dönitz goes on to describe the action around the time of Convoy HX229 and SC122. This was significant inasmuch that it became the biggest convoy battle of the war and he explains how the ships were sighted and then attacked. Two leading historians (Prof. Dr. Jürgen Rohwer and Martin Middlebrook) have written detailed books about this one single battle and it has been well covered in a multitude of other publications. So, it should not be necessary to go in to great detail here, other than to make the interesting remark that it did not appear as a great or significant event at the time and in many contemporary documents it appears as just one more bitter tit-for-tat action. From the following extract one can see that the Admiralty placed equal weight on some of the other occurrences around this time.

:: The British Side ::
The Monthly U-boat Offensive Report for March 1943 had been reproduced in its entirety here, to make it easier to judge the emphasis put on the various events. It states:

> The month was very difficult for convoys and losses were heavy. Five HX convoys and two SC convoys were attacked and in the areas west of Portugal and off the Azores there was greater activity and more display of aggressive tactics than of late. In the Caribbean, too, there was a resumption of attacks in moderate force. Sinkings of U-boats were achieved on a satisfactory scale, but there remained a debit balance at the end of the month in the form of a small increase in the number of U-boats in operational service.
>
> In the North Atlantic very large packs of U-boats appear to have operated and, considering the weight of attack developed, the convoys came through for the most part remarkably well. One HX convoy achieved an outstanding success in fighting its way through at least twenty U-boats which were in firm contact for four days in this strenuous engagement only six ships were lost, three of them being stragglers.
>
> Against the HX convoy, which lost the Senior Officer [Commander A. A. Tait] of its escort – HMS *Harvester* [protecting Convoy HX228], torpedoed when lying disabled by a successful ramming – the largest pack yet employed is estimated to have been concentrated. It seems clear that in the course of the double operation against this convoy and an SC convoy, which it overtook, at least forty U-boats must have been involved. FFS *Aconit* sank one – possibly two – in addition to the one accounted for by *Harvester*, and had the satisfaction of revenging the latter by sinking her attacker. [*U444* under Oblt.z.S. Albert Langfeld and *U432* under Kapitänleutnant Hermann Eckhardt.]
>
> Air support for North Atlantic convoys was provided with increased strength when weather permitted, but, owing to the limitations set by airfield facilities, could not always be made available when most needed.
>
> A United States convoy to Casablanca deserves mention for the achievement of its six destroyers in fighting off a pack of about fifteen U-boats during a prolonged engagement and in reducing the losses to a small proportion of the ships in convoy.
>
> Half a dozen German U-boats operated with only moderate effect off the coasts of South Africa, and one went so far afield as Lourenço

Marques; by the end of the month all are thought to have turned homeward.

It is estimated that at times the number of U-boats at sea in the Atlantic exceeded 110 and that over half of these were in the area north of the fiftieth parallel.

The Monthly U-boat Countermeasures Report adds the following:

More than three quarters of the tonnage sunk during March consisted of ships sailed in convoy, the total of such losses being, by over 100,000 tons, the highest ever recorded. The enemy's main effort continued to be in the North Atlantic but his resources were such that he was able during the month to attack convoys in the Greenland Sea, in the Indian Ocean and off the coasts of Portugal and Guiana. On 9th March five convoys were engaged, an eastbound and a westbound transatlantic convoy, a North Russian convoy, a convoy bound from Baia to Trinidad and a convoy on passage from the United Kingdom to Gibraltar.

The convoys most closely beset were SC121, HX228, SC122 and HX229, which lost between them 30 ships, excluding stragglers. It was during the passage of Convoy HX228 that HMS *Harvester* destroyed *U444* and was herself sunk by *U432*, which FF. *Aconit* disposed of in her turn. The Commanding Officer of *Harvester*, an outstanding leader of a group of British, Polish and Free French escort vessels, was unfortunately lost with his ship [Commander A. A. Tait].

Convoys HX230 and SC123 were also sighted soon after leaving Newfoundland and attracted packs of U-boats but nevertheless got through without losing any ships in convoy. SC123 was escorted by HMS *Whimbrel* (Senior Officer of Group B2) and HM Ships *Whitehall, Vanessa, Gentian, Sweetbriar, Clematis* and *Heather*. A Support Group, consisting of HM Ships *Salisbury* and *Chelsea* was in company from 0800 on the 21st March until 1400 on the 24th, and the United States auxiliary aircraft carrier *Bogue*, escorted by two United States destroyers, proceeded with the convoy until it was about 175 miles south-east of Cape Farewell.

The weather on the northerly route, which the convoy followed, made operations very difficult but on four out of six days aircraft were flown off from and successfully recovered by this small carrier.

She and her escorting destroyers parted company at 1900 on 26th March and at 1928 the H/F D/F operator in *Whimbrel* reported a transmission from a U-boat about twenty miles away and bearing 315° – the convoy's course was then 074°. Within ten minutes another U-boat was D/F'd bearing 185°, 25 – 30 miles. *Vanessa* was ordered to investigate the first and *Whitehall* the second, both ships being ordered to remain in the suspected area until dark and then to return, if not in contact.

Whitehall found nothing and was back in position at midnight, but *Vanessa* was luckier. Her first contact was obtained by Asdic at 2000 and, after an hour, was classified as 'non-sub'. *Vanessa* had just completed her investigations when, at 2056, she sighted a U-boat bearing 240°, six miles. The U-boat dived when the range was three miles and was attacked four times by *Vanessa*. She failed to regain contact and proceeded to rejoin; steering an evasive course. She was in station at 0300 on the 27th.

During the night of the 27th/28th a few more transmissions from U-boats between 25 and 30 miles from the convoy were intercepted but all appeared to come from boats astern or on the quarters; from the plot it did not seem that any were overtaking the convoy and after 0438/27th, nothing more was heard. By daylight it was fairly evident that no U-boats were in touch.

The convoy had air cover for 4 hours during the afternoon of the 27th, and at 1630 a Support Group, of which HMS *Offa* was Senior Officer, joined in a position about 250 miles east of Cape Farewell. The convoy being unmolested, the Support Group was switched to Convoy HX230, which was being threatened, and left at 1030 on the 28th.

The safe and timely arrival of the convoy was the result of the action taken during a few critical hours. In the course of the 26th/27th it probably passed through a patrol line of U-boats and was duly sighted and reported. By expert use of H/F D/F *Vanessa* was guided to the right position and dealt with the reporting U-boat so faithfully that it was forced under for a considerable time and could neither shadow the convoy nor call up other U-boats to do so. A hole was, in fact, punched in the line and the convoy passed through it.

About the same time a convoy at the other end of the world was being shadowed by two or three U-boats. This was RA53, bound from North Russia to Iceland. Three Fleet destroyers in the escort were fitted with H/F D/F and made good use of it, with the result that the position of the U-boats could be plotted within fairly accurate limits. At 0830 on 5th March two ships were torpedoed, possibly by aircraft and two more were lost later on in rough weather. One of these was a straggler and the other had been damaged in the earlier attack; both were sunk by U-boats.

HMS *Attacker* formed part of the escort of convoy CU1 [Caribbean – UK], which, arrived in the United Kingdom on 2nd April. No U-boats were sighted during the voyage. She had nine Swordfish aircraft available. During the passage 74 landings were made and only three aircraft were damaged. By daylight, aircraft were kept on deck in readiness to investigate H/F D/F bearings but night operations were not carried out, owing to the danger of the ship's position being given away by exhaust flames. Normally, anti-submarine searches made at dawn and dusk, covered an area 50 miles ahead and 30 miles on each beam and astern but, on days of greater- danger, supplementary searches were carried out in the forenoon and afternoon to 50 miles depth between limiting lines.

All flying operations were carried out inside the screen, the ship stationing herself between the leading ships of the escort or of the convoy, depending on the wind. The Commander-in-Chief, Western Approaches, considers that, to facilitate manoeuvring of the Escort Carrier, it is preferable for, the Commodore's column to contain only his ship and the Escort Oiler, thus leaving space for the Escort Carrier; to have a lane between columns in case the difficulties of station keeping for the merchant vessels.

In addition to *U444* and *U432*, sunk by *Harvester* and *Aconit* respectively, United States aircraft destroyed two U-boats during the month. They have adopted the 100-ft. spacing between depth charges, which is now also in force in Coastal Command. On the 8th March, a USN aircraft attacked a U-boat in a position 270 miles east of Barbados with 325-lb Torpex filled depth charges, which broke the vessel in two; the water was covered with debris and about a dozen men were seen swimming. Another United States aircraft, this time a Liberator of the Army Air Force, did much the same to a U-boat found near the Canary Islands, nine survivors being seen on a raft.

U-boats have tried methods of approaching to attack varying with weather conditions, visibility and the number of escorts. They have a healthy respect for RDF detection and, in a night attack, if they can reach a position ahead, which will allow of a submerged approach, they may dive through the area swept by RDF and surface between the escorts of the convoy to attack at close range. The absence of a rescue ship has again resulted in escort vessels dropping back to pick up survivors, leaving the convoy inadequately protected against subsequent attacks.

It has again been borne out that if escorts have been able to take resolute offensive action against the first U-boats to make contact with a convoy; the U-boats attacking later have not pressed home their attacks, possibly through knowing that their predecessors have been roughly handled. In other words, the Escort Commander has retained the initiative and so has avoided dispersion of effort in rescue work and protection of ships, which have dropped astern.

There is some evidence of long-range torpedo-fire by U-boats with torpedoes, which have altered course inside the convoy area. It is not known if these torpedoes alter course on reaching a certain range or if they are acoustically operated. Prisoner of war evidence suggests that the Germans are developing both types of torpedoes. [Reference to 'Curly' or FAT torpedoes – see below.]

A number of convoys running between the United Kingdom and Gibraltar have been attacked by U-boats in about 15°W after having been located by Focke-Wulf aircraft. Generally the U-boats, having placed themselves to intercept the convoy, have attacked individually and not in a pack.

Although the shipping losses for the month have been heavy, there are good reasons for hoping that the situation in the North Atlantic is improving. Advances have been made towards the provision of continuous air cover for transatlantic convoys by the use of Escort Carriers and Merchant Aircraft Carriers, either with the convoys themselves or with Support Groups. In spite of their successes, the U-boats must have received some pretty hard knocks from both aircraft and surface craft and there is every chance that quite extensive destruction and damage have been achieved, though we may have to wait some months for news to confirm our hopes.

Although it is hoped that the new Asdic sets coming into service will effect an increase in the rate of destruction of U-boats, there is little doubt that much better results are possible with existing weapons, if used by well-trained and enthusiastic teams. With the scarcity of escorts in all theatres of war, training is apt to be squeezed out but, as more escorts become available, the training periods are undoubtedly the most important necessity and give the best potential improvement in the rate of destroying U-boats.

:: Dönitz ::

Dönitz summed up the situation by quoting *The War at Sea*, where Roskill asked the question, 'How can anyone look back at the month of March 1943 and not be horrified by the results?' Fifty-six ships of more than half a million tons of shipping were sunk, forcing the Admiralty in London to seriously consider whether there was any point in continuing with the convoy system, now where it apparently was no longer providing any significant protection. Two-thirds of all the ships lost were in convoys and stragglers accounted for only a small proportion of the losses. On this occasion, the battles were brought to an end by the weather, by something worse than a mere gale, not because one side had overpowered the other, forcing it into submission. Yet, despite exceptionally awful conditions with high winds and enormous waves, where it was impossible to make use of weapons, Dönitz refused to give up, saying that such weather would also be most harmful to the opposition's shipping and could well result in masses of stragglers for easy picking off by those U-boats which remained at sea.

With the prospects for convoys looking so grim, no one at that time could have foreseen that this huge climax in the Atlantic was also Germany's last significant success at sea. Towards the end of that fateful March 1943, U-boats did find a westbound convoy but failed in getting anywhere near it because it was accompanied by an escort carrier with aircraft capable of not only using radar to locate U-boats but also carrying depth charges for sinking them and these little beasts were considerably more agile than the heavy long-range monsters from land-based airfields. Even if U-boats' anti-aircraft guns drove them off, they sent enough valuable information back to the convoy to prevent U-boats from getting close to their objectives.

Not all was as hopeless as might be assumed from reading this. Once again new innovations were already appearing at the front. One of these was mentioned earlier, although then no one was quite certain what it was. Up to the end of 1942 torpedoes travelled in straight lines and continued to do so when they missed their target, but now, on several occasions, observers had seen them change direction while speeding through a convoy. The Allies called them 'Curly Torpedoes' and this new invention gave U-boats new hope. Called FAT for Federapparat-Torpedo in Germany, the uninitiated referred to it falsely it as Flächenabsuchenenden-Torpedo meaning 'surface searching torpedo'. It could be aimed at a specific target from a long way away and if it missed it would loop through the convoy to hopefully collide with one of other ships. So, now U-boats did not have to go all that close to their objective before firing and the gloom of being repelled by aircraft was made a little sweeter by the thoughts that it wouldn't be long before this threat might be balanced out. Although the battles of March 1943 had been impressive, they didn't present anyone with a clear-cut victory and the conflict continued with new hope on both sides.

The other big problem to worry Dönitz was that many convoys were now accompanied by not only a ring of escorts but also by an additional 'Support or Reinforcement Group' of hunters, who did not just put the submarine down and then return to their position in the protective ring. Instead they had the time and patience to sit it out, often in appalling conditions, until the submarine was forced to surface and then they would hunt it to extinction.

Dönitz emphasizes that the combination of Escort Carriers, Support Groups, Very Long Range (VLR) Aircraft and the new Short-Wave Radar helped the opposition to achieve its objectives and, in many ways, the large battles around Convoys HX229 and SC122 in the North Atlantic were not really representative of what was going on. That action has often been presented as an example of a deeply horrifying event for the Allies, but in reality they were doing very well with their battle against the U-boats and one wonders whether the horror of these dreadful events was not over-emphasised to possibly cover up other shortcomings.

Dönitz goes on to explain that the Patrol Line 'Unversagt' was far more representative of the goings-on in March 1943. The group was set up on the 12th after *U130* (Oblt.z.S. Siegfried Keller) sighted Convoy UGS3 (USA – North Africa) some 500 nautical miles south-west of the Azores. The convoy was lost again very quickly because *U130* was sunk and the ships were not re-sighted by another boat until two days later. Despite there being no aircraft in this area, U-boats found themselves being forced away the moment they spotted the first indications of merchant ships on the horizon. Unable to get any closer, they remained well out of torpedo range. These U-boats were now equipped with radar detectors and were therefore fully aware how they were being discovered. These were hardly surprise attacks against them but still the escorts forced them under and then gave them a good plastering with depth charges. Dönitz reacted by ordering his U-boats to use the opposition's radar as marker for the convoy and keep so far away that they could still pick up the impulses but too far for the echo to get back to the escort. Thus U-boats were to speed on ahead of the convoy and then dive for a submerged attack. Of course, he was fully aware that such a technique incorporated considerable drawbacks and the odds were terribly high in opposition's favour of being able to avoid the wolf pack. Yet, despite these heavy odds, four ships were sunk and the action was not broken off until aircraft appeared on 19 March. Dönitz said this showed that convoys could still be attacked under favourable conditions. Although he didn't write it in his book, he was also fully aware of the fact that the results per U-boat at sea were exceedingly thin. He did make the point that almost every boat from the group was attacked and many suffered such serious damage that they had withdraw to traffic-free areas for repairs before attempting a precarious voyage back to base.

Chapter 25

Crisis Convoy – April and May 1943

:: JS ::

It is interesting to note that the period April and May 1943 has been hijacked by historians and given a slightly different twist to what was recorded by Dönitz and by the Anti-Submarine Reports. The best and most detailed account for this period has got to be the book from which this chapter heading has been borrowed. *Crisis Convoy* by Vice-Admiral Sir Peter Gretton provides a clear insight into the events around Convoy HX231, which was the first one to run into a wolf pack and drive off almost all the U-boats with hardly any losses to the convoy, despite conditions being in the U-boats' favour. The astonishing point is that the convoy left Canada at the end of March, only a few days after the largest convoy battle of all time. It might be best for this chapter to start off with how the Naval War Staff in London saw the action and then add how Dönitz saw the same events.

:: The British Side ::

The Monthly U-boat Offensive Report for April 1943 summed up the situation as follows:

> Historians of this war are likely to single out the months of April and May, 1943, as the critical period during which strength began to ebb away from the German U-boat offensive, not because of the low figure of shipping sunk which, for the whole world area, did not much exceed a quarter of a million tons; not because of the satisfactorily high number of U-boats sunk, which was again well above the average of the last twelve months ; but because, for the first time, U-boats failed to press home attacks on convoys when favourably situated to do so. There is ground for a confident estimate that the enemy's peak effort is passed. Morale and efficiency are delicate and may wither rapidly if no longer nourished by rich success.
>
> The number of U-boats operating was as great towards the end of the month as it has ever been. The U-boat construction curve still overtops

the casualties and, despite the increasing effort of our air and surface attacks, the U-boat fleet continues to grow in numbers, though more slowly than before; yet its effective strength appears on recent experience to be waning. There will still be hard knocks and setbacks but the escort groups are gaining skill and strength and have the measure of their task. With the advent of VLR aircraft to Newfoundland bases, still greater support for convoys may be expected and the mid-ocean gap where air assistance has been so sorely needed in the past should now, in favourable weather, be covered. The addition of auxiliary carriers to the protective forces is a further strategic change; since their employment will permit some convoys to travel by more southerly routes.

Apparently over half the enemy's Atlantic force operated during April in the North-West Atlantic and there appeared to be a tendency to give a wider offing to British air bases as compared with Canadian, thus producing a shift of the centre of gravity to the area west of 35°W. Probably the main scheme of patrols for the interruption of transatlantic convoys is to form up several groups of some ten or twelve U-boats on or near an arc of 600 miles radius from Newfoundland in the sector between 070° and 130° from St. John's. Pack tactics are still being used and, the size of groups tending to grow, it is thought that nowadays over twenty U-boats not infrequently make contact with a convoy. The area south and south-east of Cape Farewell has also been and will remain highly dangerous.

The U-boats were successful in finding and attacking in the North-West Atlantic eight convoys.

Off the United States there was very slight evidence of the presence of two or three U-boats, whilst in the Caribbean only one ship was sunk. Off Freetown a considerable increase of activity was marked, in particular, by an attack on Convoy TS37 [Takoradi – Sierra Leone] on the 30th April/1st May when six ships were lost. There may have been half-a-dozen U-boats in the area off Sierra Leone.

Off South Africa the sporadic sinkings, which occurred in the latter half of the month may have been caused by only two U-boats, one of them probably Italian. An increase of activity in the coastal areas between Cape Town and Lourenço Marques is to be expected.

The U-boat Countermeasures Report for April 1943 adds the following:

The enemy has clearly had some difficulty in explaining away the comparative failure of the U-boat offensive during April and the task of the apologist must have been made the more bitter by the knowledge that losses of U-boats have been heavy; as many as a dozen may have been destroyed.

Against the heavy losses the enemy can claim the sinking of 300,000 tons of shipping, a reduction of 292,000 tons as compared with last month. The falling off was not in any way due to a reduction in the enemy's effort, for large packs were operating in the North Atlantic, but individual U-boats seem to have pressed home their attacks far less effectively than in previous months. Possibly this indicates a decline in their fighting spirit, as well as some reduction in efficiency.

It seems that merely to detect the U-boats coming in to attack is to have the battle half won. All their efforts appear to tend to the avoidance of detection and once it is apparent that they have failed in this endeavour they seldom press home their attack.

Evidence is, however, accumulating, both from aircraft sightings and from the experiences of escorts, that two or more U-boats may co-operate in close company, one accepting attack while the other penetrates the protective screen. Aircraft have reported attacking one U-boat and at the same time sighting another within a mile of the first, while surface craft have detected a U-boat approaching to attack a convoy and have counter-attacked and put it down, only to find another lying a mile or two astern, ready to take advantage of the confusion caused by the counter-attacks.

Fifteen convoys were attacked and twelve lost ships. In the North Atlantic the greatest single number of casualties during the month did not exceed three, but Convoy ONS5, which had one ship sunk on the 29th; was again assailed during the first week of May and, despite the arrival of a Support Group, lost twelve more. The cost of this success to the enemy, measured in U-boats destroyed, may well have been extraordinarily high.

The passages of Convoys HX231 and HX232 are typical of the experiences of the North Atlantic convoys attacked. HX231, which sailed on the 25th March, consisted of sixty-one ships in thirteen columns and was escorted by Group B7, HMS *Tay* (Senior Officer) and HM Ships *Vidette, Loosestrife, Snowflake, Alisma* and *Pink*. First sighted on the 4th April when in 38°W it was attacked the same night. There was a strong wind and heavy swell from the north-north-west and visibility was increased by bright Northern Lights. As might be expected with a convoy eastbound under such conditions, both attacks came from the starboard side, the first U-boat from the bow and the second from the quarter. A search was carried out in each case but in each case the U-boats were not detected. The second and last attack, made next day, was a daylight one and took place about noon in excellent visibility. The attacking U-boat is thought to have come in submerged from ahead and to have fired from inside the convoy. Like its predecessors it was not detected. Air cover was provided in the course of the day but the enemy remained in contact and attacked again during the night, only to be beaten off by the surface escort. On the next day, the 6th, the Fourth Escort Group, composed of HM Ships *Inglefield, Eclipse, Fury* and *Icarus*, joined, but the enemy's main effort had already been defeated; the surface escort and the air escort, working excellently together, had each made about a dozen attacks.

Convoy HX232, which was escorted by HMS *Escapade* (Senior Officer of Group B7), ORP *Garland*, HM Ships *Narcissus* and *Azalea* and FF Ships *Renoncule* and *Roselys*, was reported, like its predecessor, in about 38°W, but the attack took longer to develop, the night after the sighting passing without incident. When the assault was made on the night of the 11th/12th April, there was a wind of Force 4 from the west and visibility was extreme, the moon being up. A number of attacks were delivered, all from the van and up moon, but all except two were frustrated and only three ships were lost. A strong pack of U-boats was still in contact on the following morning but they seemed to lose touch later in the day, by which time the weather had deteriorated. This may have been due to the arrival of air cover and of the Fourth Escort Group, but it is also possible that the convoy drew away from the U-boats after the shadower astern had been put down and an evasive turn made. In any case, the U-boats had probably acquired a respect for the efficiency of the escort.

The month showed what our countermeasures can achieve against the enemy's most strenuous efforts. Promised developments are coming to fruition. There were five Support Groups operating in the North Atlantic during the month, two of them having their own auxiliary carrier, and the number of VLR aircraft available has risen to over thirty. More important, there was a noticeably enhanced standard of group training, better use of H/F D/F was made and co-operation between the surface and air components of the escort was greatly improved. In none of the attacks on transatlantic convoys did the enemy succeed in obtaining anything like the upper hand.

The U-boat Countermeasures Report for May 1943 added:

May has been a record month for U-boat sinkings. Those known to have been sunk numbered at least twenty-four, and the probable rate of destruction was at least one a day. Our merchant shipping losses were, moreover, down to under 250,000 tons. This success is attributed to the stronger protection given to North Atlantic convoys by both shore-based and carrier-borne aircraft and to the use of escort groups as support forces in dangerous areas but these would have been of little avail without the efficiency and team-work achieved by the escorts as a result of training and experience.

At the beginning of May the enemy's U-boat fleet operating in the North Atlantic was as large as ever and in the first week of the month he concentrated against Convoy ONS5 one of the largest packs ever assembled. The resulting battle cost us eleven merchantmen out of the forty-two, which sailed but the enemy paid a very high price.

The enemy made his greatest effort in the North Atlantic against the transatlantic convoys and there suffered his heaviest losses, but he was also active in other parts of the ocean. By way of contrast with the successes just recounted was the attack on Convoy TS37 [Takoradi – Sierra Leone], which consisted of nineteen ships.

It was beset when within seventy miles of Freetown on two consecutive nights at the beginning of the month and lost seven ships. With the forces in this area working 'all out and then a bit more' under trying climatic conditions, it is still only possible to provide rather weak escorts and the losses in this area must be charged against the comparatively safe passages of the vital transatlantic convoys.

A feature of the past two or three months has been the use of anti-submarine support groups, either with or without escort carriers. They have shown that they are capable of gaining the initiative over concentrated U-boat packs and have definitely taken their place in the tactics of convoy defence. Experience is showing that a support group attached to a convoy should retain its separate entity and, to defeat a pack attack, should not normally be stationed as a reinforcement of the close escort. It appears probable that ships of a support group are best employed in putting down shadowers, following up aircraft attacks and carrying out searches on H/F D/F information; by night they should be stationed at such a distance outside the close escort that they can deter U-boats which are gaining bearing on the bows and intercept those which are closing in to attack.

Support Groups formed of Home Fleet destroyers gave invaluable service when this organisation was first instituted this year. These ships have now had to return to fleet duties and Support Groups are formed of sloops, frigates and destroyers as they come forward to join the Western Approaches Command. The Royal Canadian Navy is providing support groups to operate from the western side of the Atlantic.

To sum up, it is probable that historians will note that May 1943 was remarkable in the Battle of the Atlantic in that escorts and aircraft defeated, at least temporarily, the pack attacks of U-boats. This was achieved as much by superior leadership and tactics, quick initial action and well-co-ordinated attack and defence as by concentration of forces at the decisive points and by weapon superiority.

First Experiences with Escort Carriers

It is now possible to give some account of the experiences of the escort carriers. Very good R/T communication on H/F with Swordfish aircraft up to eighty miles allows complete control by the carrier, using fighter direction organisation, and enables her, acting on the information provided by the running commentary, to reinforce the aircraft and guide the surface escorts. The closer the control of the aircraft the greater the traffic on H/F, R/T and a TBR R/T, additional to the convoy wave is required. Escorts detached to hunt can either shift to this wave or have information relayed to them on the convoy R/T wave by the carrier.

It has been found that very close co-operation can be maintained between hunting Swordfish and hunting surface craft and that the carrier captain and the escort group commander, using R/T when out of sight, can also work closely together.

Reports from *Biter* show that the mean speed of Swordfish aircraft in depth-charge attacks was 130 knots – a higher speed than has been recommended. This was due to the aircraft either having to attack at once, if the U-boat dived, or having to close in quickly if the U-boat decided to fight it out on the surface.

Merchant Aircraft Carriers

The first merchant aircraft carrier sailed with Convoy ONS9. She is the *Empire MacAlpine*, a grain ship of 8,210 tons, and has a flight deck over her holds. Four Swordfish are carried.

:: Dönitz ::

The biggest convoy battle of the war (against Convoys HX229 and SC122) left many boats with so little fuel, provisions and ammunition that the majority had to return to their bases. As a result no one on the continent noticed a great deal of the 'Crisis Convoy' HX231 and it passed off without any significant comment. The few boats pitched against it were comparatively inexperienced and therefore it was not totally unexpected that they made only a little contact. The North Atlantic battles regained momentum towards the middle of April 1943, when Group 'Meise' was pitched against Convoy HX233. The weather had been appallingly stormy up to this period and now it was exactly the opposite. There was hardly any wind and the sea was dead calm, making it absolutely dreadful for U-boat attacks. One ship was sunk, but that cost one U-boat. *U175* was sunk in the most dramatic circumstances where a capture had almost succeeded, but failed at the last minute. These unsuitable conditions for U-boats repeated themselves for the next convoy and then Dönitz didn't even make the effort of ordering a patrol line, guessing that any attempt would be futile.

Dönitz was sure that more convoys wouldn't be long in coming and this time the B-Dienst, under Heinz Bonatz, supplied the route from decrypted signals. Convoy HX234 was found by *U306* (Kptlt. Claus von Trotha) and thee ships were sunk before it vanished into a thick fog. Astonishingly enough, *U306* maintained contact and called in a number of other boats, but all of them reported rain, hail, fog and drifting snow instead of the expected successes. The two ships sunk had to be paid for with two U-boats lost (*U189*, Kptlt. Helmut Kurrer and *U191*, Kptlt. Helmut Fiehn).

This time the southern waters were more productive and *U515* (Kptlt. Werner Henke) attacked a convoy consisting of fourteen fully-laden ships, sinking eight of them in nine attacks. What was more, all his shots were aimed properly according to the handbook. In many cases the firing process had to be carried out so quickly that there was not enough time to go through the standard firing procedures and it was a case of aiming at an overlapping group in the hope of hitting something before being driven away by zealous escorts.

Although history books keep telling us about high U-boat losses during 'Black May' 1943, the month started innocuously enough with Convoy ONS5 running right into the middle of a patrol line. Some twenty or more boats closed in from both sides sinking twelve ships totalling 55,761 GRT. Yet the opposition was noticeably aggressive, causing Dönitz to remark that it was no longer possible to attack convoys during poor visibility. Escorts with radar were then capable of detecting U-boats and fending them off with ease. A few days later he had modify these thoughts because it became clear it was no longer a case of Support Groups pushing attackers away; they were sinking U-boats very frequently as well.

According to Dönitz, this new state of affairs was finally driven home with Convoy SC129, where U-boats chasing the convoy found themselves being driven off long before they started their run-in to attack. During daylight U-boats remained so far away that anyone near the convoy could not have seen them. Yet, despite keeping this most respectful distance, they still found aircraft and ships were bearing down on them, to interrupt the shadowing. It was obvious that the U-boat had been detected even such a long way away from the convoy. The escorts and aircraft were no longer preventing U-boats from attacking, but they were hitting so much earlier that they were preventing U-boats from chasing the convoys.

Dönitz blamed radar as being responsible for the opposition finding and avoiding wolf packs, but most of the convoys circumnavigated U-boats because Bletchley Park had decrypted the positions of the individual boats within each pack and sent heavily guarded advice for clever evasive rerouting. It would appear that the most annoying contribution, as far as the

U-boats were concerned, were aircraft, especially those small string-bag type of machines being flown of escort carriers.

Dönitz said that the opposition's dominating superiority was finally shown with Convoys SC130 and HX239, which had an impenetrable ring of escorts working closely with a powerful Support Group, making it clear that convoy battles were now a thing of the past and further attacks would not be profitable. 'The coordination between the escorts and the support groups was extraordinary,' remarked Dönitz. By the middle of the month, Germany had already lost a frighteningly high number of U-boats and a few days later Dönitz took the decision to move all Atlantic boats into safer areas.

Chapter 26

The Summer of 1943

:: Dönitz ::

Dönitz goes into considerable details regarding the reasons for continuing with the U-boat war, but it was impossible to find any reference in his book of him ordering a referendum among sea-going personnel where every sea-going man was asked to vote in secret whether he wanted to continue with the battle or give up. The overwhelming support for pressing on with the war at sea finally gave Dönitz the determination to tackle the Atlantic once more. Everybody on the German side knew that it would be a while before new U-boats and superior weapons could be made available. So, during the summer of 1943 it was a case of making the best with what was available. The B-Dienst was still reading a good proportion of Allied signals and decrypted enough material to know that after May 1943 Coastal Command aircraft had been diverted for bombing raids over German cities and they took part in such horrendous raids as Operation 'Gomorrah'. These appeared to have been mass raids aimed exclusively against housing areas. The attacks on Hamburg killed as many civilians during one set of raids as died in Britain during the whole war and attacks like these provided a strong impetus for U-boat men to continue going to sea. The strange point about the massive Allied air attacks is that Winston Churchill is reputed to have said that U-boats were his most feared weapon, but very little was done to prevent them from being built by bombing the shipyards. The United States Strategic Bombing Report for the German Submarine Industry states that not a single U-boat was seriously damaged by bombing until shortly before the end of the war.

It was no longer a secret among sea-going men that the Allies had achieved air superiority in the French coastal waters. Again, this had to be counterbalanced with the U-boat Arm's own resources because there was no hope of getting any support from the Luftwaffe. The first step in overcoming this aircraft menace so close to home bases was to convert *U441* under Götz von Hartmann into an aircraft trap by fitting it out with two 20mm quadruple anti-aircraft guns and a semi-automatic 37mm. The idea was that this combination should be strong enough to shoot down even the large, fast-flying aircraft from RAF Coastal Command, rather than just scare them away. This worked exceedingly well and a four-engined Sunderland was shot down two days after the boat had set out from Brest, but one of the 20mm quads jammed and the aircraft dropped bombs so close that *U441* had to return to base.

At the same time, anti-aircraft armament of other front boats was increased from the initial single 20mm to two twin 20mm and one quadruple 20mm or a single 37mm anti-aircraft gun. *U758* under Kapitän-leutnant Helmut Manseck, the first boat with this new combination, managed to fend off eight single-engined aircraft from an aircraft carrier before it was forced to dive because two gun barrels had been put out of action by fire from the aircraft. The other new measure introduced by Dönitz was to ensure that boats leaving the French ports would do so only in groups so that they could use their combined firepower to deal with any attacking aircraft. Initially all these measures produced promising results, but it took the opposition no more than a couple of weeks to work out what was going on. Then, instead of attacking the aircraft called up others and up to four of them came in at the same time. While waiting for support the aircraft would circle so close that it was too dangerous for the U-boat to dive because in doing so it could end up with a pile of bombs on its tail. Irritatingly enough, the circling plane was also just out of reach of the U-boats' guns. So, in many ways all this new introductions did was to underline the fact that Germany was now on the defensive on all fronts.

The outcome of the half a dozen U-boats converted to aircraft traps is well known, but mentioning it here helps to underline the hopelessness of the situation. On 11 July *U441* was involved in a battle against three aircraft, which resulted in ten men killed and thirteen seriously wounded. The astonishing point about this most macabre incident is that the wounded were still being carefully brought ashore when a queue of volunteers assembled at the flotilla chief's office to take the bloodstained boat back out to sea. The so-called historians, who have made claim that Dönitz had to whip his men into action, are way off the mark. If anything, the opposite is true and the leadership at times curtailed men from heading into precarious situations.

The period immediately after May 1943 saw a dramatic change in the way the Allies dealt with U-boats. By that time Coastal Command had gained sufficient momentum to attempt a tight blockade of the French Atlantic ports and the combination of radar and Leigh Lights turned the entire Bay of Biscay into a most hazardous area, so much so that damaged boats had the greatest of problems in reaching the shelter of the huge concrete bunkers built especially to protect them. In the end, the only way to get through this danger zone was to travel submerged, turning the passage into a long, drawn-out crawl. The general situation in the French Atlantic ports continued to stew slowly until July 1943 when enough boats had been made ready to leave for operations and this time it was decided to escort them with a number of destroyers as far as 8° West. Once there, the commanders were free to decide what to do next, whether they should continue as a group or to continue on their own. Distress calls from U-boats under attack from anything up to five or so aircraft started flooding in so rapidly that Dönitz called off the entire operation and prohibited further boats from leaving port. This confirmed that there was no alternative other than to use radar detectors and to dive before an aircraft could approach close enough to attack. Once caught on the surface, there seemed to be no alternative other than total destruction with pointless loss of life.

:: **The British Side** ::
The U-boat Offensive Report for July 1943 states:

July was, if anything, a worse month for the U-boats than was May. After a marked lull in June the enemy had redisposed his forces, withdrawing them from the North Atlantic convoy routes and concentrating them in what he hoped would prove 'soft spots' – the Caribbean, off the Guiana and Brazilian coasts, and in the Freetown–Takoradi area. To withdraw from the North Atlantic was a confession of defeat but the enemy must have anticipated a rich harvest from surprise attacks in comparatively lightly protected areas.

In the event he was sadly disappointed. Shipping losses, though heavier than in the record month of June, were nevertheless much lighter than might have been expected, while the total number of U-boats sunk was nearly as high as in May. As few new U-boats are thought to have reached the Atlantic from Germany recently, the estimated total Atlantic U-boat force fell from about 180 to about 150 during July. [U-boat losses due to enemy action for each month of 1943 were as follows: Jan 7; Feb 17; Mar 14; Apr 16; May 40; Jun 17; Jul 38; Aug 23; Sep 8; Oct 26; Nov 17; Dec 8.]

The month of July opened with attacks on independents in the Caribbean sea and off the Brazilian coast as far south as Rio de Janeiro. Between 12 and 18 U-boats appear to have been operating in these areas, but they achieved little apart from an attack on a Trinidad – Bahia convoy and some sinkings of independents off Brazil, and no fewer than five of them were destroyed, mostly by United States aircraft operating from Brazilian bases.

At the same time another concentration of about a dozen U-boats operated within 300 miles of the coast between Dakar and Lagos. They behaved with considerable caution so that attacks on and by U-boats in this area were scarce. In all, less than half-a-dozen ships were lost, and one U-boat [*U135* under Oblt.z.S. Otto Luther] was sunk by HM Ships *Rochester, Balsam* and *Mignonette* near the Canaries.

The heaviest shipping losses occurred in the Indian Ocean, where about fifteen ships were sunk. After a lull in June, which may have been caused by U-boats withdrawing to refuel, there were sinkings in the Mozambique Channel and to the eastward and south-eastward of Madagascar. It is probable that six or seven large U-boats of the 'U-Kreuzer' class were responsible. Boats of this type are known to be capable of making cruises of five or even six months' duration.

A large number of attacks were made by United States escort carriers covering the passage of United States–Casablanca convoys. These were all outside the range of shore-based aircraft and must have finally convinced the enemy that he could nowhere consider himself safe from air attack. Many of the attacks were promising, and in two cases evidence in the form of prisoners was secured.

If the Indian Ocean was the best area for U-boats, the Bay of Biscay and its approaches were the happiest hunting ground for our own anti-submarine forces. Almost half the successful attacks in July were made within 300 miles of Cape Finisterre, surface forces, Coastal Command aircraft and United States aircraft all playing their part. On 30th July Coastal Command aircraft and the Second Escort Group co-operated in sinking all three of a group of outward bound U-boats which included two of the enemy's scanty force of supply U-boats. This loss will severely handicap future operations by 500-ton U-boats unless they pluck up courage to return to the North Atlantic. The perils of the passage of the Bay of Biscay, to which prisoners of war are making increasing reference, do nothing to encourage them to re-open attacks on heavily escorted convoys.

The U-boat Offensive Report for August 1943 states:

The extension throughout August of the phase of avoidance of our main shipping routes may not have been wholly intentional but to some extent forced upon the enemy by the loss in the last week of July of no less than three supply U-boats. A fourth of this type of craft, whose employment is a requisite condition of distant operations by the smaller class of U-boats, was sunk in the Iceland–Faeroes area early in August. There can be little doubt that as a direct consequence campaigns, which were then in full course in the Caribbean, off the Guianas and Northern Brazil were curtailed and the U-boats returned to base a fortnight or more earlier than they would have done, had intermediate refuelling been possible.

As a further consequence of this acceleration of departures from patrol, reliefs could not be sailed in time to maintain continuity and during the latter half of August – at least up to the last two or three days – it was estimated that almost all the U-boats at sea were on passage homeward. Naturally the tide then began to flow in the opposite direction.

The comparative freedom from U-boat danger of all areas other than the Madagascar region, where the tail end of a four-months campaign was still in evidence, is strikingly demonstrated by the facts that during August less tonnage was sunk by U-boats even than in June and that for the first time more U-boats than merchant ships were sunk.

The Bay of Biscay offensive is considered, on a statistical basis, to have achieved a measure of success equal to that of July, but in the latter part of the month its efficacy was partially defeated by the introduction of a new enemy weapon of attack from the air, which necessitated a temporary relaxation of the surface ship blockade. It was considered probable that U-boats were using a route close along the north coast of Spain and our escort groups were moved accordingly on to this route. The enemy by reacting so strongly and disclosing the new asset in his armoury gave proof of his apprehension of the danger that the groups represented.

The rate of killing remained satisfactory, having regard to the comparative scarcity of targets in so quiet a phase, and it is considered that the enemy's Atlantic operational force must have again declined during the month. Baltic sailings are, however, expected soon to replenish, to some extent, the Atlantic numbers and it is within the next two or three months, if ever, that the enemy must attempt a return to the main convoy routes. It remains to be seen whether sufficient faith can be inculcated in any new gear, which may have been installed to screw up morale to the pitch of renewing the only engagement, which can affect materially the outcome of the war.

The U-boat Countermeasures Report for July 1943 states:

There is every reason to be highly satisfied with the results for July. In May U-boat, pack tactics were defeated as the rate of loss was unacceptable for the dividend paid in June the U-boats were either withdrawn to their bases or were dispersed to widely-spread areas and attacks on shipping were few, except for an abortive effort against United States convoys to North Africa; in July, however, in spite of the dissipation of the enemy's effort over a great area and the infliction on us of shipping losses approximately equal to the average for the first half of the year, the killings of U-boats if the Italian losses are included – exceeded the record total of May. The chief credit for this achievement must be given to the aircraft of Coastal Command based in the United Kingdom and to the British and United States aircraft operating from Gibraltar and Morocco. Their crews have not only faced the increased anti-aircraft fire of U-boats proceeding in formation on the surface but they have also achieved a percentage of kills to attacks of over 25 per cent.

During the month 18 U-boats were destroyed in the approaches to the Bay of Biscay, all but two of them by aircraft unassisted by a surface force. The crowning success was achieved on the 30th when a whole group of three outward-bound U-boats was sunk, two of these being supply U-boats, of which the enemy is very short.

At 0714 on the 30th July, when the Second Escort Group was proceeding at 15 knots on a course of 149°, HMS *Wild Goose* obtained an H/F D/F bearing of 216° and the group thereupon altered to this bearing. At 0757 a signal was intercepted from an aircraft reporting herself over three U-boats in position 44°00'N, 10°35'W, this being followed at 0804 by a second H/F D/F bearing of 225°, and at 0817 by a third of 244°, this being described as 'first-class.' The group maintained its course of 240° until 0927 when more H/F D/F bearings caused an alteration of 3° to starboard. After 0817 aircraft reports were constantly being received. At 0947 what appeared to be a depth-charge explosion over the horizon was sighted fine on the port bow and the ships went to action stations, speed being increased to 18 knots. Within the next quarter of an hour definite depth charge explosions were seen ahead and the Senior Officer in HMS *Kite* hoisted the General Chase. (It is believed that this is one of the rare occasions since the days of Nelson on which this signal has been used.) At 1005 the enemy were sighted, his force consisting of two 1,600-ton U-boats and one of smaller size. *Kite* opened fire at a range of over 13,000 yards, and was quickly followed by the other ships, the group firing 121 rounds of 4-in. A hit was observed in *Kite* at 1015 and almost simultaneously the aircraft circling the position reported 'U-boat no more.' This was *U462* [Oblt.z.S. Bruno Vowel], the chief credit for her sinking going to a Halifax aircraft of 502 Squadron; her end was hastened by scuttling. *U461* [Kptlt. Wolf-Harro Stiebler] had already been destroyed by Sunderland aircraft 'U' of 461 Squadron. At 1030, when the group closed the position, it passed close to the dinghies into which the survivors were packed. [Note: the repeat of the same numbers in the previous sentence is not a printing error, but a coincidence.] The Senior Officer ordered HM Ships *Woodpecker, Wild Goose* and *Woodcock* to form a square patrol, HMS *Wren* being at the same time ordered to join him. By 1034 contact had been obtained and

Kite carried out the first attack, *Wren* following with an attack at 1040. The survivors from *U461* and *U462* were not far off from these patterns but after the water had subsided their dinghies were still to be seen rocking gently in the swell. [The third boat from this trio was *U504* under Kapitänleutnant Wilhelm Luis.]

Contact was then lost and regained intermittently until 1132 – Asdic conditions were described as very poor – but at 1149 *Kite*, in firm contact, dropped a pattern set to 350 and 550 ft. Contact was lost at 600 yards and the Senior Officer, being of the opinion that the U-boat had gone deep and had taken swift avoiding action from the three normal attacks – and could not therefore be a large supply U-boat – decided to apply the creeping attack which had been successfully used on the 24th June. At 1258, therefore, *Woodpecker* fired a 22-charge pattern set to 500 and 750 ft. under *Kite*'s direction; a quantity of oil was seen to come to the surface after the attack. *Wild Goose* made a similar attack at 1342 and contact then faded. A search made in the area revealed much oil and wreckage, which included a uniform jacket, a human lung and some well-cured bacon. The survivors from the other U-boats, who by this time had been in their dinghies for over four hours, were then collected.

To continue the story of this patrol, the next day passed quietly but at 0900 on the 1st August a signal was intercepted from an aircraft reporting herself over a U-boat in position 45°50'N, 09°40'W. The group was close to this position but, before it could close, the aircraft reported that she had to return to base owing to shortage of fuel and nothing came of the sighting. The group continued on the course of 350° to which it had altered until 1246, when a Catalina aircraft reported a U-boat bearing 132° 34 miles. Course was then altered to 180°.

This aircraft skilfully homed the group on and at 1430 two smoke floats were sighted, the guiding Catalina having dropped a fresh float close to one which was dying down. The group passed both floats on a course of 270° at Asdic sweeping speed and ten minutes later sighted a Sunderland aircraft attacking a U-boat. Very soon after the depth charges had been dropped, the Sunderland crashed into the sea and it was afterwards learnt that both pilots had been killed by the U-boat's gunfire. It seems likely that aircraft-captain died at the moment at which the depth charges were released. The group closed the position and in a few minutes was picking up survivors from *U454*.

Reference was made in the last Report to the withdrawal of U-boats to the southward and to their operations in the Azores area. Conditions in this part of the Atlantic were good during July, but if any U-boat crews were looking forward to pleasant work in good weather, they must have had some disappointments. Convoys bound to and from the United

States passed unscathed through the area, leaving behind them five U-boats sunk by aircraft from the US escort carriers, *Bogue, Santee* and *Core*. One of the five was a supply U-boat.

Further still to the southward, HM Ships *Rochester, Balsam* and *Mignonette*, who were escorting Convoy OS51, sank *U135* [Oblt.z.S. Otto Luther] in a position between the Canary Islands and the West Coast of Africa.

The result of operations still further afield must have been equally unsatisfactory to the U-boat command. Recently one of the most profitable areas for U-boats has been the coast of Brazil. During July a vigorous air offensive deprived the enemy of this 'soft spot' which he had been exploiting for some time; so powerful was the effort made by United States and Brazilian aircraft that no fewer than six U-boats were sunk in this area during the month.

There has apparently been a great reduction in the number of U-boats making the passage north on their first operational patrol. It is thought that instead of the usual monthly number of about 20, not more than five entered the Atlantic outward bound from Kiel. It will, therefore, take the enemy all the longer to recover from the blows of the past three months, which have cost the Germans over 80 U-boats. The boats of the Biscay flotillas, thinned by this slaughter, are apparently delayed in harbour while equipment and armament are being improved and increased; the U-boats, which should have started operations this month, joining the Biscay flotillas at the end of their first patrol, remain in the Baltic, perhaps for the same purpose.

Despite their losses, outward-bound U-boats are still crossing the Bay area in company and on the surface – long may they continue to do so. Proceeding in groups of three to five, often in vic-formation, they rely on tight turns at high speed and concentrated 'flak' to keep attacking aircraft at bay. The U-boat singled out for attack always endeavours, by a last-moment turn, to present a beam-on target to the aircraft when the latter is committed to her line of attack; by this manoeuvre, while still supported by the fire of her consorts, she gives full play to her own anti-aircraft armament.

This policy of fighting it out on the surface has greatly increased the hazards to be faced by our aircraft; it has also presented them with an increased number of 'Class A' targets, of which they have taken full advantage, pressing home their attacks with the greatest determination in the face of accurate fire. Many aircraft have suffered casualties and several have been shot down but the survivors of at least three of these have had the satisfaction of knowing that their gallantry has been rewarded by a kill. It is interesting that the AA fire has been more effective from single U-boats than from groups.

The U-boat is being hit and hit hard whenever an aircraft attacks her on the surface in the Atlantic; whenever a group of three or more ships can obtain contact with a submerged U-boat and have time to hunt her, her destruction is pretty well assured. The U-boat's life has indeed become precarious. There are still a few 'soft spots' where the enemy can sink a small proportion of the shipping passing through an area without being unduly worried by the accuracy of attacks by aircraft or surface forces, but in Western Approaches Command, in the Fleet and in Coastal Command in particular the emphasis on anti-submarine training has clearly borne much good fruit. Elsewhere there are difficulties in fitting in training owing to shortages and the lack of training submarines but the need is great and opportunities must be made, even if some operational commitments are not fully satisfied. A few fully efficient anti-submarine craft are worth a large number of 'fifty-percenters'.

And in August 1943:

In the last month of the fourth year of the war, for the first time, more U-boats than merchantmen were sunk. Twenty German and Italian and two Japanese U-boats were destroyed, as against 13 merchant ships sunk by U-boat attack. The month opened with the sinking in the Bay area of four U-boats in two days by aircraft of Coastal Command, but these successes (culminating in nine sunk in one week) marked the end of the six weeks' slaughter, which began in the last week of June. Fewer U-boats were subsequently crossing the Bay and those that made the passage apparently hugged the coast of Spain and surfaced only at night. Two and possibly three more U-boats are, however, likely to have been destroyed in this area of the North Atlantic. On the 25th August, HMS *Wanderer*, who was escorting Convoy OG92, sank *U523* [Kptlt. Werner Pietzsch]; this U-boat, under orders for the Far East, had had to put back for repairs and was caught as she made the passage for the second time. Three days later HMS *Grenville*, on offensive patrol to the westward of Vigo, made a promising attack on what may have been a Japanese U-boat inward-bound to the Biscay ports and, on the 30th, HM Ships *Stork* and *Stonecrop*, part of the escort of Convoy SL135, probably destroyed a German U-boat. [This was *U634* under Oblt.z.S. Eberhard Dahlhaus.]

From one of the few remaining 'soft spots' – the area south of Madagascar – came refreshing news of the destruction of a U-boat by Catalina aircraft. This is the first 'kill' reported this year from an area where losses have occurred persistently, though they have been small compared with the amount of shipping.

In August, the enemy's U-boats sank but 13 ships – only five in convoy and only one in the Atlantic north of the Equator. The sinking of so many supply U-boats has forced him to recall operational U-boats before the normal time: the weight of the offensive in transit areas has compelled him to try antidotes such as the improvement of the anti-aircraft defence and technical equipment.

Last month aircraft losses rose considerably in the Bay area, most of them probably being due to enemy aircraft and not to U-boats; and one of Germany's new 'secret weapons' – a rocket-projected glider – sank one of the ships co-operating with the aircraft. If U-boats are going to affect materially the outcome of the war, the Germans must sooner or later resume attacks on transatlantic shipping. The real battle will then be joined again. Meanwhile, the enemy is accumulating a formidable number of U-boats in their home bases, but their crews' morale must be severely strained; our power to defeat him is rising and we may now look with considerable confidence on the eventual outcome. The importance of sinking U-boats, even at the cost of a reduced scale of protection to shipping, is more than ever apparent.

The following is an excerpt from the GC&CS (Government Code and Cipher School) Naval History, written shortly after the war by Lieutenant Commanders R. J. Goodman and K. W. McMahan and Lieutenant E. J. Carpenter. This is of special interest because unlike the authors of the secret Anti-Submarine Reports, this history was written for readers who knew that Britain had been deciphering the U-boats code. Therefore they had a deeper insight into what had gone on.

While auxiliary aircraft carriers had operated in the North Atlantic since March 1943, they had not begun to impress the Commander-in-Chief for U-boats, who did not issue a warning against surprise attacks by carrier-borne aircraft until the middle of August 1943. The failure to appreciate the extension of Allied air power, especially in the form of auxiliary carrier task groups, was an essential weakness of the U-boat Command from May to July 1943. Acting upon Special Intelligence, a task group including the auxiliary carrier USS *Bogue* operated against the 'Trutz' Group before the U-boat could make contact with the expected convoy. Three U-boats in the southern part of the patrol line were bombed in rapid succession and the patrol line was cancelled at once.

Chapter 27

News from the Monthly Anti-Submarine Reports

The following reports were included in the June 1943 issue:

Coastal Command Activities

For the first time the number of sightings in a month has exceeded two hundred and the number of attacks has passed the hundred. In April there were 150 sightings and 77 attacks and in the previous record month, November, 1942, when operations off the North African coast were at their height, 147 and 86 respectively; in May the attacks were within 20 per cent, of the combined total for these two months, amounting to 136. There were 217 sightings.

In the Bay area there was the greatest activity, the sightings being almost doubled at 98, and the attacks increasing from 28 to 66, as compared with April, and it would seem likely that one out of every two U-boats crossing the Bay was attacked. It was noticeable that the operations of the searchlight-fitted Wellingtons were far less successful during May than in April, when they were obtaining one sighting for about every six sorties. Since the first week of May the results of night operations have fallen almost to nothing and those from the day sorties have greatly increased. Presumably the U-boats have been forced, as has previously happened, to take all their charge by day, considering day attacks the lesser of two evils, at any rate for the time being.

There have been a large number of successful attacks in this area and some of them have shown the results obtainable from 'follow-ups,' made possible by the increased force now operating. On the 31st May attacks by one Halifax aircraft of 58 Squadron RAF was succeeded eighty minutes later by attacks by another aircraft of the same squadron. The action was brought to an end by two Sunderland aircraft.

The sightings and attacks which resulted from operations round convoys and those made by aircraft engaged on anti-submarine patrols in northern waters were about equal in number to the results obtained in the Bay of Biscay. No ship was sunk within 600 miles of Coastal

Command bases. The greatest achievement was in the protection of Convoys HX237 and of Convoy SC129, which was following it. On the 13th four VLR Liberator aircraft of 86 Squadron were sent to escort HX237, which was then about 800 miles south-west of their base. They did not meet it but sighted five U-boats and attacked three of them. On the same day SC129, which had lost two ships on the 12th and was then about 1,200 miles from base, was receiving protection from another Liberator, which sighted two U-boats. Both of them were attacked. Three Liberators gave cover from 1440 until midnight on the 14th; two U-boats were attacked and thereafter there were no more sightings.

Another great effort was made in defence of Convoy SC130, to which cover was given almost continuously by day and night from 0817 on the 19th until the evening of the 21st. Twenty-eight sightings and ten attacks were made in this period and not a single ship was lost.

The Squid
The Squid is in principle a long-range depth-charge thrower, auto-matically operated and controlled.

It is a three-barreled mortar, electrically fired and designed to discharge bombs ahead of the attacking ship. It has been made possible to do this from the deck of a comparatively small vessel by a development in mortar design, which has reduced the size of the recoil forces. These bombs will closely resemble depth-charges in weight and explosive effect but will have four advantages over depth-charges: –

1. They will be projected with accuracy to a known point well ahead while the attacking ship is still in Asdic contact with the U-boat.
2. They will have a reliable under-water course.
3. They will have a much higher sinking speed.
4. They will incorporate a new type of fuse, which will be set automatically to the required depth with a high degree of accuracy.

The depth will be set on the fuses electrically from the new depth-prediction Asdic gear. The mortars will be fired automatically from the Asdic range recorder and there will be automatic power stabilization and control. The errors associated with the human element should therefore be very largely eliminated. The mortars will be fitted on the super-structure. The bulk of the projectiles will be stowed below but there will be a ready-use supply in a shelter on the superstructure and the projectiles will be loaded into the mortars from small trolleys, which will run on a type of mine rail. The barrels are turned over into a horizontal position and the projectiles are pushed straight into them from the trolleys. [The first 'Squid kill' occurred on 6 August 1944 when HMS *Loch Killin* attacked *U736* under Oblt.z.S. Reinhard Reff, so it took a while before this advanced weapon had an impact.]

Fitting of Asdics in Merchant Ships

Selected merchant ships of the fast cargo liner type, which normally sail independently are now being provided with Asdic for self-protection. The vessels average 7,000 to 10,000 tons displacement with speeds of 15 to 18 knots. The majority of those being fitted are new construction but opportunity is also being taken to equip existing ships of this type when the duration of refit or repair permits.

To date eight ships have been fitted; the new construction programme embraces over 80 vessels and at present two existing ships are having Asdic installed concurrently with damage repair.

At present installation is undertaken only in the United Kingdom, although in one case the bulk of the preliminary work, including the fitting of directing gear and dome, was completed in New York while the ship was under repair.

The set provided is Type 136. It incorporates destroyer-type dome and directing gear but the trunk is slightly deeper, so that the dome when housed does not project below the keel. This is necessary, since ships may often take the ground in rivers and ports abroad. Electrically, the set is primarily designed for the hydrophone effect method of detection though provision is made for echo-ranging.

A special listening operating procedure has been evolved for Type 136. If contact is obtained, the rules governing avoiding action are generally similar to those used by the larger cruisers. Since the ships make long and possibly uneventful passages, each carries a gramophone and instructional record set in order to test the proficiency and keep alive the interest of the operators. The majority of the merchantmen carry four depth charges and may later be given 'R' mines. Either can be used as an offensive or a deterrent weapon. An adequate gun armament is also mounted.

Most of the vessels fitted are still on their maiden voyages and it is, therefore, not yet possible to quote any specific cases whereby use of the set has prevented possible disaster; no doubt exists concerning the keenness of both officers and men to make the best possible use of the equipment.

Modern Trends with Anti-Submarine Attack Instruments

Modern Asdic equipment has been designed very much around ahead-throwing weapons, since it is when using these that the three primary requirements of determining the course-to-steer one's own ship, the depth of the target and the time-to-fire the charges can be most simply and efficiently fulfilled.

The equipment comprises virtually of two separate Asdic sets; the one, namely, Types 144Q or 145Q, which is fundamentally used for obtaining contact and determining course-to-steer and time-to-fire, and the other, Type 147B, for determining the depth of the target.

The weapon bearing is passed automatically from the bearing recorder to a captain's bearing instrument, where it is shown by one of four pointers equally spaced 90 degrees apart. The correct pointer is that which is most nearly right ahead when the bearing recorder is lined up and the order has been given to steer by Asdic. This pointer is followed up by a hand-controlled cursor by which means the weapon is kept trained on the correct bearing and the course-to-steer indicated on a Helmsman's Indicator. The captain's bearing instrument also shows the Asdic oscillator bearing and the ship's head and is provided with both relative and gyro scales.

The helmsman's indicator is used in much the same way as a compass; the weapon bearing is shown by a zero mark on a rotating card (in earlier models a pointer rotated over a fixed card), and the helmsman steers the ship on to the weapon bearing by keeping the zero on the card against a fixed-mark – which is the equivalent of the lubber's line.

Chapter 28

The Autumn of the U-boats – September 1943

:: Dönitz ::

The boats in the Biscay ports, mentioned in the previous chapter, were being rapidly modified by strengthening their anti-aircraft armament and adding an effective radar detector, capable of picking up very high frequency transmissions. As additional bonus, each boat was supplied with four new acoustic torpedoes, codenamed Zaunkönig (also known as T5) and the crew received special training in the use of this new equipment. The plan was to move an entire wolf pack into the North Atlantic by travelling as a group and submerging at the slightest sign of danger. This appeared to work well. The B-Dienst had decoded enough signals to inform the U-boat Command that the air activity had increased considerably during recent weeks, especially since the last effort of breaking out of the Bay of Biscay. Yet, despite this warning, there were hardly any reports of attacks. In fact twenty-one U-boats reached the open Atlantic without any serious mishaps and without the loss of a single submarine. Dönitz breathed a sigh of relief and added that this made everybody feel much better.

The 'Leuthen' Pack was ready and in position by 20 September 1943 to intercept Convoys ON202 and ONS18 and despite thick fog managed to pursue the convoy for a period of four days. Perhaps the pack was helped by the weather inasmuch that many aircraft were grounded on fog-bound airfields. Dönitz reported that the U-boats were ready; their radar detectors would prevent surprise attacks; new, improved anti-aircraft armament would cope with anything in the air and the acoustic torpedoes could sink escorts, even when these were approaching head-on at high speed. He was delighted when reports flooded in saying that twelve destroyers and nine merchant ships of 46,000 GRT had been sunk. It wasn't until after the war that he learned the correct figure was six merchant ships with 36,422 GRT and only three destroyers. One further escort was torpedoed but managed to reach port under tow. At the time of writing his book he put this massive discrepancy down to U-boats having to dive to a depth of at least 60 metres immediately after firing an acoustic torpedo, to prevent it from homing in on the boat that fired it. Post-war research by Professor Dr. Jürgen Rohwer showed that there was a major fault with acoustic torpedoes and only about 10 per cent produced any results; the failure rate was in the region of 90 per cent.

:: The British Side ::
The U-boat Offensive Report for September 1943 states:

The resumption of U-boat operations against convoys in the North-Western Approaches occurred, as anticipated, in the latter part of the month. The enemy really had no choice in the matter, since it is only in this area that the U-boats can ever materially affect the development of our war plans and to have refrained any longer from operating there would have been to confess final failure and would have completely destroyed morale at home and in the operational U-boats.

The revival has been a poor show compared with the performances of the first run. Very close studies of performers now no longer on the stage were given, but the young understudies lacked the nerve and fire of the old players. There were some new effects, which were momentarily startling but it is doubtful whether the run will be long or very successful.

The new torpedo [Acoustic torpedo of Type Zaunkönig or T5] found victims and Convoys ON202 and ONS18 had a gruelling time in a four-day pack attack by some 20 boats. Nevertheless, over a period of nearly four weeks to mid-October of this Report only four escorts and seven merchant ships have been sunk, whilst over 30 per cent of the U-boats estimated to have been used for convoy operations have been sunk.

Outside the North-Western Approaches little happened in September and during the first half of the month the only successful attack was on an Egyptian schooner.

A campaign was being prepared in the northern part of the Indian Ocean between Aden, the Persian Gulf and India and this began towards the end of the month. About five German U-boats appear to be involved. They are likely to use Penang as an operating base but to return eventually to the Bay of Biscay.

The U-boat Countermeasures Report for the same month adds:

The lull in the German U-boat campaign lasted until 19th September, although HMS *Puckeridge* had been sunk close eastward of Gibraltar and some 35–40 attacks had been carried out by aircraft and surface forces in various areas, with very little evidence on which to give provisional assessments higher than two sunk and four damaged.

On the 19th September, ONS18 (27 ships) and ON202 (38 ships) were 5.5 and 3.5 days out from the United Kingdom respectively. That evening there were indications that one or both convoys had been sighted by U-boats. Fortunately it was possible to join these two convoys on the 20th September and reinforce their combined escort with a support group. Thus was the stage set for the renewal of North Atlantic convoy battles after a four months' lull. Except for the use by the enemy of an acoustic homing torpedo fired at chasing anti-submarine vessels there was no evidence of new tactics or technical developments. The convoy attack is described later.

Escort groups working with Coastal Command aircraft in the Bay of Biscay offensive were withdrawn to support North Atlantic convoys, but the aircraft operations continued. The German countermeasures of maximum submerging tactics, accepting a long delay in making the passage of the Bay, and the routeing of a proportion of the U-boats close to the coast of Spain, achieved a measure of immunity which was increased by a spell of bad weather at bases, causing night flying to be cancelled, and by our inability to provide a sufficiently strong effort with available Wellington aircraft, the only ones fitted with Leigh Lights. This had been foreseen many months ago but there have been technical and production hitches delaying the fitting of Long Range aircraft with searchlights. There were, however, 24 U-boat sightings in the Bay and 12 attacks, of which 9 were by the Leigh Light Wellingtons. One U-boat was sunk by day and one damaged U-boat entered Vigo and has since been interned; this damage is attributed to an attack by a Leigh Light Wellington from Gibraltar.

The most profitable areas for killing U-boats are:

(a) the vicinity of convoys on which packs are massing,
(b) the refuelling areas if they can be found and the U-boats surprised,
(c) the transit areas. The first two exist only intermittently whilst the transit areas are constant probability areas.

In areas where U-boats are operating singly in patrol areas to intercept shipping, they must approach the escorts when approaching the convoys. When the U-boat has been located it is well worthwhile detaching most of the escorts and laying on as many aircraft as possible to destroy it, since the convoy is safe until it enters the next U-boat's patrol area. It is most important to destroy U-boats operating far from their bases, even at the expense of some shipping losses.

In September, although shipping losses were small, there is no certainty that we sank more than four German U-boats and caused the internment of another. In the previous four months the total score was over 100 and the enemy must be seriously alarmed. A vigorous offensive must be maintained to break his morale.

U-boats achieved a measure of surprise with their acoustic torpedo, but the weapon has many limitations such as speed, homing radius and inability to distinguish between propeller and other noises.

The outstanding event of the month was the surrender of the Italian Fleet. By the end of the month 29 Italian U-boats were under British control.

The Attacks on Convoy ON202 and ONS18

On 19th September Convoy ONS18, consisting, of 27 ships, escorted by HMS *Keppel* (Senior' Officer, Group B3), HM Ships *Escapade, Narcissus, Orchis* and *Northern Foam* and French ships *Lobelia, Roselys* and *Renoncule,* with *Empire MacAlpine* (a merchant aircraft carrier) in company, was about 475 miles west by south of Rockall, Convoy ON202 being about 60 miles to the east-north-east. This convoy of 38 ships was escorted by Group C2 (HMCS *Gatineau* (Senior Officer), HM Ships *Icarus, Lagan, Polyanthus* and *Lancer,* and HMC Ships *Drumheller* and *Kamloops*). During the day it became evident that the convoys were being shadowed and that night attacks developed against both of them. Group B3 drove off the U-boats, which attacked ONS18 persistently from about 2230 onwards and possibly damaged one of them. ON202 was attacked later that night and at about 0400/20th *Lagan* was torpedoed. She had been detached to follow up an H/F D/F bearing and had obtained a Radar contact, which had faded when the range was about 3,000 yards. She was within about 1,200 yards of the assumed diving position when she was hit by a torpedo, which blew off her stern. This was the first indication that the enemy was using a new weapon, the acoustic homing torpedo. She was taken in tow and reached harbour on the 24th.

At about 0800 two merchant ships were torpedoed one sinking almost immediately while the other was abandoned in a sinking condition.

During the forenoon the two convoys were ordered to join, forming one convoy of 63 ships, this being done during the late afternoon in poor visibility. *Escapade,* damaged by a premature explosion of her Hedgehog, had had to return to harbour, but the combined escorts were now supported by the 9th Escort Group (HMS *Itchen* (Senior Officer), and HMC Ships *St. Croix, Sackville, Chambly* and *Morden*) and throughout the day were covered by aircraft of 120 Squadron, which made eight sightings and attacked four times. That evening two of the escort were 'sunk with heavy loss of life. *St. Croix* was torpedoed at about 2100 while hunting a U-boat; she was hit again an hour later and sank.

Within two hours *Polyanthus*, who was screening the rescue ship astern of the convoy, was torpedoed while following up a Radar contact. *Itchen* was narrowly missed by a torpedo when circling the wreck of *St. Croix*.

Despite these losses, the attempts, which the U-boats made on the convoy during the night all failed, and it is thought that one counterattack by *Keppel*, *Itchen* and *Narcissus* resulted in one U-boat being seriously damaged. Early on the 21st the convoy was re-routed to the southward in order to get within range of Newfoundland-based aircraft. Owing to the previous routeing signal being received corrupt, the convoy was some 100 miles to the southward of the intended route and in the thick fog prevailing was unable to regain the route ordered. Liberators from Iceland continued to give the convoy what protection they could until prevented by the fog. This weather did not prevent another fierce night battle. The U-boats, estimated to be 15 or 20 in number, had the worst of it, for they sank nothing and in the early hours of the 22nd one of the pack was rammed and sent to the bottom by *Keppel*. *Chambly* obtained hits with her 4-in, gun on another. [The rammed boat was *U229* under Oblt.z.S. Robert Schetelig, *Chambly*'s target escaped and so did all the other U-boats attacked during this action.]

With first light on the 22nd, Liberators arrived from Newfoundland, giving cover throughout the day and making four sightings and two attacks. At about 1820/22nd the Senior Officer reported that there were still a few U-boats in contact and that they were being chased. They nevertheless attacked again that night in strength and, though many of them were driven off, the defence was twice penetrated. Just after midnight, *Itchen* was sunk, two merchantmen being torpedoed about the same time, and two more merchant ships were lost at about 0730/23rd.

The enemy did not, however, escape unscathed, as one of the 12 U-boats then in contact with the convoy was probably sunk by *Northern Foam*, one possibly sunk by *Lobelia* and three probably damaged by *Chambly*, *Renoncule* and *Northern Foam* respectively. The U-boats kept in contact during the 23rd but the attacks made by the escorting Liberators from Newfoundland, which again gave cover throughout the day, so deterred then that their attacks on the night of 23rd/24th were half-hearted and they probably lost another of their number, as a result of attacks by *Sackville*, without causing any loss to the convoy. After this they lost touch with the convoy and the number of attacks on Atlantic convoys was small and the losses inflicted negligible.

The enemy's propaganda has continually stressed the point that his attacks on our shipping have resulted in such heavy tonnage losses that they are beyond our shipbuilding capacity to replace. It may, therefore, be of interest that at the beginning of October, United Nations merchant ship construction had wiped out, not only the accumulated tonnage losses caused by enemy action since 3rd September, 1939, but the marine losses as well. United States shipyards have played, and are playing, the major part in this highly satisfactory performance. Their share of the total new construction at the end of September, 1943, was about 74 per cent; that of the United Kingdom about 20 per cent; and Canada about 6 per cent.

Enemy propaganda claims of Allied shipping losses continue to be of a grossly exaggerated character, for example, on 13th October, 1943, the German Telegraph Service (DNB) put out the following: – 'During the past few weeks the naval war situation has developed considerably. Since 1st August, German naval and air forces have sunk no fewer than 140 vessels of 785,000 GRT and damaged 284 vessels of 1,370,000 GRT; some of these were damaged so heavily that their total loss may be assumed, and the others will be out of commission for some time, so that Anglo-US available shipping has been decreased by 424 vessels of 2,155,000 GRT.'

So long as the net increase of United Nations merchant shipbuilding continues to be over 1,000,000 gross tons per month, as at present, they can face even such claims with equanimity.

:: JS ::

Acoustic Torpedoes – Mark 24 Mines – 'Fido'

Whilst there is a good deal of information about German acoustic torpedoes, it would appear that virtually nothing was released about the Allied version until long after the war. I have not found any references to Allied acoustic torpedoes in the secret Anti-Submarine Reports. This is understandable inasmuch that 'silent drive' in submarines had already become an accepted part of everyday operations by the beginning of the Second World War and this could easily render an acoustic weapon entirely useless. An emergency or alarm dive was usually carried out by the surfaced submarine increasing speed before flooding the tanks and then continuing as fast as possible with electric motors to get far away from any possible depth charge blasts. Thus, an attacker with a torpedo capable of homing in on noise was in an ideal situation to use the weapon, but this high-priced item could be rendered useless if the submarine went into 'silent drive'. So, it was of utmost importance to keep this weapon under close wraps for the duration of the war. The 'Cold War', the hostilities between the western Allies and the Soviet Union, started before May 1945 and so, no doubt it was necessary to develop this highly secret weapon further for a possible conflict with the Soviets.

The following notes come from papers left by Hanns Parsch, second watch officer of *U760*, who was attacked with an acoustic torpedo on 12 August 1943. The boat survived but was too heavily damaged to make it back to France and it put into Vigo (Spain) on 8 September, where the crew was interned. Hanns Parsch wrote that it would appear as if trials with the American acoustic torpedo were completed towards the end of 1942 and the first production models arrived in Britain in April 1943. Working out exactly how effective they were is most difficult because the majority of aircraft carried a number of different weapons and no one is sure which one was responsible for actually sinking the target. For example, a Liberator with rockets, depth charges and an acoustic torpedo attacked *U514* under Kapitänleutnant Auffermann, but it is not known which weapon was responsible for actually sinking the boat. The few 'definites' such as *U160* (Kptlt. Gerd von Pommer-Esche), *U509* (Kptlt. Werner Witte) and *U43* (Kptlt. Hans-Joachim Schwantke) can be determined because small carrier-based planes were responsible and these worked in groups, with one forcing the U-boat to submerge and another then dropping an acoustic torpedo in its wake. Aiming for the release point was made easier by marking the position where a submarine submerged with smoke buoys.

Chapter 29

After the Crash of September 1943

:: Dönitz ::

Dönitz writes very little about the continuation of the U-boat war after the autumn of 1943, other than to emphasise that the objective of tying up the opposition's forces in the Atlantic, to prevent the aircraft there from being unleashed against German towns, was most successful. Decrypts from the B-Dienst, observations made by U-boats, reports from agents and other sources all indicate that there was a steady increase in anti-submarine forces throughout the following months. Dönitz goes on to say this battle to tie up enemy forces was especially hard for U-boat crews. A third of them never came back from their missions and the exceptionally high losses were accepted because Germany had no other way of keeping so much destructive enemy potential tied up in far-off waters. The losses and deaths in Germany due to Allied bombing were far worse than what was being experienced by the U-boat Arm. There was a considerable discrepancy with numbers because the Germans thought that the Allies had such huge resources that they were patrolling all possible areas of the Atlantic where U-boats might be operating, but this was not true. Both Britain and America used Special Intelligence to send their anti-submarine forces to those areas where they knew that U-boats were definitely operating.

:: The British Side ::

The U-boat Countermeasures Report for November 1943 starts with the words:

> The renewal of the U-boat offensive in the North Atlantic, which started in September, has proved a costly failure to the enemy, who appears to have adopted new tactics which have greatly reduced his attacking power. It is now so rare an occurrence for a U-boat to be sighted on the surface in daylight that it may safely be assumed that U-boats now spend the hours of daylight in avoiding our air patrols by remaining submerged, surfacing only at night to charge batteries and to follow up and attack any

convoy within reach. To compensate for this loss of mobility, enemy long-range aircraft are, it seems, being used to locate our convoys and it is likely that small groups of U-boats will be disposed along their probable course. As most of the enemy's long-range aircraft are based in France, the routes between the United Kingdom and Gibraltar saw the greatest activity.

The U-boat Offensive Reviews provide a good summary of how U-boat operations influenced the Allies, and state:

A fundamental change in U-boat tactics was manifested during November 1943. Whilst still concentrating in packs to attack any convoy encountered, the U-boats appeared to remain submerged by day. The negative evidence provided by the absence of sightings of surfaced U-boats in daylight is convincing proof of this change of habit, at any rate in the area between the Azores, Ireland and Portugal, where the month's only activity occurred. It should be emphasized that it is only with regard to this area that the deduction of a change of procedure can safely be drawn; in the North Atlantic, between Ireland and Newfoundland, insufficient evidence is available to justify an assumption that the appreciation will hold good for that area.

Ubiquity of air cover, now that we have flying facilities in the Azores, has compelled the adoption by the U-boats of a mode of existence, which favours their survival rather than their effective employment against shipping. The U-boats are now behaving by day and in part by night as submarines and no longer, as in their hey-day, moving and attacking like torpedo boats or E-Boats. Mobility is correspondingly reduced and the threat of cumulative pack attack, beginning with a force of two or three U-boats and swelled night after second or third night by the addition of fresh boats, is diminished.

Several convoys on the Gibraltar – United Kingdom run were intercepted, but in each case strong support by escort groups and land-based aircraft brought the convoys safely through concentrations of U-boats, which probably represented the larger part of all boats at sea.

Two convoys in either direction between Iceland and North Russia encountered no opposition despite the probable presence of half a dozen U-boats in the Bear Island area.

In the Indian Ocean Japanese U-boats were troublesome and sank three ships in the Gulf of Aden and one to eastward of the Seychelles.

The Mediterranean was rather more active, particularly off the North African coast and it is probable that one or two arrivals from the Atlantic have brought the U-boat force up to about 15.

Of a world total of 12 ships, aggregating approximately 80,000 tons, sunk by U-boats in December 1943 none was in the Atlantic one ship was however, torpedoed on 31st December south-west of Iceland when straggling, and was sunk by a further attack on 3rd January. [The 7,359 GRT *Empire Housman* was torpedoed by *U545* under Kptlt. Gert Mannesmann and later sunk by *U744* under Kptlt. Heinz Blischke.]

The Atlantic campaign still conformed to the recent pattern, though in the first half of the month there was no activity on the routes between Gibraltar and the United Kingdom. This area became active again in the latter part of the month and it seems that the enemy intend to maintain a group of boats there. It must be admitted that they have a nuisance value and tend to force convoy routes to the westward with a resultant strain on escorts through increased sea time and reduced layover. A serious effect on convoy cycles and ship lift is involved and it is likely that in future shorter routes will be adopted and encounters with the U-boat patrols will be proportionately more numerous. Such a development will be acceptable as escort strength improves.

In the North-Western Approaches, such scanty indications as there were, in so quiet a month, of the whereabouts of the U-boats pointed to an almost complete disregard of the whole of the area west of 30°00'W and to a fairly dense concentration between longitudes 25°W and 20°W. Some of the 20 or more U-boats estimated to have been in the last-mentioned area may have penetrated even closer to Ireland, and it is considered possible that, under the spur of the necessity of finding convoys, an occasional U-boat may come really close in to the North Channel to act as a scout.

The impression made by the W/T behaviour in recent weeks is one of sporadic and wide-spread dispositions throughout the range of latitude from 50°N to about 62°N in the longitudes indicated, and it seems likely that, when a convoy is intercepted, no large number of U-boats will operate against it.

In January 1944 the U-boat campaign assumed a new aspect in the North-Western Approaches. The main disposition comprising some two dozen U-boats apparently moved gradually towards the West coast of Ireland and the North Channel, starting perhaps from approximately longitude 25°00'W and closing, as a string bag is drawn together to its neck, until they were within some 350 miles of Slyne Head [Connemara – Irish Republic]. This reconstruction of apparent movements was well evidenced by aircraft or other sightings despite the prevalence of appalling weather: it was, of course, to the weather that the U-boats owed their relative immunity despite their proximity to air bases. It is considered that the necessity to find targets compelled the enemy to make this move towards the North Channel.

In the North Atlantic two merchant ships and one escort vessel were lost during the month. The total casualties due to U-boats were not heavy but were increased this month by the loss of three ships in a convoy to North Russia. There was considerable activity by about a dozen U-boats in the Bear Island area against this convoy and against a second convoy, which reached Murmansk without losing any merchantmen. One destroyer was sunk and another damaged.

During February 1944 the most difficult area from the point of view of the U-boat campaign was the Indian Ocean. We suffered serious casualties in this area in the course of a campaign by six U-boats, which sailed from Penang and are expected to return to Biscay ports. It is appreciated that half a dozen 740 tonners, now outward bound from the Bay of Biscay, may be intended to renew the eastern campaign and that two or three boats of the 1,000-ton type may also be on passage to the same area.

The outstanding feature of the Indian Ocean incidents was the impunity with which U-boats operated in focal areas well within air range of shore bases and without any interference in dark hours. The contrast was very marked in the North Atlantic where the initiative has been retained by our forces, both air and surface, and, subject to the handicap of bad weather, has been vigorously wielded to harry and subdue the far larger number of U-boats attempting to attack shipping.

In early January the disposition in the North-Western Approaches had apparently been close into the North Channel but about the end of the month it was withdrawn to about 25°W, probably as a result of the weight of air attack which had been brought to bear.

No pack attack of the type familiar a year ago was developed and it is thought that the enemy spread his U-boats more sparsely and relied on fast travel by night to bring together sufficient for attack on any convoy reported by a U-boat or aircraft. Co-operation with enemy reconnaissance aircraft flying west of Ireland was a feature and it is noteworthy that such a technique is valid for attack on outward rather than on homeward convoys; it is therefore unsuitable for any concentration of effort against our military preparations. U-boats for the most part remained dived by day to minimize the risk of attack from the air.

The type of operation, familiar in the late autumn, conducted by a series of small packs co-operating with aircraft on the Gibraltar convoy routes to the eastward of the Azores was not in evidence: it had been anticipated that in such an area the U-boats would find the cost of aggressive operations unacceptable.

The coastal areas of West Africa have been troubled by two bold U-boats and some apprehension is felt lest this comparatively soft spot may be further exploited. Brazil was left severely alone, presumably in deference to the strong air patrols encountered by U-boats operating in this area last summer. The Caribbean and U.S. seaboard have been inactive but may soon experience a renewal of U-boat patrols.

It is satisfactory to observe that as yet there is no indication that the enemy has increased his U-boat forces to meet any military invasion.

During March 1944 the tonnage of Merchant Shipping sunk by U-boat action rose considerably above the figure for February, but the number of U-boats disposed of remained satisfactory.

Losses were again heaviest in the Indian Ocean where Japanese U-boats achieved several successes, which were often accompanied by brutality to the survivors. German U-boats were probably seriously inconvenienced by the sinking in the Southern Indian Ocean of two tankers, one in the latter half of February and the second in the middle of March. U-boats were seen near both ships, so refuelling operations were probably in progress.

Another setback for the Indian Ocean campaign was the sinking by USS *Block Island* in the Cape Verde Islands area of two U-boats. One of these, from which survivors were rescued, was of the VIIF or torpedo-carrying type [*U1059* under Oblt.z.S. Günther Leupold]. She may well have been taking a stock of torpedoes, including 'Gnats' [British term for acoustic torpedoes of Type Zaunkönig or T5] to the Penang base [Yes, she was]. A U-boat was also sunk by aircraft south of Cape Town, by a series of well co-ordinated attacks by aircraft. Despite these misfortunes it is unlikely that either the Germans or the Japanese will altogether abandon one of the few areas where the rate of exchange of U-boats and merchant ships is still much in their favour.

Subsidiary operations by one or two U-boats, presumably intended to cause us to disperse our forces, continued off West Africa, where three ships were sunk, and in the Caribbean, where one ship was lost. There was also evidence of minelaying at St. Lucia and possibly off San Juan, Puerto Rico. Single U-boats appear to have been operating off the coast of Virginia and in the Nova Scotia and Newfoundland areas, but without achieving much success.

Dispositions in the North Atlantic appear to have been widely scattered between 46°00'N and 60°00'N, mostly between 30°00'W and 15°00'W. Only a small number of U-boats are thought to have been involved and probably areas were difficult to estimate. The enemy cannot have hoped to achieve much with such slender forces and in fact only one merchant vessel was lost. One American and two British escort vessels were sunk, probably all of them by 'Gnats', but in two instances the U-boats concerned were themselves subsequently destroyed. Over one-third of the U-boats sunk in March were accounted for in this area, most of them by hunting groups, which again demonstrated their value.

One of the periodical attempts to reinforce the Mediterranean U-boat force may have been partially successful.

The enemy's biggest reverse was in the Arctic. At the beginning of the month an outward-bound convoy to Russia arrived without the loss of a single ship despite a heavy concentration of U-boats against it, while the homeward bound convoy only lost one ship. Five U-boats appear to have been sunk in this double operation and others were probably damaged. A large share of the credit for this must go to the aircraft of HMS *Chaser*. The month closed well with a kill by the Second Support Group, supporting the next outward-bound convoy. The U-boat concerned was probably on passage to the Atlantic and was unlucky to have encountered trouble so soon after leaving the peaceful waters of the Baltic.

During April 1944, when shipping losses by U-boat attack throughout the world were the lowest for four years, more than twice as many U-boats as merchant ships were sunk.

It is remarkable that so much should have been achieved against U-boats which were clearly being husbanded in anticipation of a major effort in the summer months, for all the indications by bulk of W/T traffic, infrequency of encounters and the immensity of shipping in the North Atlantic pointed to the fact that patrol dispositions must have been sparse and wide flung. Numerous U-boat transmissions were intercepted of a regular type and form which almost certainly were weather reports, and it seems that, during this period, great importance was attached to obtaining meteorological information, probably in aid of military and air planning.

As a corollary to the economy in employment of U-boats in the North Atlantic, there was a noteworthy increase of effort in areas far afield where diversionary effects might be hoped for in dispersion of our forces. It is considered that half a dozen or more boats of the larger types were on passage through the Central and South Atlantic towards the Indian Ocean, and that several of these were involved in refuelling operations west of the Cape Verde Islands, in the course of which kills were obtained by United States escort carriers.

The enemy continued to maintain a strong force of U-boats in Arctic waters but they achieved little against the North Russian convoys.

Patrols off Florida and Nova Scotia were in evidence and in the latter part of the month there may have been two or three U-boats off West Africa.

In the Mediterranean the U-boats have apparently shown increased reluctance to attack and a greater caution in the use of W/T, which has naturally resulted in a decrease in the number of locations of U-boats. During the latter part of the month there were five U-boats operating. The main effort seems to have been off the East coast of Sicily, where probably two U-boats maintained a patrol for two or three weeks, but without making any attacks. The third was operating off the Algerian coast and the fourth in the Naples/Anzio area. The only boat to achieve anything was the fifth boat, which, operating of the Cyrenaican 'Hump,' torpedoed two ships in Convoy UGS37 [*U407* under Kptlt. Hubertus Korndörfer].

On the night of 20th/21st April the Germans made an unsuccessful attack with human torpedoes off Anzio. Both prisoners and craft were taken.

Chapter 30

Weapons used against U-boats

The Monthly Anti-Submarine Reports for early 1944 include information on the following new weapons used against U-boats.

The Shark Anti-Submarine Projectile
A projectile has been developed for use in 4 inch guns for the attack of U-boats on the surface. During development the projectile was known by the camouflage name of 'Shark'. ['Shark' was also the British codename for the four-wheel Enigma Code, which was introduced for U-boats in February 1942 and was not broken into by Bletchley Park in England until after 30 October 1942, when men from HMS *Petard* captured the necessary machine and code books from *U559* under Kptlt. Hans Heidtmann.] Its official name will be 'Projectile, 4 inch, Anti-Submarine'. The 'Shark' is intended to hit the water just short of the U-boat and strike the boat underwater when the water tamping will make its detonation more effective.

The purposes underlying development are that: –

When attacking U-boats on the surface the target in a vertical plane, on which lethal damage can be done, is very small. Even if this small target be hit, SAP [semi-armour-piercing] shell are likely to glance off the pressure hull.

If these shells hit the conning tower, they often go on before bursting and, even if they burst, are unlikely to prevent the boat diving. HE [high explosive] shell will detonate if they hit the target anywhere but only under exceptional circumstances will the fragments from a 4 inch shell hole the pressure hull. Larger calibres are more successful.

The 'Shark' is heavy and unwieldy but its AP [armour-piercing] head enables it to pierce tanks or superstructure before bursting. It is immune from ricochet, at all angles greater than 4°, which means that, if fired from a gun mounted not less than 15 feet above the waterline, it will not ricochet at any angle of gun elevation. Its fuse gives sufficient delay to permit penetration and its charge, 25 lbs of Torpex, will cause a large hole in the pressure hull.

On hitting the water the 'Shark' continues to move substantially along the same trajectory but loses its velocity rapidly. It follows that the 'Shark' is essentially a short-range weapon, because the greater the distance the more steeply is the trajectory inclined downwards and the projectile will miss under the U-boat unless it falls very close to it.

Owing to the unhandiness of the projectile, the rate of fire will be slow particularly with motion of the ship. Starting with the gun loaded, it would be a smart crew that fired three rounds in a minute.

The muzzle velocity is only 500 feet a second, which means that the 'forecast' to be applied by the gun layer when there is motion on the ship would need to be five times that required by an ordinary shell. This would be so difficult to assess that it is advisable to restrict firing to the end of the roll towards – there may be insufficient depression to be able to fire on the roll away – when no forecast will be required. This is unlikely to reduce the rate of fire further than it is already reduced by the unhandiness of the projectile and in any case the small number of rounds carried will preclude a high rate of fire.

The present projectile can be fired from all marks of 4-inch gun, but each mark requires a different propellant charge. It is anticipated that a small number of these projectiles will be available for Western Approaches by the end of March, 1944. A larger order will begin to mature in May. Other possible uses of the projectile, such as for sinking small merchant vessels, will no doubt receive consideration. 'Sharks' are also being designed for 3-inch, 12-pdr, 4.5-inch, and 4.7-inch guns. For the two former it is not yet established whether the weapon will be lethal or not.

Radio Sonic Buoys

General Description

The ERSB (Expendible Radio Sono Buoy) is a method of providing aircraft with a means of listening to underwater sounds. The two principal parts of the equipment consist of the ERSB and a receiver in the aircraft. The ERSB, which is launched by the aircraft, weighs 14 lbs and is about 45 inches, long by 6 inches diameter. It consists essentially of the following: –

(a) a hydrophone which is released from the base of the buoy when this strikes the water and is suspended some 24 feet below the surface;

(b) a transmitting set contained within the buoy and a short antenna by means of which sounds picked up-by the hydrophone are transmitted by radio to the listening aircraft.

The buoy has an operational life of 4 to 8 hours, after which it will sink. Those in use at present have a non-directional hydrophone, but a directional model is being developed. In order that the aircraft may know which buoy is transmitting sounds they are made in six frequencies, each buoy being painted a distinctive colour corresponding to its frequency.

Range of detection of submerged U-boat sounds depends upon the speed of the U-boat and upon sea conditions and are approximately as follows: –

U-boat speed 2 knots. Range of detection 300 – 1,000 yards.

U-boat speed 4 knots. Range of detection 1,000 – 6,500 yards.

U-boat speed 6 knots. Range of detection 3,000 – 10,000 yards.

The range of the radio transmitter is 35 miles, when aircraft is flying at 5,000 feet altitude and 30 miles at 3,000 feet.

Tactical Uses

These are manifold and include: –

1. the evaluation and assessment of attacks by aircraft against U-boats;
2. to ascertain counter-measures employed by U-boats;
3. tracking a submerged U-boat;
4. investigation of MAD (Magnetic Airborne Detector) contacts;
5. investigation of oil slicks.

The method of tracking a U-boat seen to submerge by aircraft with sono-buoys is as follows: –

At the last point of submergence an ERSB is dropped together with a visual marker, e.g. a smoke buoy. The aircraft then flies 2 miles in any direction from that point, preferably along the estimated course of the U-boat, and then proceeds to fly a square of 4 miles on each side, dropping a different coloured ERSB at each corner.

On completion of this operation, which takes about four to six minutes, the operator of the receiver in the aircraft tunes in to the frequency of each buoy according to its colour and, knowing the location of each of these, is able by tuning from one to another to evaluate the proximity of the U-boat to any particular buoy.

At present supplies are limited, but it is hoped that it will be possible to step up production to meet the increasing demands for the Radio-Sono-Buoy.

Ships in the Vicinity

Shore based aircraft working on their own with sono buoys will endeavour to attack the U-boat should its position be found with sufficient accuracy. It is important, therefore, that ships should ascertain the situation from aircraft, which may be hunting with sono buoys. Until full information has been obtained, escorts should keep well clear of the sono buoy area. In this connection it should be remembered that high speed will interfere with the aircraft's sono buoy reception at a considerable distance.

Magnetic Airborne Detector (MAD) and Retro-Bombs

This [MAD] is a device installed in aircraft for the purpose of locating submerged submarines by detecting the small local changes produced by submarines in the magnetic field of the earth. It is in fact a form of flying indicator loop. The normal range of detection (aircraft to target) varies from 400 to 700 feet. That is to say, an aircraft patrolling at 100 feet should theoretically be able to detect a U-boat 300 feet below the surface. It will also detect wrecks or other fairly large iron or steel objects.

The equipment includes a recorder, which produces a continuous trace on a moving tape and magnetic oscillation appears as a distortion in the trace. MAD equipment (the weight of a typical installation is about 135 lbs) has been installed and is in operational use in some United States Catalinas, and tests are being made in other types of aircraft

Retro-Bombs

To increase the effectiveness of MAD it has been necessary to develop a weapon which can be released at the moment a strong signal is received, and in order to ensure that the weapon will hit the water above the target a rocket propelled bomb is projected backwards with a speed equal to the forward speed of the aircraft so that the backward motion of the missile will neutralize the forward speed of the aircraft There are two variations of this:

1. by giving the bomb excess backward velocity, or
2. by giving it a downward component of velocity so as to reduce the time of fall.

This weapon is known as the Retro-Bomb which is similar to the Hedgehog projectile in size and weight, but has a rocket motor attached. The bombs have contact fuses.

MAD Tactics

MAD is probably most value as a means of tracking a U-boat whose presence is already known or in narrow waters such as the Strait of Gibraltar. Here, on 16th March 1943 a very promising attack was made on a U-boat by surface ships after initial detection and attack by MAD equipped Catalinas of the United States Navy. [The U-boat was not sunk.]

In tracking a submerged U-boat the MAD equipped aircraft flies over the area in circles completing two circles on each side of the probable course of the U-boat, and dropping a marker during each circle when a signal is received. Towards the completion of the fourth circle, the aircraft will prepare to carry out its bombing run between the lines of markers. The retro bombs are launched either manually or automatically when the MAD signal is received.

Illumination for Night Attacks on U-boats by Aircraft, June-August 1944

The two types of illuminants proven to be of value for night attack on the U-boat are the Leigh Light and the 4-inch high intensity flare. There is also the 1.7-inch, high intensity flare, which has not yet been used against a U-boat.

The Leigh Light

The Leigh Light in the Wellington has proved itself to be an effective means of delivering night attacks on U-boats. The manoeuvrability of the Wellington, with its good pilot's view, combine to make it very suitable for this type of attack. Nevertheless, good crew drill, with a high state of ASV homing efficiency, are also essential to achieve success. The candlepower of the Leigh Light is approximately 22 million.

The Leigh Light in Liberator aircraft is a newer project, which requires a higher state of crew training than with the Wellington. The reason for this is the lack of manoeuvrability inherent in larger aircraft, which renders it less simple to make last minute corrections during an approach. The pilot's view forward is restricted by the long nose, and if the target is picked up on the starboard beam it may be impossible for the pilot to see it.

The Anti-Submarine 4 inch Mark I High Intensity Flare

This method of night attack was adopted operationally in late 1943 when two Halifax squadrons became available for night anti-U-boat operations. Here again a high state of training is necessary to achieve success. The method used for attack is briefly as follows: –

The aircraft homes by ASV on to the U-boat and releases a stick of three flares from 750 feet at approximately 1.25 miles, or slightly less from the target. The aircraft then decreases height as quickly as possible, consistent with safety; on picking up the target visually a normal low-level attack is made.

The 1.7 inch High Intensity Flare

The 1.7 inch high intensity flare is the latest addition to illuminants for night attacks, and trials show great promise. These flares burn for approximately three seconds, giving 3 million, candlepower. They are dropped by hand down the tube, one at a time, and the fuse is set off electrically on passing over contacts near the base of the launcher. The flare, then falls clear of the aircraft and ignites after a delay of 1 to 2 seconds.

Trials have been carried out in both a Halifax and a Sunderland, while at the present time, 58 Squadron of Halifax and 228 Squadron of Sunderland aircraft are equipping with this gear and carrying out all fittings with station facilities on the spot.

The results achieved with the 1.7 inch flare have been most satisfactory. Apart from the simplicity of this method of attack there are also these advantages: –

1. Unlike the parachute flares the illumination can be continued or stopped at will.
2. The aircraft is not committed to remaining at a height where the U-boat radar cover is bound to pick them up.
3. The aircraft is in a position to lose height gradually during the approach instead of making a steep approach as is required with the 4-inch A/S flare after release.

It has been strongly recommended that the 1.7 inch flare be adopted for night attacks on U-boats in aircraft which are not equipped with Leigh Lights. Each type of aircraft has points both in its favour and against it with regard to its suitability for night attacks.

Anti-Submarine Weapons in use by Fleet Air Arm and Coastal Command Aircraft

The anti-submarine weapons employed by Fleet Air Arm and Coastal Command aircraft fall into two main groups: –

1. Those which depend for their effect on exploding within a certain distance from the target, according to the kind and amount of explosive; and
2. those effect of which depends on hitting and penetrating the pressure hull.

The first group comprises the depth charge and the A/S bombs, which are fired by hydrostatic pistol or fuse. These have a lethal radius against a typical German U-boat ranging from about 8 feet in the case of the 100 lb bomb up to about 28 feet in the case of the 600 lb bomb.

In view of the fact that the chance of placing the depth charges or bombs within lethal range or the target falls off rapidly after a U-boat has been submerged for more than 15 – 30 seconds, these weapons each have a setting fixed to explode at an appropriate depth and adjusted to the explosive charge.

The depth charge, Mark XI, is the most generally used weapon. It contains 185 lbs of Torpex, giving a lethal radius of 19 feet and is fired at a depth of about 25 feet. Height and speed of release are limited to a maximum of 1,000 feet and 250 knots, respectively, by reason of the possibility of it breaking up on impact if released above those limits.

The 100 lb A/S bomb, Mark VI, has recently been introduced for use by the Fleet Air Arm, for which it is especially suitable as the bomb load can be adjusted flexibly to meet conditions of takeoff from carriers. It has not yet been used operationally. Maximum height and speed of release are, at present, 150 feet and 130 knots.

The 600 lb A/S bomb, Mark I, is a Coastal Command weapon, which is used to a somewhat limited extent. It can be released at heights from 100 to 2,500 feet without restriction as to speed.

The second group consists of the RP [rocket projectile] and the six-pounder gun. Both weapons have been introduced during the past two years, and are intended for use against visible and, in the case of the RP only, very recently submerged submarines. The projectile, in the case of both weapons, consists of a solid steel head, which is capable of penetrating the pressure hull if certain conditions of attack are observed. In the case of the RP, penetration of the pressure hull can occur when the RP has travelled as much as 150 feet underwater.

In Coastal Command the employment of RP is at present confined to certain Liberators, which are fitted with retractable launching rails for two rounds on each side of the fuselage, into which they can be withdrawn for re-loading. This operation takes about two minutes in flight. In naval aircraft the RPs are carried on the under sides of the wings, usually four on each, and cannot be reloaded in flight. Developments are in hand to increase the hitting power.

The six-pounder gun (57 mm) is fitted only in some Coastal Command Mosquito aircraft. The magazine carries 24 rounds which are automatically loaded and the rate of fire is 60 rounds per minute, but usually only about six rounds are fired in each attack which is opened at about 2,000 yards range, the aircraft diving at an angle of 25° to 45°.

Chapter 31

The Radio War

[The following report was released shortly after the end of the war in the Monthly Anti-Submarine Reports.]

This paper, condensed from the very great bulk of material available, concerns itself mainly with the German reaction to our conduct of the radio war. Many detailed figures and dates have been omitted to avoid overloading the text and to produce a broad and general review. Where it has been necessary to examine some situation in greater detail, this has been done as far as possible by quoting from a document which reveals the state of mind of those concerned: for, as will be seen, this highly technical subject is just as dependent upon the personal qualities of individuals as are the classical modes of warfare.

It is a truism to state that one of the most valuable qualities of the U-boat is its relative invisibility; this applies not only to the period when an operation is in progress but to passage to an operational area and to the phase of recuperation ready for the next operation.

Throughout the war the aim of the U-boat hunter has been by any means to discover the elusive quarry. Our methods available at the beginning of the campaign, though applicable to small areas where the U-boats might be expected to congregate, such as the neighbourhood of a convoy, were not, however, applicable to the wide spaces of open ocean where they spent the period intervening between operations. The use of radio technique has provided two complementary solutions to this problem – H/F D/F and radar.

H/F D/F (High Frequency Direction Finder)

Some time before the beginning of the war the Admiralty appreciated the need for a shore H/F D/F organization and the important part that it might play in operations. The extensive use of H/F D/F as an anti-U-boat device could not, however, be foreseen until the U-boat Command showed its hand towards the end of 1940 after acquiring the French bases.

In the early stages of the war, indeed, H/F D/F was not much concerned with U-boats. The location of German naval shore stations, an occasional raider or merchant ship and, surprising as it may now seem, enemy aircraft were the main objectives.

The small number of H/F D/F stations, combined with the fact that enemy transmissions were mostly in home waters, made it seem at the end of 1939 that the art had nearly been mastered; positions were estimated not to degrees but to minutes, and one enemy aircraft was plotted and eventually shot down by a patrol which had been directed on as a result of H/F D/F.

Even in those days, there were signs that the apparently simple process might become not simpler but more complicated. So it proved. As more H/F D/F stations became available round the Atlantic shores and as U-boats started to operate in numbers on the Atlantic trade routes, it became clear that a given set of bearings plotted on the chart did not produce a point of intersection, nor even the 'cocked hat' of the textbooks; it produced a plan view of a large and untidy bird's nest.

So the sad truth was learnt that the shore H/F D/F organization could only produce an indication of area and, at best, could do no more than provide a warning for a threatened convoy, and so assist evasive routeing; no considerable improvement could be expected, although from time to time the available resources in men and material were picked over yet again to see if anything had been missed.

In the summer of 1940 the pattern of the U-boat tactics in attacks on shipping became discernible, with the thread of communications running through as an essential part of the design. It soon became obvious that, if shore stations could give an indication of area, H/F D/F in the Convoy escorts themselves might do a great deal more – might even find the U-boats before they could launch their attack.

The first requirement was a H/F D/F outfit for ships, which was quick and easy to operate, those previously fitted in warships being neither. Accuracy had to be of secondary importance, because a ship is far from ideal as a site for H/F D/F but, by careful placing of the aerial, an adequate accuracy should be – and was – obtained.

The equipment was designed and put into production but production was slow at first, nor did the results from the few ships that were fitted during the second half of 1941 give much encouragement. Gradually, however, as the new technique was learnt and applied, it was realized what a powerful aid was available: successes became more frequent and by November 1942, H/F D/F was accepted as an essential part of the equipment of escort craft. In the April, 1942 Report it was stated: 'the combination of a warning from shore and a line of bearing (from the escort), both based on the same U-boat H/F transmissions, gives the escort information of the greatest value. The warning indicates that a U-boat may be within visibility distance of the convoy. The line of bearing gives its approximate position relative to the convoy.'

The German appreciation of the use of H/F D/F against U-boats appears to have both overrated and underrated the danger. They overrated the accuracy of shore H/F D/F (which they must have known to be operating against them), but for a long time they underrated – indeed, ignored – the danger of ship-borne H/F D/F. This was reflected in their communications, which seemed to be conducted on the principle that W/T silence was to be strictly kept until contact was made with the enemy but might be completely relaxed thereafter; in other words, they were afraid of revealing their dispositions but saw no danger from the transmissions of individual U-boats once the battle was joined. During the attack on Convoy SC118 [4th–9th February 1943], for example, the U-boats concerned made 108 transmissions during the period of 72 hours.

It is difficult to understand why it took the Germans so long to realize the threat from ship-borne H/F D/F. They must have had many reports – and perhaps photographs – of escorts equipped with the characteristic aerial which could really have had no purpose other than H/F D/F; nevertheless, the credit for the enemy's enlightenment goes to the first of the 'Y' parties [listening/interception teams] to put to sea in a U-boat, which heard D/F intercommunication on 2,410 kc/s. Whatever the cause, the effect was to make the task of U-boats attacking convoys increasingly difficult. The U-boat command connected their diminishing success to some extent with their communications, and cleaned things up considerably. The length of messages was reduced, the frequencies in use were changed more often and, for special jobs, a system of changing frequency two or three times a day was introduced. These shifts, while they made H/F D/F both ashore and afloat more difficult, did not seriously affect its use or effectiveness.

Affairs had reached this stage when, for reasons quite unconnected with communications, the whole German naval radio effort came under new direction. This new direction produced interesting technical solutions to the problem of devising a means of communication, which would put the U-boats a jump ahead of reception and D/F by existing means. These devices, however, came too late to affect the operational use of H/F D/F during the German war and it will be more convenient to consider them later on.

Granted the solution of the many technical and operational problems involved, the plot and counterplot of communications and H/F D/F have been simple and easily discernible throughout but H/F D/F could do no more than bring the escorts, if all went well, close enough to the U-boat to allow other and more accurate means of location to be used. When the U-boat Command turned its attention to radar, the scene became unruly indeed.

Radar and GSR (Group Search Receiver)

The wavelength of the early radar sets was long and, in consequence, the aerial had to be very high above the surface of the sea before any considerable range could be obtained on small objects. This limited the effectiveness against U-boats of the early radar sets in ships, but not in aircraft, and the value of ASV as a U-boat detector soon became apparent. Its operation was unaffected by conditions of visibility and by its use large areas of sea could be swept and any contacts investigated. This led to an increase in air attacks and sinkings of U-boats not only around convoys but also in other areas, and it became apparent to the Germans that aircraft were appearing much too often for their presence to be due to visual sightings. The Germans were fully alive to the possibilities of metre wave radar (in some aspects their development was ahead of ours in 1939), and had two ASV sets planned, the FuG 200 (lowest in number of all airborne radars) and the FuG 213; they were also aided by the capture of a Mark II ASV set in Tunisia in the spring of 1942. They accordingly concluded that ASV was causing the trouble and tests in the summer of 1942 confirmed that the transmissions were easily detectable by a simple receiver and aerial.

Grand Admiral Dönitz, never a man for half measures, ordered the speediest equipping of all boats with makeshift equipment. The aerials of wood and cable (Biscay Crosses) were easily made but it must be assumed that all the production of the German radio firms was concentrated on the German Air Force, as the choice of receiver fell on the Paris firm of Metox, which turned out the R600, the first and, for more than six months, the only standard U-boat GSR (Group Search Receiver). This set had many shortcomings, the more serious being the less obvious. On the one hand, although the lower limit of its wavelength cover was 130 cm, it purported to receive lower wavelengths on harmonics of the local oscillator, and a chart showing these down to 30 cm was fixed to the front of the set. As the aerial plug was connected to the mixer valve by a piece of twisted flex, the technical report on the first of these sets to fall into our hands stated: 'The reception of the lower wavelengths can hardly have been a serious objective of the design.'

On the other hand, had it been designed as a transmitter, it could hardly have radiated more power from the valves provided. Its operational success was, however, undeniable: ASV fitted aircraft could be detected at ranges which enabled U-boats to dive before they approached; the set gained the confidence of the U-boat captains, and soon in the Mediterranean no one would put to sea without a search receiver in working order. When the installation was standardized with a fixed aerial and the loose wooden cross type reduced to a standby, the R600 remained the chosen receiver. All appeared to be well and the pitfalls for the unwary remained hidden.

Centimetric Radar

Meanwhile, all unobserved by the U-boat Command, the storm was beginning to gather. The Germans were far from unaware of the possibility of generating radiations of wavelength around 10 cm. In the early 1930's they had produced such radiations in sufficient strength to employ in signalling and, using them, had developed a very narrow beam system of point-to-point telecommunications. They had, however, never succeeded in producing any considerable power and it was the British invention of the strapped magnetron in the spring of 1940 which made this possible; from this seed sprang many valuable pieces of radar equipment up to Types 275 and 277, ASV Mark V; and, later, the 3-cm equipments. [The strapped magnetron was a special form of radio valve capable of generating powerful centimetric radiations.] This invention first impinged on the U-boats in February to March 1943, in the form of ASV, Mark III. As has been mentioned, the GSR set in use, the Metox R600, was peculiarly unsuited to detecting these very short waves, even by accident, and the sightings and attacks on U-boats began a steady increase, while the proportion of aircraft approaches undetected by the U-boats rose. When this was noticed, the first possible explanation, which occurred to German technical intelligence was that we were employing supersonic modulation, producing vibrations in the headphones above or below the limit of audibility; they accordingly fitted the Metox R600 GSR with a visual tuning indication of the 'Magic Eye' type, familiar on the more elaborate types of broadcast receiver. Fortunately naval aircraft operating from Gibraltar at this time were employing this very device and at first the 'Magic Eye' met with some slight success – enough at least to divert attention from one of the fundamental causes of the Germans' steadily mounting losses. For another couple of months they were lulled into a sense of false security. It then became painfully apparent that the 'Magic Eye' was in fact no solution and a search for an alternative began. The next two blind alleys to be explored appear to have been suggested by reports of observations from operational U-boats; one was infra-red, the other supposed that we were using an anti-interception technique in operating our ASV, only switching it on for very short periods.

Many U-boat men became convinced that Allied aircraft were using some sort of infra-red detecting device, nature unspecified: the U-boat Command appears to have received numerous reports of dull red glows from attacking aircraft and this idea occupied them for some time. Their reaction was along the obvious lines – an infra-red detector was carried by some U-boats in an attempt to confirm the hypothesis. Fortunately the difficulties of operating the device used were such that negative reports were not convincing and, throughout the summer of 1943, the fruitless attempt to escape this child of their imagination continued. Many U-boats were coated with a special paint intended to give no reflections of infra-red rays. The sinkings of the U-boats went on.

Their other supposition of the use of anti-interception technique in ASV operation was an eminently reasonable one. It was the counterpart in radar of the use of short signals in H/F communication, which the Germans were already extending as one means of escaping from our H/F D/F. It is common knowledge that in radar interception this method is easily defeated by using a specially designed receiver, sweeping rapidly and automatically through its whole wavelength range several times a second and presenting the result on a cathode ray tube. There is then visible across the face of the tube a horizontal line of light, from which a vertical line shoots whenever a transmission within the wavelength range is intercepted. This has great advantages from the operator's point of view: it requires less concentration to watch this than to listen to headphones and there is no strain on the wrist from the continual movement of tuning controls.

The German technicians were still engaged with these phantoms when the crash came at the end of May 1943, and it can safety be assumed that this gave great impetus to their researches.

Appreciations, June and July 1943

Viewed from the Allied side, there was at this time no logical reason why the Germans should not solve their puzzle within a very few weeks. Taking an impartial survey of every conceivable method of detecting U-boats, it seemed that they must inevitably be led to the correct answer – shorter wavelength radar. Authorities were resigned to the inevitable discovery and the principal feeling was one of astonishment that the secret had been kept for so long. Subsequent intelligence has not altered the salient features of an appreciation of the possibilities inherent in the situation at that time, prepared for the Naval Staff to date 1st June 1943, and published in the Anti-Submarine Report for that month:

There are indications that there is now a crisis on the Search/Counter Search competition, similar to that which ten months ago produced the German search receiver. Up to the beginning of June there had been minor modifications, but no fundamental change of policy.'

In the last few batches of prisoners of war, two trends have been noticeable:–

1. A progressive lessening of confidence in the German Search Receiver, while recently positive dissatisfaction has been expressed.
2. An increase in gossip and rumours both about the means of U-boat detection which we are employing and the proposed German counter measures. Although each individual statement is flimsy enough, an impression is created of something substantial in the background.

Operational reports from Coastal Command indicate that a major change of surfacing tactics has taken place, reversing those previously in use. In the Bay of Biscay, at least, U-boats now surface during part of the day and submerge at night. This preference for surfacing at a time when search by aircraft is simplified appears to indicate distrust in the performance of the existing German Search Receivers.

If this in fact reflects the policy of the German authorities, we may assume that they are aware of our use of a method of detection, which cannot be picked up by existing German Search Receivers. Their reaction may be expected to be vigorous; and there are two possible courses open to them: –

1. The discovery of how our new U-boat detection device works, followed by the production of a suitable telltale. This would continue the old German search receiver policy, which is dependent on picking up radiations from aircraft or surface vessels. There are as yet no signs of German success here.
2. The production of an independent aircraft detection device (such as radar) to be fitted in U-boats. This has the advantage of working whatever means of detection we employ.

Only if both these fail is it likely that the problem will be abandoned and reliance placed only on increased anti-aircraft armament, such as has recently been reported.

It has been urged that the use of anti-aircraft radar is unlikely on account of the careful observance of radar silence by the Germans and their evident fear of our use of search receivers. There is, however, less reason for observing radar silence in a restricted area such as the Bay of Biscay, through which boats must pass, and the possibility of attracting aircraft outside detection range is offset by obtaining sufficient warning for a safe dive.

The most likely requirement is an all-round-looking radar set of relatively small range and not necessarily giving any indication of bearing. Such a set need not have an elaborate aerial array. It might be possible to meet the requirement by using the existing U-boat radar set with an aerial system alternative to the directional array with bearing indication now fitted.

Operational experiences of our own submarines have confirmed that these were the avenues for mimicking for the U-boats and it was on this basis that countermeasures were planned. It was fortunate at our technical lead at that time left us enough margin to produce suitable counters. In the event the year drew to a close without them being needed; the German reaction had been much overestimated.

On 6th July 1943, the Director of the Naval Communications Division, German Naval War Staff, wrote: –

Appendix to Most Secret, Reg. No. 2074, of 6. July 1943
Surface-watching Radar Service

1. Result
The enemy's location service does at least afford the inferior party an opportunity of using his interception service as a means of warning; the successful use of this on our side quickly brought our superior foe to the necessity of generally introducing a procedure into his location to render our radar interception service as difficult as possible. Our interception service followed suit by discovering the enemy's new location procedure and increasing its own tenacity and skill to correspond. Our opponent again retaliated with great initiative, by means of which he succeeded, months ago, in locating and attacking us by surprise again, using new methods, which have so far proved almost inaccessible to interception.

The great superiority thus shown by the enemy in location, jamming and recognition service, together with the depreciation of our own warning service (radar interception service) has eliminated the element of surprise in U-boat and E-Boat warfare, and in mining operations by aircraft in the enemy's coastal waters.

Thus the only offensive branch of Axis warfare against the Anglo-Saxon enemies – the war on their imports – is severely prejudiced and its very existence imperilled.

2. Objectives
In the sphere of enemy control of the sea and superiority in the air, first importance must be given to: – Preventing and obstructing the enemy's location of our own units, especially U-boats and E-Boats, and of minelaying by the Luftwaffe.

According to our success in this, the significance of our tactical warning service will increase or decrease but it will always be of fundamental importance, independently of its temporary usefulness as a tactical warning service. With its help we must discover and analyse the organization, technical and tactical procedure of the enemy in his location service, as well as his methods and ways of working. This is necessary from many points of view, if we are to strive successfully towards our principal object and attain it.

Outside the sphere of marked enemy superiority, our foremost aim must be superior, active location. This applies specially to U-boats, E-Boats, defence forces and coast defence. In the case of U-boats and E-Boats, their small elevation is a hindrance; moreover, in their operational sphere, sudden changes in the tactical situation must always be expected, owing to the enemy's systematic and extensive pursuit by air and naval forces. Our own location apparatus in these boats must, therefore, be made to produce results with the shortest possible time of operation.

3. Conditions of the Specialist Service

Measures for the prevention and obstruction of the enemy's location are not yet all ripe for operation. The measures planned cover camouflage, jamming, and deception. The tactical warning service is a serious failure at present, chiefly because the enemy is now continually locating and attacking us by surprise, using new methods beyond the reach of the present equipment of our warning service. The supplementing of our equipment by corresponding means of interception lags decidedly behind, owing to the theoretical and practical superiority of the enemy's physical research and technology.

Our location service is at present particularly in want of an efficient location set for defence forces and light naval forces, especially E-Boats. The sets in use in units of the naval forces, in U-boats and on the coast, are either only partially satisfactory in their performance compared with the enemy's, or else – especially in the case of U-boats – they are extraordinarily liable to defects, owing to defective fitting.

The development work, mostly very praiseworthy, carried out by Communications Research Command [NEK – Nachrichtenmittel-versuchskommando], was often sent straight to the front, to save time, without undergoing an operational test by Communications Testing Command [NVK – Nachrichtenmittelerprobungskommando]. Many obvious results since obtained show this to have been wrong.

The extensive tasks of production imposed on Communications Research Command have restricted its capacity for research and development.

Failure in appointing a section head in the Communications Technical Department (NWa) of the Supreme Command of the Navy, and the extensive cutting down of many offices in the matter of auxiliary workers, have proved very detrimental, having regard to the ever increasing burden of work and the problems connected with it.

There were at first no properly trained personnel for fitting and repairs. Often, after gaining sufficient experience, these were drafted into the Army. Mistakes in fitting and repairs, affecting naval forces and U-boats in particular, were the result.

4. Building up

The research required for the radar service has been placed on a broader basis by transferring the existing naval organization to the Reichs Organization of the Reichs Representative for High Frequency Research.

The development side of Communications Research Command has now been strengthened by transferring production to the technical organization and to industry. Communications Testing Command is in the process of being rapidly built up for radar service purposes, especially with regard to personnel.

A section for 'Surface-Watching Radar Service' is being built up, forming part of the Supreme Command of the Navy/Naval War Staff/Naval Communications Division.

The first promising measures for preventing location by the enemy will soon be ready for operation, as their development is finished and their production has been begun. (The work is based on the intensive preparatory work of the last half-year). Further measures are being developed with the assistance of the Luftwaffe.

The gaps to be filled in the Radar Interception Service, first in the matter of equipment with sets and then in the work of interception itself, can shortly be dealt with. But this will demand a great deal of energy and adaptability on the part of the radar personnel. As a locating set for defence forces, there is now at disposal a limited number of Lichtenstein sets, which are satisfactory for the most urgent purposes.

But above all, the C-in-C of the Navy has promised his special support to the rapid and energetic advancement of surface-watching radar. On this basis further expansion is in preparation.

5. General Principles of Further Development

The most important points are stated in Section 2, Objectives (above).

All officers, ratings, civil servants, employees and workmen who have worked in the surface-watching radar service up to now must have seen from the way it developed that the heads of the Navy were following events with an unusually critical eye. The increasingly obvious superiority of the Anglo-Saxon opponent gave rise to ever sharper criticism, the substance of which was salutary in the long run, in that it thoroughly exposed the dangers of our inferiority.

Every reinforcement of the Officer Corps for the conduct of surface watching radar, especially by energetic personnel used to the sea, is most valuable. The better we succeed in this, the more change – and need – we shall have of ensuring and utilizing independence. With reference to this, special attention is drawn to Section 2 of this work, on keeping to the organization ordered and its official channels. This is the only way of avoiding an inflation of correspondence, a paper war. The enemy's lead must be wrested from him!

The Great Radiation Scare

When search receivers were first introduced into U-boats at the end of 1942, our experts had considered the possibility of homing on to the receiver radiations. Unless special precautions in design are taken, the average receiver produces sufficient radiation to be detected at a distance of several miles, as any one knows who has suffered from whistles in his broadcast receiver while a neighbour is tuning in. Some experiments were made but difficulties lay in the continual change of frequency of the receiver radiations as the operator tuned through the receiver's range, and this, combined with the difficult operating conditions in patrolling aircraft, made this method impractical as a means of detecting U-boats. The Germans had also considered this property of their GSRs in the autumn of 1942 and had likewise discarded it as not dangerous to the U-boat.

We may never learn what reminded the German technical intelligence officers of GSR radiations again in the middle of 1943, but in fact they abandoned the logical examination of the problem (which as already mentioned must have led them to the correct answer) in favour of this will-o'-the-wisp. Tests were made on the Metox R600 receiver and it was discovered that it produced very powerful radiations. Hastened by a statement of one of our prisoners in German hands, the R600 was withdrawn from service and after a short delay the Wanz G1 search receiver, manufactured by Hagenuk was introduced.[1] [Wavelength covered 120–180 cm.] This had been designed to counter our supposed use of short ASV

---

1 2nd U-boat Flotilla Command, Western Area
8th August 1943
Registration Number Most Secret 1247
   To All Boats: –
   Subject: – Prohibition of the use of Metox.

transmissions and worked on the principles already discussed. It so happens, however, that the application of these principles also produces a receiver, the radiations of which are very much more difficult to detect – about in a ratio of 25 to 1 in the case of the Metox R600 and the Wanz G1. The introduction of this receiver should accordingly have set the Germans' minds at rest on the score of dangerous radiations, and left them free to tackle the real problem. It did not. Under pressure of continued sinkings of U-boats a mental stampede began and what followed can only be described as pathological.

The Wanz G1 was withdrawn from service in order that an elaborate and hastily conceived apparatus to reduce radiations still further might be built in.

It may be remarked that the only result of this modification was to increase the complexity of the set and make breakdowns much more frequent.

The use of one after another of the standard U-boat communications

---

(A) The tests made by the Radar Experimental and Training Detachment on the order of the Director of Naval Communications Service have shown that radiation front the oscillator of the Metox receiver can be detected by an aircraft with a suitable search receiver (and to a certain extent with the receiver of the 'ASV' set) at 25 km from a height of 500 metres, at 35 km from 1,000 metres and at 50 km. from 2,000 metres. A target run-in on the basis of this radiation appears also possible. When searching. i.e., when continually turning receiver-tuning of Metox detection and target run-in is harder, but it appears still to be possible if the enemy is skilful.

(B) An English pilot, a prisoner, stated during an interrogation on 13th August that the ASV set was scarcely used because a run-in on U-boat's leak radiation was possible. ASV only being used for a short time to establish the range. It was alleged that leak radiation could be detected at range of up to 90 miles from a height of 1,000 metres.

(C) The prisoner's statement is accepted as true, although the range is improbably long and could only be obtained with a particularly sensitive receiver. It must be assumed that the enemy will have the best possible sets. The extent to which searching with Metox renders the enemy's task more difficult is not certain.

(D) Since in the existing situation it was better to accept a known danger (location run-in by the enemy without warning because Metox not used) rather than expose the boats to a danger the extent of which is not known (exploitation of the radiation from Metox by the enemy) the use of Metox was forbidden in all sea areas.

(E) The new radar search receiver (Hagenuk – wave indicator) by reason of its construction has considerably less leak radiation than Metox. After the first trial its radiation was estimated as carrying for 1/5th the distance of that from Metox. Further exhaustive tests, with every possible means, are proceeding. The modification of Hagenuk so that, for all practice purposes, it is free from radiation, has been successfully begun. There is at present no restriction on the use of Hagenuk.

Signed: C-in-C, U-boats Ops.

Most Secret 5133

Communications Department.

End of Message

receivers was banned while extensive tests of their radiations were made and, as sinkings continued, U-boats in the Bay of Biscay were ordered to receive W/T routines submerged, using VL/F and their D/F loop aerial. It would then be a complete theoretical impossibility for any radiation to reach the air above the surface of the sea, let alone a patrolling aircraft. The sinkings still continued.

Serious as were the immediate effects of these errors of judgment for the Germans, they have extended far beyond their original limits. They engendered in the minds of U-boat captains a fear lest they should produce some radiation, which would betray their presence, as well as a distrust of Admiral Dönitz's technical advisers. This had the immediate effect of paralysing the use of radar as an anti-aircraft warning – the effects of this persisted even at the end of the German war – and more than a year later only a minority of U-boat captains appreciated the true value of their radar as a means of preventing surprise by aircraft.

Another effect of this extraordinary aberration was in turning the minds of the German scientists in the direction of the detector receiver. These receivers generate no radiations, but those with memories of the days of crystal sets will recall how remarkably insensitive they are compared with the modem superheterodyne receiver. Nevertheless the Germans decided to accept this drawback on account of their complete lack of radiations and produced the 'Borkum' set, which is still carried by U-boats as part of the standard GSR equipment. Here for the first time was a set, which could conceivably give in indication of a 10 cm transmission. It had no tuning control but was designed to accept all signals with the band 75 – 300 cm. Outside this band sensitivity falls off, but a strong enough signal well out of the band would nevertheless produce a response. It has an audio frequency amplifier similar to that used in a radio gramophone and presents the received radar signal as a whistle either from a loudspeaker or headphones. June, July and August 1943, passed away for the Germans in the futile pursuit of these phantoms. We do not know exactly by what means the conclusion was reached, but in September the U-boat command became aware that 10 cm radar was in use against them. It is tempting to suppose that this may have resulted from a piece of inter-service co-ordination. Apparently owing to the increasing strain on the German radio industry, Professor Esau was appointed to coordinate the radio and radar policy of the German Navy and Air Force. Soon after this happened the murder was bound to be out – in March 1943, the German Air Force had captured the blind bombing aid H2S working in the 10 cm band. [Also known as Rotterdam Radar, after the place where the first set was captured from a crashed aircraft.] All its salient features had been described in a technical intelligence summary circulated by the German Air Ministry under date 6th June 1943, which, it will be noted, was some weeks before the great radiation scare began.

From September 1943, then, the Germans were aware of our use of 10 cm radar. A situation developed thereafter which was highly diverting to a disinterested spectator: the enemy had the right answer and for a long time he refused to believe it.

Naxos

To understand how this came about it is necessary to go back to the detector receiver. 10 cm radiations are not only difficult to generate, they are also difficult to receive. Under the best conditions they are not easy to detect, and in fact at that time the Allies themselves had not produced an adequate search receiver in this region. As the simplest means, and still under the influence of their obsession, the Germans produced a detector receiver, the 'Naxos,' for the 8 to 12 cm band. In the simple form in which it was first designed, the maximum theoretical range of this type of receiver on Mark II ASV was about 5 miles – no more. Some loss of efficiency under operational conditions was inevitable and it is obvious that there was no room for this. The Naxos was a very delicate instrument: it was not pressure tight and had to be passed below before diving: it had a long coil of flexible cable which was liable to damage: in the early forms spray caused a marked loss of efficiency; and, furthermore, any or all of these defects could easily pass unnoticed by the operator. However efficient the set was, unless a source of 10 cm radiation was very close nothing would be heard. A large drop in sensitivity did not alter the normal silence and the operator could not be forever testing the set. The net result was that the U-boats continued to be surprised successfully and the Germans continued to believe the problem to be more complex than it really was.

Once again we overestimated our enemy. In the October 1943, Report it was said of Naxos: 'It is likely that such an arrangement would respond to a very wide band of frequencies, and, although it would be much less sensitive than previous receivers, it may be expected to give sufficient warning in the majority of cases.' Pressure for the production of counter-measures continued, and it was not until three months later that we wrote 'the U-boats continue to be surprised successfully and it is apparent that the efficiency of the 10 cm GSR equipment is low. Every effort is presumably being made to produce a better set'. It was indeed. By this time the U-boat command had emerged from its trance.

The Effects on Morale

The workings of the brains at headquarters, however, only became apparent to the U-boat captains and crews through their effects. After the collapse of the offensive in May 1943, they observed with increasing misgiving the withdrawal of the Metox R600, the introduction and almost immediate withdrawal of Wanz G1, the ban on the use of W/T equipment which had been standard throughout the war, and finally the collapse of the much-heralded return to the offensive in September when someone had been foolish enough to say that technical parity with the Allies had been regained. 'Naxos' was then introduced but the situation did not improve. It was made worse by the programmes of the so-called 'German short-wave transmitter Atlantik', much listened to by U-boat crews on account of its excellent dance music. This station, which appeared to be extraordinarily well informed as regards the genuine grievances of the U-boat man, kept up a running fire of commiseration, criticism of high policy and denunciation of the effete technicians who played around ineffectually ashore while crew after crew of the U-boats went to a watery grave. 'Atlantik' was in fact a British political warfare station and these subversive naval programmes were directed by the Admiralty.

The lowest point of the depression was reached when at last the U-boat command took the long-anticipated step of sending to sea a U-boat fully equipped to investigate every type of Allied radar, and carrying one of their best technicians with operational experience, Dr. Greven. He sailed from St. Nazaire in *U406* [Kptlt. Horst Dieterichs] on 5th February 1944, and was captured when the U-boat was sunk by HMS *Spey* on the 18th. The worst fears of 'Atlantik' were realized. *U473* [Kptlt. Heinz Sternberg], which was similarly equipped and left Lorient on 27th April 1944, had an even shorter career, being destroyed by HM Ships *Starling, Wild Goose* and *Wren* after nine days at sea.

Even as late as the 5th March 1944, a German Naval Staff officer, preparing a précis of a long paper circulated by the Director of the Communications Division to all German Naval Commands, made the following illuminating notes:

The U-boat's own radiation intercepted by the enemy is probably to be attributed to the Metox receiver. Tests to detect other radiations transmitted from the U-boat have been negative. Detection of Metox radiations was probably easy for the enemy, since this apparatus, which was built in France, is certain to be well known to him.'

In the meantime non-radiating GSRs have been built and introduced (Wanz).

The enemy location operating in centimetre range, according to the enclosed report, is increasingly approaching the limits of optical visibility, while radar interception ranges cannot be increased. The result is that radar interception warning is no longer possible before the enemy locates.

The following are decoys against enemy location: –

(a) Short-term, which are released from the ship.

(b) Longer-termed, which are put out and float in the water as an apparent target.

(c) Decoys on board, which distort the location picture and give the impression of another target. The first measure is called 'Aphrodite,' the second 'Thetis' and the third is still being developed and has no special name.

It is interesting that the note of hopelessness vis-a-vis our S-band radar remained and that, at staff level, faith was still being placed in decoys as the only way out.

Radar Decoys

In some ways the deception technique adopted for the German U-boats makes almost as curious, though much less complicated, a story as their GSR measures. The first device to appear – in July 1943 – was 'Aphrodite', the Radar Decoy Balloon, oddly enough coinciding almost exactly with the first operational use of 'Window' by Bomber Command of the Royal Air Force. Fortunately, owing to the opportune capture of a document, it was possible to inform ships about these devices by an Admiralty general message before the decoying had begun and the element of surprise in their use was minimized. In the event, though it caused some slight difficulties at first, it was never a serious nuisance.

Consideration of 'Thetis II C,' the Radar Decoy Spar Buoy (RDS), again takes one into the realms of the imagination. Designed against metre-wave radar, this device was not introduced into operations until about February 1944, by which time the U-boat staff were well aware that 10-cm radar was the real danger, an efficient GSR had still not appeared and despondency and alarm among the U-boat men had reached a high level. A considerable effort was put into the sowing of these decoys, which a moment's reference to the standard German radar manual would have shown to be valueless. They took up a good deal of much-needed space in the U-boat and were quite awkward to assemble and launch. RDS has never been known to have produced an echo on Allied radar. From the first it was anticipated that it would not be a nuisance to us, but no one anticipated that it would be quite as inefficient as it has proved to be, and, in fact, the only specimen to be recovered from the sea was sighted visually. There is no evidence that the morale of the U-boat men improved.

A New Approach

So far the story has been one of ever deepening gloom for the Germans and, though it was not to be anticipated that matters would continue at this low ebb indefinitely, yet recovery must have been slow in the absence of the most drastic action on the part of Grand Admiral Dönitz. After a time it must have become clear to him that the midsummer reorganization was paying no dividends, and that the rearrangement of existing posts was not an answer. As already stated, it was about Christmas 1943, that the U-boat Command emerged from its trance, and it now remains to follow a story of informed and co-ordinated scientific and developmental effort, which, carried through under increasing difficulties, within 17 months trans-formed the situation in every aspect. It is clear that the Director of the Communications Division was incorrect when he referred on 6th July 1943 to 'the theoretical and practical superiority of the enemy's physical research and technology.' The blame must be laid at the door of the German Naval Intelligence and Planning staff.

The solution proposed by Grand-Admiral Dönitz was true to the 'Führer principle.' He invited, an eminent physicist, Professor Kuepfmüller, to take charge of the whole technical conduct of the radio war. On the 12th December 1943 he wrote as follows to all Commanders-in-Chief: –

Top Secret.
Berlin, 14th December 1943.
Subject: Creation of Naval Scientific Directional Staff
For some months past the enemy has rendered the U-boat war ineffective. He has achieved this object, not through superior tactics or strategy, but through his superiority in the field of science; this finds its expression in the modern battle weapon – detection. By this means he has torn our sole offensive weapon in the war against the Anglo-Saxons from our hands. It is essential to victory that we make good our scientific disparity and thereby restore to the U-boat its fighting qualities.

I have therefore ordered the creation of a Naval Scientific Directional Staff, with its headquarters in Berlin, in addition to other measures already taken. I have nominated Professor Kuepfmüller as head of this staff and directly subordinate to myself.

Professor Kuepfmüller is invested by me with all necessary authority for the execution of his duties.

All naval authorities are ordered to give every assistance to the head of the Naval Scientific Directional Staff, his staff and subordinates.

Signed DÖNITZ.

Much could be written on what Professor Kuepfmüller achieved but only a brief account can be given here. Every aspect of the radio war was surveyed and practical steps proposed to meet every contingency. U-boats were specially equipped to make observations under operational conditions

– the fate of *U406* and *U473* has already been mentioned – and a dozen special teams were constituted to carry the practical steps into effect.

A New Appreciation

Broadly speaking the problems before Professor Kuepfmüller can be considered under four heads – communications, location methods, guided missiles and navigational aids. Little need be said of the two latter. The ability to guide one's own missiles without interference from the enemy was of small importance as their use by the German Navy – as opposed to the German Air Force – was not proposed and, although one of the dozen teams worked on the complementary question of interference with enemy missiles, their labours were, in the event, unnecessary. The navigational aids already in use, particularly the German Air Force's 'Sonne' – its British cover name was 'Consols ' – were considered sufficient without further work at high priority.

As regards communications, there had to be an efficient method which allowed the enemy the minimum opportunities of interception and, particularly, of D/F, together with, for tactical use, facilities for the interception and D/F of the enemy's communications.

With regard to location methods, the problems were, first, to construct a U-boat which could at will remain invisible for indefinite periods, secondly, to equip such a U-boat with efficient methods of locating the enemy either by radar or by interception of the enemy's radiations, and thirdly, to devise facilities for confusing the enemy's location methods so as to create a favourable tactical situation.

Jammers and Decoys

The last requirement covers jammers and decoys and two of the special parties worked on these. Jammers do not need to be considered further as their use was to be confined to surface warships: in decoys, however, they had likely projects coming into production at the end of the war in the form of 'S' band corner reflectors. This had been considered a likely development since the summer of 1944 and indeed the risk of exploitation by the Germans had been accepted when the large-scale deployment of light folding reflectors for air/sea rescue work began. The Germans had, however, devised not only a simple folding reflector, which could be put together by hand, known as the 'Thetis S,' but also an automatically opening type (Thetis US), which could be launched when submerged through the SBT tube; another type could be dropped from aircraft. All these were intended to simulate the echo from a schnorkel uncamouflaged. Apparently none were ever used in operations but in theory they could have been a considerable nuisance both in narrow waters and around convoys.

Work on these devices was, however, on relatively low priority. The first priority went to GSR and anti-radar coverings, the second to ship radar, especially for gunnery, and the third to more secure communications with U-boats. There are thus four main threads to follow through before the complex pattern can be completely traced, and of these it will be convenient to take first GSR, which has already been followed in some detail beyond the time when Professor Kuepfmüller was appointed.

GSR

It was apparent that the first necessary step was to provide the U-boats with an improved search receiver against 10 cm which, even if only a makeshift, would at least give ample warning and provide a margin of sensitivity against inevitable losses of efficiency under operational conditions. There were available in December 1943, a small number of tunable magnetron receives, the 'Korfu', covering 8 to 12 cm. This was tried in four U-boats, but it required skilled operators and its use was abandoned. As it happens, the receiver radiates strongly and its use was inhibited for this reason as well. The Germans remained faithful to the detector principle and produced an aerial of much greater sensitivity (the 'Cuba 1a,' or 'Fliege') by using a vertical section of parabolic reflector like a slice of an electric fire. The effect of this is to retain sensitivity over a wide azimuth, while restricting it in zenith to an angle from horizontal to some 5 to 10 degrees above the horizon. From the point of view of search, however, this is immaterial, and under the best conditions the device increased the range of 10 cm GSR up to 35 miles against Mark-V ASV in an aircraft flying at 1,000 feet

In the form described above, this new aerial does not appear to have been ready for Dr. Greven's ill-starred expedition in early February 1944 – he carried one specimen of a less effective model. The improved type began to appear in service in April 1944, and in the Anti-Submarine Report for that month it was said: 'It is to be expected that this is more sensitive than the original Naxos aerial, but it still suffers from the disadvantage that it must be unshipped every time the boat submerges.'

Meanwhile the enemy had obtained from crashed aircraft our 3-cm airborne radar in the form of the blind bombing aid H2X. It was first used in a raid on Berlin in November 1943. Already on the alert, they soon discovered the new frequency from the fragments, and work on the production of a GSR to cope with the use of this frequency in anti-U-boat operations began. Though this is a more difficult task than the reception of 10 cm, by the end of May they had the search receiver 'Mücke' ready for operational use. This has an electromagnetic horn aerial instead of the parabolic reflector of the 'Fliege', but the effect is the same. The two were soon combined in the standard U-boat equipment 'Tunis'.

In order to obtain the necessary sensitivity with these aerials, the Germans had to sacrifice the desirable property of all-round looking and the aerials had to be continuously rotated by the bridge watch. The directional property can, however, be put to a useful purpose in determining the direction of approach of an aircraft or surface vessel using radar and it has been claimed that these bearings have been used to train the guns in the direction of an approaching aircraft before it has been sighted.

In the longer-term programme, however, this requirement for all round looking still held, together with the requirement for pressurizing already mentioned. The detector receiver must, however, have a directional aerial if its range is to be sufficient for useful tactical employment. One system used the high-speed spinning aerial 'Naxos ZM' (FuMB 23 and, improved, FuMB 28), which rotated at about 1,300 rpm. The results were presented on a cathode ray tube. By an ingenious device a spot of light was made to rotate round the edge of the tube in synchronism with the rotation of the aerial and the spot was then suppressed except when a signal was being received. The result was that all signals received appeared as bright spots round the periphery of the CRT, which was calibrated in degrees and from which the relative bearings could be read off. This device was fitted in some E-Boats, but the U-boat version had not become operational by the end of the German war.

The second possible system involves several separate aerials directed to different points of the compass – in practice four are found to be enough. The idea went through three different versions before a fully satisfactory type was evolved. The first, the 'Cuba II,' was not pressurized; the second, the 'Cuba III,' was pressurized but only covered S-band radar; the final set, the 'Athos,' had both S- and X- band aerial heads, one above the other; the remainder of the set had four separate amplifiers and again gave continuous presentation of bearing on a cathode ray tube. This last had reached operational trials in one U-boat by early May 1945.

The necessity for a fully pressurized S-band GSR aerial had been becoming more and more urgent as time went on and it became apparent that the mere use of Schnorkel by itself did not render a U-boat immune from attack. It was stated in the September, 1944 Report:

There can be no doubt that the Germans were doing their best to produce such an aerial, and that concentration on schnorkel-fitted U-boats has lent an impetus to their efforts. Equipment, which in the case of GSR carried on the bridge merely adds a few seconds to the crash-diving time (though in some circumstances this can be of course serious enough) becomes a complete prohibition to fitting as a Schnorkel GSR. In fact the only search receiver aerial which the Germans have so far fitted is the old standard 'round dipole' type, designed to cover meter wave radar.

The 'Athos' aerial and associated equipment met this requirement in full and it is interesting that Professor Kuepfmüller did not intend to be caught again. The whole apparatus was so designed that, had we started to use another centimetric waveband not covered by the S- and X-band heads already supplied, a further head could have been supplied and readily fitted to extend the cover as required.

The Problem of Invisibility

The idea of using some device to reduce radar echoes is not a new one – it was indeed being canvassed in this country in 1939 – and the German naval technicians had been working on it for some time before Professor Kuepfmüller assumed control. The earlier position can be summed up by another quotation from the September Report:

> The large scale appearance of Schnorkel may well have lent an impetus to another device on which the Germans are known to be working, that of the anti-radar screen or camouflage, the object of which is to prevent an object from giving a radar echo at all, or at least to reduce the size of the echo produced. In some circumstances even a small reduction in detection range may be all that is required.
>
> Such devices may operate on two general principles, either the reflection of the radar rays in some direction away from the radar receiver (just as a mirror reflecting a torch beam in a dark room will be almost invisible unless the beam is returned into the eyes of the man holding the torch), or the absorption of the radar rays by some suitable substance, in the same way that visible light is absorbed by a matt black paint. There are various possibilities in applying either – principle, but the difficulties of producing a device that will work under operational conditions are very great. There are numerous reports of U-boats being covered with anti-radar netting which washed away as soon as they submerged, and experiments with an absorbent plastic covering are also said to have been going on.
>
> As far as we are aware no operational U-boat has ever been fitted with a complete anti-radar outfit of either of these types: and it is quite likely that the experiments may have failed simply because it has not been mechanically possible to produce a device large enough to cover the U-boat and at the same time strong enough to resist wave action. But Schnorkel presents a much easier problem: not only is it much smaller, it is also a simple shape. We should accordingly be prepared for great efforts on the part of the Germans to produce an anti-radar covering for Schnorkel.

The original objective of the Germans – the camouflage of an entire ship – was not, of course, practicable under operational conditions with the means available; but the introduction of the schnorkel provided in fact an alternative solution to the development of special coverings – here the surface of the sea is used in effect as an anti-radar screen for the bulk of the U-boat, and the echo from the remainder is at once reduced to about a fifth of that from the fully surfaced U-boat. At the same time the practical difficulties of camouflaging the residual area above sea level are reduced to manageable proportions. Encouraged by this, the technicians pressed on and by the end of the war were within sight of their goal – a U-boat which could not be distinguished by radar from the surrounding waves. They had in fact produced a covering, which had been widely fitted to operational boats and which produced a small reduction in the schnorkel echo – not indeed very much but then the gap separating them from complete invisibility was becoming so small that the difficulties of the radar operator multiplied out of all proportion. The covering, which was claimed as the final answer to the radar in use by the Allies had been developed and production was beginning, but it was apparently never fitted to any operational boat. This would have afforded protection against radar sets on wavelengths from 3 cm upwards and, as the schnorkel echo was to have been reduced to less than that from a wave, no increase in power of the radar set would help detection at all.

U-boat Radar

The barriers, both of material and psychology, which prevented the U-boat captains from making effective use of their earlier radar sets have already been mentioned. These sets had been originally made by the firm of Gema which manufactured all the early German naval radar but, being at once heavy, bulky, and subject to frequent breakdown, they were finally abandoned in the autumn of 1943 in favour of a modified version of the German Air Force ASV set FuMG 200, or Hohentwiel, which was manufactured by Lorenz. Until the end of the war this remained the standard equipment, using a small extensible mattress aerial housed in the bridge fairing, and rotatable from below through 360 degrees. Various refinements and simplifications were introduced but there was no change of principle and no great improvement in the enthusiasm of the users, although there is no doubt that latterly they possessed as useful a set as the Type 291W, which stood our own submarines in such good stead. As in all other fields new solutions were being pressed on though on lower priority than the anti-radar devices. These solutions were two, taken over by Professor Kuepfmüller from the earlier reign of Professor Esau. Instead of a single all-purpose U-boat radar set it was proposed to have two – one specialized for air warning and the other for surface watching.

This idea reflects the general backwardness of German radar equipment. Although realizing that advance lay in the centimetric field, their inferior valve development made it impossible for them to produce really high powered sets. Indeed, it was necessary for them to make a copy of a British magnetron in order to get a centimetric radar going at all, with the undesirable result that their early sets were in the Allied waveband. A low-powered centimetric set is useless for air warning and so, if the U-boat wanted this as well as surface watching, two entirely different sets were needed. It is unnecessary to point out the numerous complications and disadvantages, which this entails in so cramped a vessel as a U-boat.

The air warning set, the 'Lessing', was almost exactly on the lines we forecast earlier; it was modified from the common German Air Force radar 'Freya', and had as aerial a single vertical dipole, giving complete all-round cover without bearing indication and using the simplest possible aerial. It would, however, have been as heavy and cumbrous as the earlier Gema set, with which the electrical circuits have many affinities. Like its predecessor Hohentwiel, the surface watching 'Berlin' radar was also modified from an original German Air Force airborne design, which (faute de mieux) was coming into extensive use by the German Navy for almost every conceivable purpose. It had an interesting aerial system but, owing to the low power, its range on surface vessels was probably not very much greater than Hohentwiel though the target resolution would of course be much improved. It was, however, so far from operational use that it is not necessary to speculate on the probable repercussions, which would have followed its introduction.

H/F Security

The system which was to put the Germans 'a jump ahead of interception and D/F by existing means' was called by them 'Kurier'. It involved a transmission from the U-boat of very short duration (a signal of about seven letters – in 2/5ths of a second) and a continuously varying schedule of frequencies. Such a signal is too short to interfere with W/T communication by normal methods on the same frequency and the whole H/F band is thus available. The result is that, whereas the authorized recipient can readily set up special equipment on the predetermined frequency at the receiving end, the listening enemy is faced with a task very like looking for a needle in a haystack. In practice things are not as bad as they might be for the opponent. To ensure good communication it is necessary to have a shore transmitter near to the frequency being used in order to determine whether propagation conditions are suitable, so that the difficulties of interception are somewhat eased. D/F at sea, however, becomes virtually impossible. The apparatus used at the transmitting end is a small attachment to the standard U-boat transmitter, which is simple, robust and easy to operate. There is no doubt that the idea is good but it must not be assumed that ordinary W/T is by any means outmoded. An important disadvantage is that the receiving gear is much too complex to carry in a U-boat, so that the method can be used only for ship to shore transmissions, with the consequent necessity for rebroadcasting messages, which must reach other boats. Even within these limitations the Germans had not developed their new system into operational use, though it had survived extensive trials and five U-boats had been fitted with it.

Professor Kuepfmüller had not overlooked the interdependence of secure communications and anti-radar requirements, for the former would be of much less value if the aerial could readily be located. Extensible rod-aerials were developed for the Type XXI and Type XXIII boats, which made transmission at schnorkel depth possible. It is clear that these devices were far from perfect, the main complaint during trials in the Baltic having been of damage to the cabling during raising and lowering and consequently water logging. These teething troubles were no doubt rapidly being overcome.

This aerial was relatively secure from radar detection but, in order to leave no loophole, experiments were being conducted on a floating aerial lying along the surface of the sea. This gave an adequate signal strength on the reflected wave with negligible ground wave and the radar reflection was expected to be well below the sea returns. Another solution also being actively pursued was the use of an extendible transmitting buoy, which could be released from the U-boat and would make a predetermined signal some time later. Neither of these last two devices had passed the experimental stage.

'Y'

The success of the first German 'Y' party to put to sea in a U-boat in connection with the compromise of our ship-borne H/F D/F has already been referred to. Fortunately their successors did not live up to this early promise. It seems that the information that they provided on the tactical situation proved merely confusing to the U-boat Command directing the battle from ashore, and in the autumn of 1943 they went into eclipse. A further trial early in 1944 was of negligible value to the Germans, but most useful to us, for not only did it provide an assurance of the ineffectiveness of the German methods, but, quite incidentally, it supplied a vital link in the chain of intelligence leading to the destruction at the end of May of the main German Naval 'Y' station covering the area of the Normandy landings. After this not very encouraging beginning 'Y' in U-boats was even further hampered by the policy of maximum submergence and nothing more was heard of it. Professor Kuepfmüller was, however, determined that this important field should not be left untilled for lack of suitable machinery. As in so many other instances, he produced an interim measure to make a quick if slight improvement to be followed by a more fundamental improvement. The former was an attachment 'Presskohle' enabling a standard U-boat receiver to be used for taking bearings in the band from 1,500 to 3,000 kc/s, which had not been possible before. The latter involved the ingenious idea of crossed D/F loops fixed to the Schnorkel head underneath the new type of anti-radar covering. This is almost completely transparent to the wavelengths used in H/F communication, and the loops can thus be kept in continual use while schnorkeling without danger of their detection by radar. This aerial and the associated equipment were coming into production but it had not been used on operations.

Conclusion

The great developments described were going on almost entirely in the German laboratories and experimental establishments during the last 18 months of the war. They did not in fact pass unnoticed but the intelligence problem presented was an essentially different one from that of the earlier developments. Then we were following the enemy's struggles through an astonishing series of illogical vagaries but the illogicality was compensated for by our access to the large body of U-boat men who were concerned in all these hand-to-mouth expedients. The later phase, however, concerned a much smaller public – the laboratory and planning staff – and those relatively inaccessible. Indeed the elucidation of enemy research and development work is notoriously one of the most difficult intelligence problems. Here we were assisted by two factors – our extensive knowledge of the position on both sides in December 1943, when the second phase began, and the scientific logic of the Germans approach – and, when Dr. Greven was captured, we were privileged to obtain a momentary glimpse or a corner of the laboratory as it was in January 1944.

Our position was similar to that of a solver of jigsaw puzzles given 20 pieces from a 200 piece puzzle. From the solution of many previous puzzles the expert solver can place most of the pieces in their relative positions and, the painter of the picture being identified from the scraps, a knowledge of his methods enables the rest of the composition to be inferred, even to the postulation of the existence of objects in the whole picture of which no vestige appears on any individual piece. So it was in our case. 'The Germans must devise a means of communication which will put them a jump ahead of reception and D/F by existing means. The need for this must by now be obvious to them. The future success or failure of the U-boat war may well be weightily influenced by the speed with which the Germans can solve this problem.' 'There can be no doubt that the Germans are doing their best to produce a pressure-tight centimetric GSR aerial, and that concentration on Schnorkel-fitted U-boats has lent an impetus to their efforts.' '. . . We should accordingly be prepared for great efforts on the part of the Germans to produce an anti-radar covering for schnorkel, ... they may later on produce an effective radar decoy.' The story was carried a stage further in March 1945, when it was stated with reference to the earlier conclusions that 'it has since become clear that the U-boat Command was in fact working along all these lines . . . Their efforts seem, however, to be accumulating in the background, for few of the devices considered here appear to have been used in operations up to the present.' Professor Kuepfmüller was not the only one who was worried about his inability to keep to his planned dates.

This knowledge of the enemy's proceedings enabled considerable thought to be put into the development of suitable counter-measures, some of which reached an advanced stage before the European war ended; those concerned were already beginning to speculate what the Germans' reactions to these countermeasures would be. This is as it should be, for when it is remembered that the entire U-boat campaign was stultified and the most damaging losses were incurred by the Germans for nine months for the lack of a cheap and simple apparatus which can be packed into a large suitcase, it is apparent how easily the success of an active operation may depend on the possession and efficient use of the right equipment.

The prerequisites of success in these matters are early and accurate intelligence, imaginative forward planning, rapid production and fitting, and efficient operation – the whole process being carried through against a time factor, which allows of no relaxation.

Addenda
Veterans meeting at the Arctic Convoys Museum (www.russianarcticconvoymuseum.co.uk) by Loch Ewe in May 2013 confirmed that ships were allowed to keep the secret monthly Anti-Submarine Reports for any length of time and each ship had an officer responsible for destroying the material after it had been read by the officers. A radar officer and a radar operator also confirmed that Short Wave Radar or Centimetric Radar (mentioned in detail on page 173) was capable of picking up the head of an extended periscope at 2,000 yards (1,800 metres).

Glossary

AP = armour-piercing (shell)

A/S = anti-submarine

ASV = Air to Surface Vessel (radar)

B-Dienst = German radio monitoring service

CAM = Catapult Aircraft Merchantman (ship)

D/F = Direction Finder (Radio)

ERSB = Expendable Radio Sono Buoy

FAT = Federapperat-Torpedo (erroneously also known as Flächenabsuchenden-Torpedo)

Fregkpt. = Fregattenkapitän = Captain (Junior Grade)

'Gnat' = British name for German Zaunkönig or T5 acoustic torpedoes

GRT = Gross Registered Tons

GSR = Group Search Receiver

HE = high explosive (shell)

Hedgehog = British ahead-throwing A/S mortar

H/F = High Frequency

H/F D/F ('Huff Duff') = High Frequency (Radio) Direction Finder

Korvkpt. = Korvettenkapitän = Commander

Kptlt. = Kapitänleutnant = Lieutenant Commander

Kpt.z.S = Kapitän zur See = Captain (Senior Grade)

MAD = Magnetic Airborne Detector

Mousetrap = U.S. rocket-propelled ahead-throwing A/S weapon

NEK = Nachrichtenmittelversuchskommando – German Communications Research Command

NVK = Nachrichtenmittelerprobungskommando – German Communications Testing Command

Oblt.z.S. = Oberleutnant zur See = Lieutenant (Senior)

RDF = Radio Direction Finder (radar)

RDS = Radar Decoy Spar Buoy

RP = rocket projectile

R/T = radio telephony

SAP = semi-armour-piercing (shell).

Shark = (1) British designation for new four-wheel Enigma code
    introduced for U-boats in February 1942. (2) 4in shell developed by the
    British for attacking U-boats on the surface
Squid = British long-range three-barrelled depth charge mortar
TBR = Technisches Beschaffungsamt = Technical Acquisition Office
VLR = Very Long Range (aircraft)
W/T = Wireless Telegraphy
Y = radio listening/interception

British Ocean Convoy Routes

HG   Gibraltar – UK
HX   Halifax – UK
JW   Britain – North Russia
OB   Liverpool – outwards
OG   UK –Gibraltar
ON   UK – Halifax
ONS   UK – Halifax
OS   UK – Freetown
PQ   Iceland – North Russia
QP   Russia – Iceland or UK
SC   Halifax – UK
SL   Freetown – UK
TM   Trinidad – Gibraltar
UG   USA – North Africa

Further Reading

Beesly, Patrick, *Very Special Intelligence*, London: Hamish Hamilton, 1977 and New York: Doubleday, 1978. (An interesting read and probably one of 'the' most significant books of the war, dealing with Admiralty intelligence by an officer who served there as the Deputy Head of the Submarine Tracking Room.)

Brennecke, Jochen, *Jäger – Gejagte*, Jugendheim: Koehlers Verlag, 1956. (One of the great early classics about life in U-boats, written by an ex-war correspondent.)

Brown, David K, *Atlantic Escorts (Ships, Weapons & Tactics in World War II)*, Barnsley: Seaforth Publishing, 2007. (Well illustrated with useful information and a great aid when trying to visualise what Dönitz has written.)

Busch, Harald, *So war der Ubootskrieg (U-boats at War)*, Bielefeld: Deutsche Heimat Verlag, 1954. (Another great early classics about the U-boat war written by an ex-war correspondent.)

Busch, Rainer and Roll, Hans-Joachim, *Der U-Boot-Krieg 1939 bis 1945*. Vol 1, *Die deutschen U-Boot-Kommandanten*, Hamburg, Berlin, Bonn: Koehler/Mittler, 1996. Published in English by Greenhill as *U-boat Commanders*. (Brief biographies produced from the records of the German U-boot-Archiv. Sadly, the English edition has been published without the numerous corrections recorded by the Archive.)

_____, *Der U-Boot-Krieg 1939-1945*, Hamburg, Berlin and Bonn: E. S. Mittler & Sohn, 1999. (German U-boat losses from September 1939 to May 1945 from the records of the U-Boot-Archiv.)

Compton-Hall, Richard, *The Underwater War 1939-45*, Poole: Blanford, 1982. (The author was the Director of the Royal Navy's Submarine Museum and this is by far the best book describing life in submarines.)

Connel, G. G., *Fighting Destroyer – The Story of HMS Petard*, London: William Kimber, 1976. (One of the early books dealing with the capture of the German four-wheel Enigma machine from *U559*.)

Creveld, Martin van, *Fighting Power: German and US Army Performance, 1939-45*, Westport, Connecticut: Greenwood Press, 1982. (Deals with armies rather than navies but most interesting especially as the author works at the Hebrew University in Jerusalem and presents some unexpected and surprising facts about the performance of the German armed forces.)

Delmer, Sefton, *The Black Boomerang*, London: Secker & Warburg, 1962. (Essential reading because this outlines how many accepted stories about the war originated with British Black Propaganda and the British Political Warfare Executive rather than being based on real happenings.)

Dönitz, Karl, *Ten Years and 20 Days*, London: Weidenfeld & Nicolson, 1959. Reprinted in

2012 by Frontline Books, London and Naval Institute Press, Annapolis.

_____, *Mein wechselvolles Leben*, Göttingen: Muster-Schmidt, 1968. (An account dealing with Dönitz's life before and after the Third Reich.)

Frank, Wolfgang, *Die Wölfe und der Admiral*, Oldenburg: Gerhard Stalling Verlag, 1953. Translated as *Sea Wolves – The Story of the German U-boat War*, London: Weidenfeld & Nicolson, 1955. (An excellent book, one of the early classics by an ex-war correspondent.)

Franks, Norman L. R., *Search, Find and Kill*, Bourne End: Aston Publications, 1990. (A record of Coastal Command's successes against U-boats.)

Görlitz, W., *Karl Dönitz*, Göttingen: Muster-Schmidt Verlag, 1972. (A small book giving a good general introduction to Dönitz.)

Gretton, Sir Peter, *Convoy Escort Commander*, London: Cassell, 1964. (A most significant book about the convoy war, especially Convoy HX231, where the author was commander of the escorts.)

Hadley, Michael, *U-boats against Canada*, Kingston and Montreal: McGill-Queen's University Press, 1985. (This and the following book are both useful accounts of the war at sea by a highly respected historian.)

_____, *Count not the Dead*, Montreal, Kingston and London: McGill-Queen's University Press, 1995.

Harbon, John D., *The Longest Battle*, Ontario: Vanwell, 1993. (The Royal Canadian Navy in the Atlantic 1939–45.)

Herbschleb, Axel, *Vom Schiffsjungen zum U-Boot-Kommandanten*, Würzburg: Flechsig Verlag, 2009. (A fantastic book with many brilliant photographs in what looks like a rather cheap edition, but most interesting. Probably one of the best memoirs-type of book.)

Herzog, Bodo, *60 Jahre deutsche Uboote 1906-1966*, Munich: J. F. Lehmanns, 1968. (A useful reference book with much tabulated information. Contains a lot of technical information.)

_____, *U-boats in Action*, Shepperton and Podzun, Dorheim: Ian Allan, n.d. (A pictorial book with captions in English.)

Hessler, G. and others, *German Naval History: The U-boat War in the Atlantic 1939-1945*, London: HMSO, 1989. (Written by Dönitz's son-in-law immediately after the war for the Royal Navy. An essential and most useful aid for anyone wanting to study the war at sea. With a useful introduction by Lieutenant Commander Andrew J. Withers, RN.)

Hinsley, F. H., *British Intelligence in the Second World War*, London: HMSO, 1993. (When reading casually about the war at sea, the abridged edition is easier to digest than Hinsley's three-volume official history. Most interesting, useful and an essential companion for anyone studying the war.)

Hirschfeld, Wolfgang, *Feindfahrten*, Vienna: Neff, 1982. (The secret diary of a U-boat radio operator compiled in the radio rooms of operational submarines. A most invaluable insight into the war.)

_____, *Das Letzte Boot – Atlantik Farewell*, Munich: Universitas, 1989. (The last journey of *U234*, surrender in the United States and life in prisoner of war camps.)

_____, and Geoffrey Brooks, *Hirschfeld – The Story of a U-boat NCO 1940-46*, London: Leo Cooper, 1996. Reprinted by Frontline, Barnsley, 2012. (A fascinating English-language edition of Hirschfeld's life in U-boats.)

Kemp, Paul, *U-boats Destroyed*, London: Arms and Armour Press, 1997. (Parts of this book are now out-of-date but the author used the Secret Anti-Submarine Reports as a source and those actions where the U-boat was identified at the time of the sinking are of special value because Paul Kemp provides more details than in the majority of other similar publications.)

Konstam, Angus and Showell, Jak P. Mallmann, *Spearhead: 7ᵗʰ U-boat Flotilla – Dönitz's Atlantic Wolves*, Hersham: Ian Allan, 2003.

Lowe, Keith, *Inferno*, New York, London, Toronto and Sydney: Scribner, 2007. (The fiery destruction of Hamburg in 1943. Well written with most useful background information. This book helps to explain why U-boats continued going to war when the odds were stacked so heavily against them.)

Middlebrook, Martin, *Convoy*, London: Allen Lane, 1977. (A personal account of the largest convoy battle – SC122 and HX229 as seen through the eyes of some survivors.)

Milner, Marc, *North Atlantic Run*; Naval Institute Press, Annapolis, 1985.

Moore, Captain Arthur R., *A Careless Word ... a Needless Sinking*, Kingsport, NY: American Merchant Marine Museum, 1983. (A detailed and well-illustrated account ships lost during the war.)

Morgan, Daniel and Taylor, Bruce, *U-boat Attack Logs*, Barnsley: Seaforth Publishing, 2011. (A complete record of warships sunk by U-boats during the Second World War with a foreword by Prof. Jürgen Rohwer. An excellent book with a lot of useful explanatory notes and a summary of the war. Most helpful for anyone wanting to understand German log books.)

Morison, Samuel Eliot, *The Battle of the Atlantic*, Boston: Little, Brown and Company, 1947. (Fifteen volumes dealing with the history of United States naval operations in World War II.)

Mulligan, Timothy P., *Neither Sharks Nor Wolves*, London: Chatham Publishing, and Annapolis: United States Naval Institute Press, 1999. (An excellent book about the men who manned the U-boats.)

Nesbit, Roy Conyers, *The Battle of the Atlantic*, Stroud: Sutton Publishing, 2002. (Contains a vast number of brilliant photographs with informative text. Most useful.)

Niestlé, Axel, *German U-boat Losses during World War II*, London: Greenhill Books, 1998. (Although now in urgent need of revision because the author's on-going research has turned up a lot of new information, this is still the most up-to-date book about U-boat losses.)

Paterson, Lawrence, *U-boat Combat Missions*, New York: Barnes and Noble, 2007. (Contains good photographs and many first-hand accounts of U-boat life.)

_____, *U-boat War Patrol*, London: Greenhill Books, and Mechanicsburg, Pennsylvania: Stackpole Books, 2004. (The secret photographic diary of *U564* under 'Teddy' Suhren, written from the boat's war diary and illustrated with interesting photographs.)

Pfefferle, Ernst (ed), *Kammeraden zur See*, Altmannstein: Ernst Pfefferle, several volumes from 1985 onwards. (A most fascinating series of personal recollections and some brilliant articles not available elsewhere.)

Price, Alfred, *Aircraft versus Submarine*, London: William Kimber, 1973. (One of the early classics. Well written and most useful.)

Raeder, Grand Admiral Dr. Erich, *My Life*, Annapolis: United States Naval Institute Press, 1960.

_____, and Dönitz, Karl, *Führer Conferences on Naval Affairs 1939-1945*, London: Greenhill Books, 1990. (An essential reference book for anyone studying the war at sea.)

Robertson, Terrance, *The Golden Horseshoe*, London: Pan Books, 1966. (One of the early classics, written at a time when information was still extremely hard to come by.)

Rössler, Eberhard, *The U-boat*, London: Arms and Armour Press, 1981. Translated from *Geschichte des deutschen U-Bootbaus* (2 vols), Bonn: Bernhard and Graefe Verlag, 1996. (An excellent technical book about the development of U-boats from 1850.)

Rohwer, J., *Axis Submarine Successes of World War II 1939-45*, London: Greenhill, 1998.

_____, *The Critical Convoy Battles of March 1943*, Weybridge: Ian Allan, 1977. (An interesting account of the biggest convoy battle of the war, when HX229 and SC122 amalgamated to fend off some eighteen attacking U-boats.)

_____, and Hümmelchen, G., *Chronology of the War at Sea 1939-1945*, London: Greenhill Books, 1992. (A good, solid and informative work. Well indexed and essential for anyone studying the war at sea.)

Roskill, Captain S. W., *The War at Sea* (4 vols), London: HMSO, 1954, reprinted 1976. (The official history of the war at sea, 1939-45.)

_____, *The Secret Capture*; Collins, London, 1959.

Sarty, Roger, *War in the St. Lawrence*, Ontario: Allen Lane, 2012. (The forgotten U-boat battles on Canada's shores. An interesting book.)

Savas, Theodore P.; *Hunt and Kill – U505 and the U-boat War in the Atlantic*, New York: Savas Beatie, 2004. (This book is of special interest because at least eight distinguished authors contributed specialist information to provide an in-depth history of this well-known capture.)

Showell, Jak P. Mallmann; *The German Navy in World War Two*, London: Arms and Armour Press, and Annapolis: United States Naval Institute Press, 1979, and published in German as *Das Buch der deutschen Kriegsmarine*, Stuttgart: Motorbuch Verlag, 1982. (Covers history, organisation, the ships, code-writers, naval charts and a section on ranks, uniforms, awards and insignia by Gordon Williamson. Named by the United States Naval Institute as 'One of the Outstanding Naval Books of the Year'.)

_____, *Hitler's Navy*, Barnsley: Seaforth Publishing, 2009. (A revised version of *The German Navy in World War Two* with additional text and new photos.)

_____, *U-boats under the Swastika*, Shepperton: Ian Allan, and New York: Arco, 1973, and published in German as *Uboote gegen England*, Stuttgart: Motorbuch, 1974. (A well-illustrated introduction to the German U-boat Arm.)

_____, *U-boats under the Swastika*, Shepperton: Ian Allan, and Annapolis: United States Naval Institute Press, 1987. (A second edition with different photos and new text of the above title.)

_____, *U-boat Command and the Battle of the Atlantic*, London: Conway Maritime Press, and New York: Vanwell, 1989. (A detailed history based on the U-boat Command's war diary.)

_____, *Germania International*; Journal of the German Navy Study Group. (Now out of print.)

_____, *U-boat Commanders and their Crews*, Marlborough: The Crowood Press, 1998.

_____, *German Navy Handbook 1939-1945*, Stroud: Sutton Publishing, 1999.

_____, *U-boats in Camera 1939-1945*, Stroud: Sutton Publishing, 1999.

_____, *U-boats at War – Landings on Hostile Shores*; Hersham: Ian Allan, and Annapolis,: United States Naval Institute Press, 2000. Published in Germans as *Deutsche U-Boote an feindlichen Küsten 1939-1945*, Stuttgart: Motorbuch Verlag, 2002.

_____, *German Naval Code Breakers*, Hersham: Ian Allan, 2003.

_____, *The U-boat Century – German Submarine Warfare 1906-2006*, London: Chatham Publishing, 2006. Published in German as *Geschichte der deutschen U-Boot-Waffe seit 1906*, Stuttgart: Motorbuch Verlag, 2008.

_____, *The U-boat Archive Series*, Milton Keynes: Military Press 2001 – 2007. (www.miliarypress.co.uk – a set of seven reprints of secret wartime material essential for studying the war at sea.)

_____, *U-boats Attack!*, Stroud: Spellmount and imprint of The History Press, 2011.

Smith, Constance Babington, *Evidence in Camera*, Newton Abbot: David & Charles, 1957. (One of the early accounts of British Photographic Intelligence by an author who worked there throughout the war. Most interesting.)

Smith, Michael and Erskine, Ralph, *Action this Day*, London and New York: Bantam Press, 2001. (One of the best books written about code breaking at Bletchley Park.)

Taylor, John A., *Bletchley Park's Secret Sisters*, Dunstable, The Book Castle, 2005. (Psychological warfare in World War II.)

Thompson, H. K. and Strutz, William L., *Dönitz at Nuremberg: A Re-Appraisal*, Torrance, California: Institute for Historic Review, 1983. (Very interesting, with quotes and comments about Dönitz from many famous leaders.)

U-Boot-Archiv, *Das Archiv* (German language), *The U-boat Archive* (English language). (A journal now published once a year for members of FTU, Deutsches U-Boot-Museum, D-27478 Cuxhaven-Altenbruch. (www.dubm.de) (www.militarypress.co.uk)).

Verband Deutscher Ubootsfahrer, *Schaltung Küste*. (Journal of the German Submariners' Association.)

Watts, Anthony, *The U-boat Hunters*, London: MacDonald and Jane's, 1976. (One of the first books about anti-U-boat forces. Well written.)

Witthöft, Hans Jürgen, *Lexikon zur deutschen Marinegeschichte*, Herford: Koehler; 1977. (An excellent two-volume encyclopaedia.)

Wynn, Kenneth, *U-boat Operations of the Second World War*, Vol 1 and 2. London: Chatham Publishing, 1997 and 1998. (An essential reference work listing the majority of U-boat operations and other useful information.)

Index

Daydawn, 18
Deptford, HMS, 83
Deutschland, 5
Devonshire, HMS, 38
Dianthus, HMS, 117
Dinaric, 78
Dorsetshire, 38
Drumheller, HMCS, 151
Eclipse, HMS, 129
Eglantine, HNoMS, 81
Emden, 1
Empire Housman, 157
Empire Hudson, 47
Empire MacAlpine, 131, 151
Empire Rainbow, 47
Escapade, HMS, 129, 151
Eulota, Dutch, 7
Exe, HMS, 83
Fame, HMS, 84, 89
Folkestone, HMS, 79
Fury, HMS, 129
Garland, ORP, 129
Gatineau, HMCS, 151
Gentian, HMS, 120
Gneisenau, 59
Gorleston, HMS, 79
Grenville, HMS, 142
Hainaut, 78
Hannover, 47
Harlingen, 16
Harvester, HMS, 18, 119, 120
Havidar, 29
Heather, HMS, 120
Hesperus, HMS, 90
Highlander, HMS, 18, 114, 115
Hurricane, HMS, 18
Icarus, HMS, 129, 151
Inglefield, HMS, 129
Itchen, HMS, 151
Kamloops, HMCS, 151
Kashmir, HMS, 5
Keppel, HMS, 151 , 152
Kingston, HMS, 5
Kite, HMS, 139
Königsberg, 29
Lagan, HMS, 151
Laurelwood, oiler, 83
Laurentic, armed merchant cruiser, 18
Leamington, HMS, 46
Lobelia, HMS, 151
Loch Killin, HMS, 146
Londonderry, 115
Loosestrife, HMS, 128
Mackay, HMS, 19
Mignonette, HMS, 137, 141
Montbretia, HNoMS, 81
Moosejaw, HMCS, 45
Morden, HMS, 151
Narcissus, HMS, 129, 151
Nordmark, 18

Norfolk, HMS, 5
Northern Foam, HMS, 151
Oakville, HMCS, 108
Offa, HMS, 121
Orchis, HMS, 151
Ottawa, HMCS, 83
Patroclus, Armed Merchant Cruiser, 18
Pentstemon, HMS, 80
Petard, HMS, 102, 162
Pink, HMS, 128
Planter, 18
Polyanthus, HMS, 151
Potentilla, HNoMS, 81
Prinz Eugen, 33, 59
Puckeridge, HMS, 149
Python, 38, 47
Rabbit, USS, 66
Renoncule, FFS, 129, 151
Restigouche, HMCS, 114
Rhododendron, HMS, 18
Rochester, HMS, 34, 137, 141
Roper, USS, 64, 66
Roselys, FFS, 54, 129, 151
Rother, HMS, 83
Sabre, HMS, 83
Sackville, HMS, 151
Saint Dunstan, 29
Saladin, HMS, 83
Salisbury, HMS, 120
Salvonia, 18
Santee, USS, 141
Saracen, HM Sub, 28
Sardonyx, HMS, 83
Scharnhorst, 59
Scimitar, HMS, 93
Scotstoun, Armed Merchant Cruiser, 9
Scottish Maiden, 18
Shemara, HMY, 110
Sherbrooke, HMCS, 114
Siroco, French destroyer, 5
Skeena, HMCS, 45
Snowflake, HMS, 128
Spearfish, HM Sub, 10
Spey, HMS, 83
St. Croix, HMCS, 78, 151
St. Germain, 18
Stanley, HMS, 48
Stonecrop, HMS, 142
Stork, HMS, 48, 65, 67, 83, 142
Stuart, HMS, 109
Tay, HMS, 83, 128
Vanessa, HMS, 120
Vanoc, HMS 27
Veronica, 18
Vetch, HMS, 65, 67
Veteran, HMS, 46
Viscount, HMS, 81, 89
Victoria, 18
Vidette, HMS, 128
Vimy, HMS, 113